Love: A Good Medicine

The Saga of the Elixir of Life

(Introducing 'LoveOlogy')

Books Published by Allied Publishers for Dr. Siddhartha Ganguli

1. Live Happily, Work Happily - 2009
2. SUCCESS Can be Planned and Earned - 2010
3. Greying Gracefully: Planning for Retirement and Old Age Happiness - 2011
4. Conscious Management - 2011
5. The Making of a Winning Child - 2012
6. Smart Leading and Parenting of Teenage Kids in the Digital Era - 2021
7. Music is Magic Music is Medicine: Impact of Music on Body, Brain, Mind & Soul - 2023
8. The Four Moons in the Human Body - The Mysterious Tales of the Bauls of Bengal (Introducing 'BaulOlogy') - 2023

Love: A Good Medicine

The Saga of the Elixir of Life

(Introducing 'LoveOlogy')

Siddhartha Ganguli, *PhD*

(Special contributions on 'Love' by Stellar Maestro Dr Leonid Timoshenko PhD from Russia and multi-talented gynaecologist & obstetrician Dr Gouri Kumra MD from India)

ALLIED PUBLISHERS PVT. LTD.

Noida • Mumbai • Kolkata • Chennai • Bangalore

ALLIED PUBLISHERS PRIVATE LIMITED

D-5, Sector-2, **Noida**–201 301
Ph. Nos.: 0120-4320295/2542557/4352866
E-mail: delhi.books@alliedpublishers.com

17 Chittaranjan Avenue, **Kolkata**–700072
Ph.: 033-22129618 • E-mail: cal.books@alliedpublishers.com

15 J.N. Heredia Marg, Ballard Estate, **Mumbai**–400001
Ph.: 022-42126969 • E-mail: mumbai.books@alliedpublishers.com

No. 25/10, Commander-in-Chief Road, Ethiraj Lane (Next to Post Office)
Egmore, **Chennai**–600008
Ph.: 044-28223938 • E-mail: chennai.books@alliedpublishers.com

P.B. No. 9932, No. 15, 3rd Floor (Next to Vijaya Bank), 5th Cross, Gandhinagar,
Karnataka, **Bangalore**–560009. Ph.: 080-41530285 / 22386239
E-mail: bngl.journals@alliedpublishers.com / apsabng@airtelmail.in

Website: www.alliedpublishers.com

ISBN: 978-93-90951-86-4

The background mosaic for the front cover of the book has been designed by the author's close friend Stellar Maestro Dr Leonid Timoshenko PhD, ace pianist, astrophysicist, composer & philosopher from Russia whose name has a place in the Guinness Book of World Records.

Published by Sunil Sachdev and printed by Ravi Sachdev
at Allied Publishers Pvt. Ltd., D-5, Sector-2, Noida–201 301

This book is

dedicated to

the scholars of

love

of

all ages

The Trigger

What prompted me to take up this book project on 'Love: A Good Medicine'? What was the trigger? It was a marvellous 'love song' by the Japanese singer Satsuki.

Satsuki is a Japanese vocalist who sings to 'heal' the 'soul'. When she sings to a bowl of water, the water turns into beautiful crystals; such is the impact of her sonic vibrations. It reminded me of the experiments of the Japanese scientist Masaru Emoto (References 1, 2 & 3).

Satsuki's singing brings harmony in the mind and body; it repairs a broken heart! Thus, when she sings a love song, the love that she spreads all around her in the environment, acts as a good medicine. Having authored world's first authentic epic volume (600 + pages) on 'Bio-musicology', I could not resist the temptation of listening to one of Satsuki's emotionally-packed love songs. (Reference 4)

[Incidentally, 'Bio-musicology' is a term coined by me. It deals with the study of the impact of music on body, brain, mind and soul. It is a very important division of 'Neuro-management' or 'NM' – a totally new and novel multi-disciplinary domain that I have been dedicated in developing since 2015.]

I was introduced to Satsuki and her love songs by my Japanese music composer friend 'Tsutsumi Hideki' who is based at Fukuoka, Japan, at the moment.

Let me share with you one of Satsuki's most touching love songs. She is the songwriter & singer (the original song is in Japanese; she has translated it into English for me) and the composer is Tsutsumi Hideki.

The song goes like this:

> *"I will let my flower of soul bloom as long as I am alive*
> *You made promise on the bottom of my heart*
> *In a shower of cherry blossom (in past life)!*
> *We do fulfil the promise*

That transcends time and space now and here
Celebrate the joy of meeting again.
Sing Dance on this planet
Play Smile even in sadness
Your beautiful scar veiled with kimono
Turn into the brilliances that light up the world
Sing Dance on this planet
Play Smile even in suffering
Your warm teardrops that fall on your bare skin
Turn into the love that embraces this planet!!"

The context of the song is no less interesting factually!

In old Japan, there were so many girls who had to sell themselves as call girls and prostitutes because of poverty. If they tried to escape from the brothels, they had to receive heavy punishment, sometimes even death. They could not get married to the persons they loved. Unfulfilled love was filled with sadness. When they were devastated by very strict restrictions or even a death sentence, they promised to get united in the next life, when reborn. The song says: "We will definitely meet again and be joined together. And, if the dream came true, we will celebrate – sing and dance in joy. All the past suffering and sorrow would turn into extra-bright light that would make the world shine."

All over the world, due to differences in social status and poverty, there are so many people who can't be with their loved ones. Hope that kind of pain would be healed. May the sadness would turn into joy.

It is a love song filled with hopes and prayer!!

References

1. *Masaru Emoto* – Wikipedia.
2. "Dr Masaru Emoto and Water Consciousness" – *TWE: The Wellness Enterprise*, 23rd March 2017
3. "Water Experiment by Dr Masaru Emoto" – *alive water*, World Living Water Systems Ltd.
4. Siddhartha Ganguli, *Music is Magic/Music is Medicine*, Noida: Allied Publishers Pvt. Ltd., 2023.

Gratitude

In conceiving ideas, thinking about the possible contents and writing this book, I've become unknowingly indebted to my wife Utpala and our three kids Abhishek, Abhirup and Ishita for their silent good wishes!

No doubt, I am awfully grateful to Pervez Alam for his incessant technical help and cooperation throughout the lap top to printing press stage movement process. Great many thanks go to my publishers Allied Publishers Pvt. Ltd. – especially Jagdish Singh of the Editorial Dept. and his colleagues who have been involved throughout with a 'Just In Time' and 'Zero Defect' spirit.

Much kindness has been showered on me by Dr Leonid Timoshenko PhD, the great astrophysicist-philosopher-music composer-ace pianist-painter, from Russia, for allowing me to use one of the products of his imagination – the theme design that I've used for the front cover of the book. The special contribution by the Stellar Maestro sharing his thoughts on the Venus, the Planet representing the Goddess of Love, and what we can learn about 'deep love' from the music of the galaxy and the stars has added immense value to the contents of the book.

Dr Gouri Kumra, MB BS, DGO, MD, one of the top gynaecologists & obstetricians of India today, who has magic in her hands and fingers the way she delivers a baby from the womb and performs complicated surgeries in the female private parts, has contributed her thoughts in an illustrated article regarding the most controversial topic "Child of Lust versus Child of Love" which has been annexed with this volume. I am indeed indebted to her for stealing time from her most hectic clinical schedule to comply with my request. Her article is a most valuable input for my readers.

I must not forget the encouragement that I receive from my thousands of readers from all over the world who offer smart comments and shoot pertinent questions. Dr. Douglas Werner from Tampa, Florida, USA, Ennio Manfredi, Stefano Vagnini and Giorgia Ragni from Italy, Greg Sauzet and Fraulein Ursula Hasenbusch from France, Toss Levy from The Netherlands, Dr Norbert Ammerman, Samira Saygilli, and Carsten Wicke from Germany, Clem Alford and Paul Lefty Wright from the UK, L V Erick from China Avi Sheikh, Rabiul Karim Apon and Md Sagar Islam Miran from Bangladesh need very special mention.

Finally, I thank, most profusely, the most talented music composer Tsutsumi Hideki and the songwriter-singer Satsuki – both from Japan, who served as 'triggers' for me to delve deep into the nuances of 'love', its different facets, aspects and characteristics including its 'medicinal' values.

Gift

I am making a gift of this precious work of mine to my most beloved wife and life-companion Utpala with the wishful dream that we will be united and tightly bonded together again and again in all our future lives on this planet or on any other star, with the right dose of 'Love: A Good Medicine'.

Contents

CHAPTER 1

We Want to Feel Good Always (The Drive for 'Pleasure')

"Mark Lavon 'Levon' Helm (1940–2012) was an American musician who achieved fame as the drummer and one of the three lead vocalists for 'The Band', for which he was inducted into the Rock and Roll Hall of Fame in 1994. Helm was known for his deeply soulful, country-accented voice, multi-instrumental ability, and creative drumming style." (Reference 1)

Helm had earned many accolades in his lifetime as a drummer, vocalist and as a movie actor, but I remember him while penning my saga of 'Love' because of one of his popular songs whose underlying message fits in here absolutely snugly.

It goes like this:

> *"Feelin' good, feelin' good*
>
> *All the money in the world spent on feeling good!"*

I would say: we want to feel good always because that need arises from our inherent drive for 'pleasure' (Reference 2). And, to earn 'pleasure' we not only spend money as the writers of the Levon Helm song, J.B. Lenoir and J.B. Lenoir say. Money appeared with the uprise of consumerism. Humans have been hungry for 'pleasure' and 'feeling good' ever since the first man and woman appeared on this planet in their birthday suits. For earning 'pleasure' and 'feeling good', man has been devoting his precious time, spending the energies of his body and brain, putting in physical, emotional & mental efforts, and dedicating all his economic and other resources.

One of the basic sources of 'pleasure' and 'feeling good' for man has been LOVE. The other day, I bumped into a post which said that the

English word 'love' has got some link with the word 'lubh' which exists in the ancient Indian Sanskrit language.

James Robinson Cooper writes on 7 February 2017 under "Sanskrit – The Language of the Gods" (Reference 3):

> "The Sanskrit 'lubh' has been described as 'to release (l) strong (u) vital energy (bh)'. The dictionary defines 'lubh' as 'to desire greatly' 'to long for' 'to enchant' 'to seduce the mind' 'to allure' 'to entice' 'to covet' 'to excite lust'."
>
> "'Lubh' becomes 'lubdha' meaning 'covetous' 'greedy' 'lustful' it becomes 'lobha' meaning 'cupidity' 'avarice' 'greed' it becomes 'lobhana' meaning 'attraction' 'alluring' 'temptation' and it becomes 'lobhita' meaning 'seduced' 'allured' 'enticed'."
>
> "A favourite pastime of Lord Krsna was entering the homes of the gopis and stealing the yoghurt and curds. One of his partners in crime was the mischievous monkey named 'dadilobha' who along with Madhumangal performed all kinds of mischievous pranks. 'Lobha' as mentioned means 'greed' and 'dadhi' means 'curd' and so 'dadilobha' is an intimate associate of Lord Krsna, a mischievous monkey who was always 'greedy for curds'."
>
> "In Europe, 'Lubh' becomes the Latin 'Lubido' meaning 'erotic desire', it becomes 'Libido' meaning 'passion' 'lust' and it becomes 'luxury' meaning 'sexual intercourse'."
>
> "From 'Lubh' comes the English word 'Love'. It leaves the shores of Sanskrit and travels throughout Europe as the Proto Germanic 'Lubojan', the Slavonic 'Lubu', the Old English 'Lufu', the Norse, Frisian and Dutch 'Lof', the Old Saxon 'Liof', the Gothic 'Liufs', and eventually ot becomes the word 'Love'"
>
> " 'Lubh' is seen throughout the European languages – Polish – lubic – Slovak – lubit – Belarusian – liubic – Bosnia – ljubav – Bulgaria - ljubov – Croatia – ljubav – Macedonia – ljubov – Russian – lyubov – Serbia – ljubav – Slovenia – ljubiti – Ukraine – lyubov – German – liebe – Yiddish – leiba – All meaning 'love',

'passion' and all pointing towards the Sanskrit 'Lubh' as the source of the word 'love'."

"In English, the word 'love' is derived from Germanic forms of the Sanskrit 'Lubh' meaning 'desire'." (Reference 4)

So, from an elaborate analysis of the term 'love' from different languages and cultures, one can see that 'Love' is an universal instinctive emotion.

Love: Its Origin in Human Life

All creatures are born to fulfil the twin basic objectives of life: 'survival' and 'replication'. We, humans, are no exceptions. 'Love', in its purest form, is essential for healthy and happy survival. For survival and healthy growth of the foetus, the pregnant mother's love travels to it through the umbilical cord in the form of invisible vibrations. (Reference 5) The Maoris of New Zealand follow the custom of burying the umbilical cord connected with the placenta in the soil as they believe that we all are children of Mother Earth. They don't treat those parts as biological waste as we, non-aborigines, do. (Reference 6)

A physically and mentally healthy and happy mother showers 'pure love' neuro-transmitter 'Oxytocin' to the newly born by exchanging positive eye contact and smile at the moment of birth, at the first sight. The 'Oxytocin' supply gets increased during nursing and breast-feeding. 'Impure' and 'erotic love' raises its head with the onset of sexual drive and libido in the growing child, instigated primarily by the male sex hormone 'Testosterone'. The biological root cause is the second of the twin objectives – 'replication' or 'reproduction' governed by the 'Selfish Genes' whose only motto is to propagate them generation after generation, in their original or in altered, mutated forms. (Reference 7). 'Erotic love' is a typical feature of 'pre-human' existence when there was no custom of bonding through social marriages. The lovers engaged in physical relationship used to earn only 'Dopamine' which is a transitory, 'earn-enjoy-exhaust' biological chemical which does not last for long.

Classification of 'Love'

This is the right time for me to classify 'love' into three categories, from my experience. The first one is 'Smart Love' – which is a temporary, transient situation. You like someone, you mix for a few days – both of you earn the brain's reward chemical 'Dopamine' and then get disassociated. Memories of that relationship also fade away from your mind. The second one is 'Short-lived' or 'Short Love' where, although you are no longer close to that person, but the memory lingers. 'Dopamine' is released inside your brain whenever memory traces flash on your mind's screen. The third and the last one is 'Sustained Love', which is long-lasting, based on closely bonded relationship. 'Sustained Love' leads to a good level of the neurotransmitter 'Oxytocin' in the bloodstream of the two persons in loving relationship.

As the quality of love in an opposite-sex or same-sex relationship progresses from infatuation and physical attraction to intimacy and finally to commitment, the biochemical releases also keep changing from 'Dopamine' and 'Testosterone' to 'Serotonin' and 'Oxytocin'.

Any of the three types of 'Love' that I've described between a male and a female may involve physical intimacy leading to pregnancy.

Parthenogenesis

Parthenogenesis (Greek 'parthenos' – 'virgin' + 'genesis' – 'creation') is a natural form of asexual reproduction in which growth and development of embryo occur in just either the egg or the sperm without the sperm of the male fusing with the egg of the female. It thus means that the embryo develops from an individual sperm or an individual egg. (References 8 & 9)

Parthenogenesis is common in plants, algae, and invertebrate animal species and a few rare vertebrates, such as some fish, amphibians, reptiles and birds. Parthenogenesis is unknown in human beings. Left on their own humans cannot reproduce asexually. (Reference 10)

Birth of Jesus

Jesus came from the womb of his mother Mary who was a virgin betrothed to Joseph. Jesus's father was God. God's spirit had made virgin Mary pregnant. Mary was human. Jesus, being born in her womb, grew into the one who saved the mankind by uniting men to all creation.

> "……..We begin our lives, tethered to our mothers – who feed us before we ask and who (when all is well) bless us before we enter the world. Not one of us is 'self-made', but generation after generation, we are made and formed by the women who accepted us and shaped us, as best as they could; who formed our bodies in their wombs, formed our souls in their love, formed our character by the examples they gave us in their lives." (Reference 11)

Mary, a young virgin, was chosen by God to conceive Jesus through the Holy Spirit. After giving birth to Jesus in Bethlehem, she raised him in the City of Nazareth in Galilee, and was in Jerusalem at his crucifixion and with the apostles after his ascension. God chose Mary because she was of the right lineage. She was from Nazareth, she was engaged to a man whose lineage set up a trip to Bethlehem; she was a virgin, and she was a young woman of good character. The virgin birth was important because the Son of God could not be born into sin. Every human is born into sin and every human being freely commits sin in a male-to-female relationship. By Jesus being born to a virgin also attested to Jesus being the Son of God. No mere man would be born to a virgin. That kind of 'parthenogenesis' is impossible and unimaginable in the human society.

When the Holy Spirit entered virgin Mary's womb, she must have been flooded with 'Oxytocin' as it was a case of 'Divine Love'. The same thing had happened when Gadadhar's (later, 'Ramakrishna Paramhansa') mother had a feeling that a bundle of divine energy is entering into her womb and when young prince Siddhartha's (later, 'Lord Buddha') mother dreamt of giving birth to a divine soul.

The parents of Ramakrishna are said to have experienced supernatural incidents and visions regarding his birth. In Gaya, his father Khudiram had a dream in which Bhagawan Gadadhara (a form of Lord Krishna) told him that he would be born as his son Ramakrishna. (Reference 12)

The 'Sacred Embryo' ('Shengtai')

Taoist Internal Alchemy practitioners developed the term 'shengtai' ('sacred embryo' or 'embryo of sagehood') with a complex process of symbolic pregnancy generating a spiritually perfected duplicate of oneself within oneself, which later become synonymous with the elixir of immortality in External Alchemy. (Reference 13)

All sentient beings are born with a Buddha-nature potential to become enlightened. The renowned Daoist Zhang Boduan (984–1082) was first to use the expression 'shengtai' ('sagely embryo') in a context of physiological neidan (or, Internal Alchemy), and neidan adepts. (Reference 14)`. He developed prolonged meditation techniques through which one can supposedly become pregnant, gestate, and give birth to a spiritually perfected 'doppelganger' (an apparition or double of a living person).

Virgin Mary was not married yet. She was only betrothed to Joseph. After Joseph found out she was pregnant, he thought to 'put her away privately' so the she would not be stoned for adultery. An angel visited Joseph, who told him how things stood, and then Joseph married her (Matthew 1: 19-21). Thus whether it was a case of 'Parthenogenesis' or "Golden Embryo", I am not sure. The latter was the most likely happening.

The Story of 'Pandu' in Mahabharata

King Vichitravirya was the official father of Pandu, but Veda Vyasa was the biological father. Pandu was born with the help of the 'Niyoga' practice where an impotent aristocrat's wife would be impregnated by a respectable wise man or a sage to become pregnant.

Karna, son of Kunti was born before she was married to King Pandu. Once Kindama, a Brahmin had taken the form of a deer to make love with his wife, who also took the form of a doe (a female dear) in a deep forest, King Pandu, the socially acknowledged father of the Pandavas, shot them. Though it was no accident, the Brahmin died, but before dying he cursed the King that he would also die if he engaged in intercourse with any woman.

Due to the curse, Pandu had to remain unable to be the father of any child in the normal biological process and it was established that Pandu was impotent. Even though after that curse of inability, King Pandu had five sons. Among those five, except Yudhisthira, the other four were born through the boons of different gods. Pandu's wife Kunti, in her youth, had satisfied Durbasha, a very ill-tempered sage, with her power, prayer and dedicated service; and, being pleased, he granted her the power to invoke Gods so that, each God, if invoked, would give her a child. (Reference 15) Yudhistir, was born by the boon of God 'Dharma' or 'Righteousness', Bhim (by 'Pawan' or 'air'), Arjun (by Indra – the King of Gods), the twins Nakul and Sahadev (born to Pandu's second wife Madri by Ashwini gods).

Why did Pandu kill the deer during the sexual act? He had a very restrictive upbringing concerning sex, which had contributed to his negative attitude towards sex. The traumatic sexual experience that his mother had with his biological father Veda Vyasa, which he had internalised – had led to the unconscious feeling of hostility, fear, and guilt. (Reference 16)

Due to the unfortunate death of Chitrangada and Vichitravirya, Satyavati sought the help of her untold and unrevealed son Vyasa to beget heirs to the kingdom and Vyasa made Ambika and Ambalika beget sons by name Dhritarastra and Pandu. In Vedic texts, it was allowed to have children with the help of another man in case the husband was either dead or he was not fit to procreate. Many times, kings would take the help of sages with high ascetic merits.

As the legal father of Pandu and Dhritarastra had died without leaving any successor, Satyavati and Bhimsa decided to take the help of some great men. She suggested her first son Krishna Dwaipayan Vyasa. Vyasa agreed but on the condition that, Ambika and Ambalika should be able to face him with his ascetic appearance.

Ambika could not keep her eyes open during the intercourse so Vyasa cursed her child to be born visually handicapped; that child was congenitally blind Dhritarastra. And, Ambalika was so much under stress that although she kept her eyes partially open, her face became pale as all the blood had shifted to her limbs with her brain's 'freeze-fight-or flight' switch on. So, the Rishi said your child will be pale in complexion as you've become pale in fear......and his name will be 'Pandu' (meaning 'pale'). So, both Dhritarastra and Pandu did not carry 'Kshatriya' blood – their blood was more Brahminical. (Reference 17)

Love: As Discussed in Plato's 'Symposium'

The 'Symposium' by the legendary Greek philosopher was a dialogue between a few distinguished men who came to attend a banquet. In ancient Greece, traditionally, the post-meal session in a specially invited gathering was a banquet when drinking for pleasure was accompanied by music, dancing, recitals, speech-making and conversation. The wine-drinking participants would be in an altered mood, inclined to say things they would not say otherwise or elsewhere when sober. Socrates the eminent philosopher and Plato's teacher, nevertheless, was an exception as no one had ever seen him in a drunken state. (Reference 18)

The invitees were: Socrates; Phaedrus: an Athenian aristocrat associated with the inner circle of Socrates; Pausanius: the legal expert; Eryximachus: a physician; Aristophanes: the eminent comic playwright; Agathon: a tragic poet – the host of the banquet that celebrated the triumph of his first tragedy; Alcibiades: a prominent Athenian statesman, orator, and general.

Phaedrus had made a suggestion that they should all make a speech in praise of 'Eros', the God of 'love' and 'desire'. He opened the symposium by saying the 'Eros' was the oldest of gods – highlighting that, for humans, 'love' and 'desire' are basic needs.

Next, Pausanius contrasted common desire with a 'heavenly' love between an older man and a young lad (before the age when the adolescent's beard started to grow), in which the two exchange sexual pleasure while the older man imparts wisdom to the younger one. While this is virtuous love, Pausanius said that the love between an older man and a very young immature boy was forbidden as intelligence had not yet developed in the kid. He might not take this kind of 'love' in the proper spirit.

Eryximachus, the next speaker, suggested that 'Eros' encouraged 'sophrosyne' – a soundness of mind and character.

Aristophanes narrated a comic, fantastical story about how humans were one time two people conjoined, but as this was seen as threatening to the gods, Zeus – the god of sky and thunder, cut every human being into two halves like a fish is neatly cut into two equal halves, separating those from the spine bone. He spoke highly about the confidence, courage, and manliness in one half (the masculine characteristics) and praised the positive emotions such as love, affection, compassion, empathy, understanding and fellow-feeling (the feminine characteristics).

The next speaker, Agathon, saw 'Eros' as youthful, beautiful and wise, and as the source of all human virtues.

When Socrates's turn came, he related a story he was told by a wise woman called Diotima. According to her, 'Eros' was a spirit that mediated between humans and their objects of desire. 'Love' is the desire for things that are beautiful. It is practically expressed through either physical 'procreation' and 'propagation' or emotional-mental-spiritual 'creativity'.

Alcibiades crashed into the discussion, fully drunk, and said Socrates had no interest in physical pleasure. Agathon, the host, laid down next to Socrates much to Alcibiades's chagrin,

The party became wild and drunken, with the symposium coming to an end.

References

1. *Levon Helm* – Wikipedia.
2. *Pleasure Principle (Psychology)* – Wikipedia.
3. James Robinson Cooper, "Sanskrit – The Language of the Gods", 7th February 2017.
4. Alexander Moseley, "Philosophy of Love", *Internet Encyclopaedia of Philosophy*.
5. Joanne Lewsley, "How love blossoms between you and your child", *babycentre* (My Baby & Pregnancy Today)
6. HT Correspondent, New Delhi, "Newborn gets clicked with attached umbilical cord spelling out 'love'", *Hindustan Times*, 9th January 2016.
7. Richard Dawkins, *The Selfish Gene*, Oxford: Oxford University Press, 30th Anniversary Edition 2006.
8. *Parthenogenesis* – Wikipedia.
9. *Parthenogenesis and Its Types* – Video presentation on YouTube.
10. Abdelmonem Awad Hegazy, Aiman Ibraheem Al-Qtaitat and Raafat Awad Hegazy, "A new hypothesis may explain human parthenogenesis and ovarian teratoma: A review study", *International Journal of Reproductive Medicine*, Vol. 21, No. 4, April 2023, pp. 277-284.
11. Fr. John Whitney, SJ, "Umbilical Cord of Love", St. Ignatius Parish, 10th May 2023.
12. *Ramakrishna* – Wikipedia.
13. *Shengtai* – Wikipedia.
14. *Neidan* – Wikipedia.

    ('Neidan' or 'Internal Alchemy' is an array of esoteric doctrines and physical, mental and spiritual practices that Taoist initiates use to prolong life and create an immortal spiritual that would survive after death.)
15. Chinmoy Prasun Biswas, "Mysterious fathers in Mahabharata (Part One)", *daily sun*, 15th October, 2023.
16. Satya Chaitanya, "The Puzzle of Pandu", *Boloji*, 15th October 2023.
17. Rajib Shraban, *Mahakabyer Antarale Janma Rahasya (in Bengali)*, Kolkata: Lalmati Prakashan, 2023.
18. *Symposium (Plato)* – Wikipedia.

CHAPTER 2

Professor Albert Einstein on 'Love'

'Head' is on the top of our body, the 'survival outfit' – the digestive system and the 'reproductive outfit' the genitals and associated organs are located below. 'Heart' which represents 'love' is in the middle of these two regions. It is the mediator.

Professor Albert Einstein was a man of the 'Head'. He was also a ladies' man, active in the 'heart' region. There are umpteen references available regarding what his thoughts were regarding the physical sciences. We hardly come across what his thoughts were on 'love' – how his heart used to 'feel' about this emotion.

In the late 1980s, Lieserl, the daughter of the famous genius, donated 1,400 letters, written by Einstein, to the Hebrew University, with orders not to publish their contents until two decades after his death. This is one of them, for Lieserl Einstein.

> ......"When I proposed the theory of relativity, very few understood me, and what I will reveal now to transmit to mankind will also collide with the misunderstanding and prejudice in the world. I ask you to guard the letters as long as necessary, years, decades, until society is advanced enough to accept what I will explain below.
>
> There is an extremely powerful force that, so far, science has not found a formal explanation to. It is a force that includes and governs all others, and is even behind any phenomenon operating in the universe and has not yet been identified by us.
>
> *This universal force is LOVE.*
>
> When scientists looked for a unified theory of the universe they forgot the most powerful unseen force.
>
> *Love is Light, that enlightens those who give and receive it.*

Love is Gravity, because it makes some people feel attracted to others.

Love is Power, because it multiplies the best we have, and allows humanity not to be extinguished in their blind selfishness. Love unfolds and reveals.

For love, we live and die.
Love is God and God is love.

This force explains everything and gives meaning to life. This is the variable that we have ignored for too long, maybe because we are afraid of love because it is the only energy in the universe that man has not learned to drive at will.

To give visibility to love, I made a simple substitution in my most famous equation if instead of $E = mc^2$, we accept that the energy to heal the world can be obtained through love multiplied by the speed of light squared, we arrive at the conclusion that love is the most powerful force there is, because it has no limits. After the failure of humanity in the use and control of the other forces of the universe that have turned against us, it is urgent that we nourish ourselves with another kind of energy......

If we want our species to survive, if we are to find meaning in life, if we want to save the world and every sentient being that inhabits it, love is the one and only answer.

Perhaps we are not yet ready to make a bomb of love, a device powerful enough to entirely destroy the hate, selfishness and greed that devastate the planet.

However, each individual carries within them a small but powerful generator of love whose energy is waiting to be released.

When we learn to give and receive this universal energy, dear Lieserl, we will have affirmed that love conquers all, is able to transcend everything and anything, because love is the quintessence of life.

I deeply regret not having been able to express what is in my heart, which has quietly beaten for you all my life. Maybe it's too late to apologize, but as time is relative, I need to tell you that I love you and thanks to you I have reached the ultimate answer!"

Your Father Albert Einstein

I'm a little perplexed to get exposed to these thoughts of Albert Einstein (1879–1955) on 'love'. Perplexed because he himself had a chequered love life. He was not that fond of matrimony to begin with. He had a live-in relationship with his first wife Mileva Maric and had a child before they got married. However, he had been unfaithful to Mileva and eventually left her to marry his mistress, Elsa Einstein, who was also his cousin. After divorcing Mileva and marrying Elsa, he soon resumed having relations with numerous other women as well.

He had very strong views about monogamy. In a June 1953 letter, Einstein tried to console a female friend who had discovered that her husband was having an affair, by advising her that she should not take it personally.

"I am sure you know that most men (as well as quite a number of women) are not monogamously endowed by nature", he wrote according to a translation from the original German published decades later. "Nature will come through even stronger if convention and circumstances are putting resistances in the way of the individual."

Einstein seemed to prefer what we would call today 'free love'. He used to say: "one should do what one enjoys, and won't harm anyone else". He had extra-marital affairs with several women including his personal secretary Betty Neumann and a Berlin socialite Ethel Michanowski.

In a letter to Betty Neumann, he had even fantasized about having her live with him and his second wife Elsa in a big house; and, when Betty, his extra-marital lover dismissed the idea, he admitted that she had more appreciation "for the difficulties of the triangular geometry than I".

Einstein told the son of his best friend from college, Michelle Besso: "What I admire in your father is that, for his whole life, he stayed with only one woman. That is the project in which I grossly failed, twice."

His biographer, Walter Isaacson writes: "When confronted with the emotional needs of others, Einstein tended to retreat into the objectivity of his science".

Einstein had found his 'True Passion' in 'Physics' and not in love towards the opposite sex. (References 1 & 2)

References

1. Patrick J. Kiger, "Genius Einstein's Theory of Infidelity", *natgeotv.com/za/special.*
2. Walter Isaacson, *Genius: Einstein – His Life and Universe*, New York: Simon and Schuster, 2017.

CHAPTER 3

The Bower of the Better Halves Where Love Blossoms

A Live Case Study: 'Ginni Kunja'

For thirty-five long years until 2018, I used to roam about like a moving minstrel with my team in different corners of India and her neighbouring countries conducting workshops with the goal of turning 'Human Resource' into 'Human Capital'. Whenever I used to get a little breathing time, being a very active person, I did not laze about on my free days, I used to wake up early and go for long morning walks in and around the Lakes in South Kolkata.

As I was walking along the long stretch of Purna Das Road, suddenly my eyes got stuck at the name plate of a house. I had an utter surprise. The name of the house was 'Ginni Kunja' (in Bengali). The English translation would be 'The Bower of the Better Halves'. Very strange….. very unusual!! I must explore. The 'Seeking System Circuit' ('SSC') inside my brain got activated. (References 1, 2 & 3)

I did not wait. I rang the doorbell. The door was opened by a gentleman who was fat and round. Most respectfully he smiled at me and the smile carried a message: "May I help you Sir?" I said: "I'm very sorry to bother you so early in the morning. I'm very curious to know what is the background of naming your three-storeyed residential house "Ginni Kunja"? The man displayed the same sweet smile again and told me: "You're most welcome to come inside and have a cup of tea while I tell you the story." He took me in and offered me a seat in the living room; went inside for a couple of minutes, and came back – ready to narrate the story to me. One lady, very tall, slim and lanky with long upper and lower limbs and a face that was of the shape of an inverted triangle appeared in a couple of minutes with a steaming hot cup of tea and a plate full of assorted biscuits for me. The gentleman introduced himself as 'Samir' and the lady as his wife 'Sabita'. Quite a contrast in body morphology – husband was short and plump like an apple and the wife very tall and lean like the trunk of a tree.

Samir now started: "We are three brothers – all married, living with our wives. None of us have any kid. I am the youngest. I'm very well-matched with my wife. We are deeply in love with each other. I stay on the ground floor with my wife. The middle brother and his wife occupy the 1st floor. And the eldest brother and his wife are on the 2nd floor. We all live independently, having separate professions and separate kitchens. The house property is also not joint. Each floor had been bequeathed by our father separately to each brother before he passed away."

Samir now said: "Doctor, please enjoy another cup of tea, I'm going to call my other two brothers and their wives to get introduced to you." He used the intercom telephone to request his two elder brothers and their wives to come down; and meanwhile, Sabita came with another cup of steaming tea for me and some buttered toasts and a stuffed egg omelette for me!

I got introduced to the middle brother Soumen and his wife Sohini as they came in and what a coincidence! They were of the same height and totally athletic in body type with well-proportioned body segments. Soumen & Sohini both said together that they were so deeply in love with each other that they did not want to share the orange of love with anyone else – even their own child. Both were competition swimmers and water polo players. The top floor resident eldest brother Souren and his wife Seema, constitutionally, were just opposites of Samir and Sabita. Souren was six feet tall and lean whereas Seema was short, round-faced and her body was pear-shaped. Seema got a little emotional when to answer my question, she said: "We are so deeply in love with each other that I have never been to my parents' house ever since we got married fifteen years ago as I cannot stay a single moment without him. We both work in the same office and our work stations are placed side by side.

I was simply awe-struck with the three made-for-each-other couples, who are head-over-heels in love with their respective spouses.

My last question that I asked all of them being present together was: "Do you not have any illnesses?" Prompt came the answer: "Nothing very serious at all – only very trivial ones like cold, cough, headache, running nose and so on."

I could anticipate this answer as, if you're so deeply in love with your lover or spouse, you have mutual microbial harmony. (References 4, 5, 6 &7)

Love Acts as a Good Medicine Without Any Bad Side Effects!!

Loveology: A Sweet Song

I was exposed to 'Ginni Kunj' decades ago but the exposure was so unique that the episodic memory got stored permanently in one corner room of my mind. The 'key' phrase that was live in that corner room was the 'power of love'. It will flash on my mind's invisible screen whenever I was not otherwise preoccupied. I had saved it up for researching and writing on it during my winter years when time would be ripe for working out my life's 'love balance sheet' – the income and expenditure of love – whether the end result would be 'profit' or 'loss'. When the time came to be devoted to such a task, I thought it would be too personal and thus silly. Towards the end of my existence on this planet, I must share general instead of personal information with my readers so that they derive some benefit and apply some tips for planning the love-linked activities of their lives judiciously.

If someone would ask: what am I researching on, what would be my answer? Since I had coined terms like 'Bio-musicology' and 'BaulOlogy', what came readily to my mind was: 'LoveOlogy'. The next step for me was to search if the term was totally new and unused or it has been used already. Google helped me to discover a most unusual yet melodious music called 'Loveology' by Regina Spektor (References 8, 9 & 10).

The 'Loveology' song's lyric (Reference 11) goes like this:

"Oh, an incurable humanist you are; Oh, an incurable humanist you are; You are, you are you are;
Oh, an incurable humanist you are; Oh, an incurable humanist you-oo-oo-oo are; are, are, are;
You -oo-oo-oo are, are, are, are.

Let's go to the movies; I will hum you a song about nothing at all
Let's go to the movies; I will hum you a song about nothing at all;
Let's go to the movies, let's go to the movies; Nothing at all, nothing at all;
Nothing at all, nothing at all.

Oh, an incurable humanist you are; Oh, an incurable humanist you-oo-oo-oo are,
are, are, are, are; You-oo-oo-oo are, are, are, are.

Let's go to the movies; I will sing you a song about nothing at all;
Let's go to the movies; I will sing you a song about nothing at all;
Let's go to the movies, let's go to the movies; Nothing at all, nothing at all;
Nothing at all; nothing at all.

Sit down, class, open up your textbooks to page 42;
Porcupine-ology, antler-ology, Car-ology, bus-ology, train-ology, plane-ology;
Mama-ology, Papa-ology, you-ology, me-ology;
Love-ology, kiss-ology, stay-ology, please-ology;
Love-ology, love-ology, I'm sorry-ology, forgive me-ology;
Love-ology, love-ology, love-ology, love-ology.

Let's study, class, let's study, class, sit down
Love-ology, love-ology, I'm sorry-ology, forgive me-ology
Love-ology, love-ology, I'm sorry-ology, forgive me-ology.

Oh, an incurable humanist you are; Oh, an incurable humanist you are;
I'm sorry, forgive me, I'm sorry-ology; Forgive me, I'm sorry, forgive me-ology;
Forgive me, forgive me, forgive me-ology."

Regina Spektor (full name: Regina Ilyinichna Spektor, 1980-born in Moscow) is a Russian-born American singer-songwriter and pianist. She has composed the lyric of the song 'Loveology'. Her music is associated with the anti-folk scene centred on New York's East Village. (References 12 & 13)

She studied classical piano from the age of six. She was also exposed to the music of rock and roll bands such as The Beatles, Queen and The Moody Blues. The Spektor family left the Soviet Union in 1989 and after living for a while in Austria as well as Italy, got finally settled in the Bronx, New York. In N.Y., she got a firm grounding in piano; but since they could not bring their piano from Russia, she practiced in ingenious ways. She started writing songs from the age of 16 and had advanced musical training in USA as well as UK.

Loveology: A Book

Google also helped me to discover that there has already been a book written on Loveology. And who was the author? The author was one 'John Mark Comer'. (Reference 14) John Mark Comer is the founding pastor of Bridgetown Church in Portland, Oregon, a teacher and writer of multiple best-selling books.

Let us see what Comer has to say about 'love'.

It is stated in the 'Genesis 2v 15–25' that the Lord God took the lone man, Adam, in the Garden of Eden to work it and take care of it. And he commanded the man: "You are free to eat from any tree in the garden; but you must not eat from the tree of the knowledge of good and evil, for when you do it, you will certainly die".

The Lord God said: "It is not good for the man to be alone. I will make a helper suitable for him". So, now he created all the wild animals and all the birds in the sky. He brought them to the man to see what he would name them. The man gave names to all of them, but for him no suitable helper was found.

So, the Lord God caused the man to fall into a coma-like deep sleep; and, while he was sleeping, he took one of his main ribs and then closed up the place with flesh. Then the Lord God made a woman from the rib he had taken out of the man and brought her to Adam. Adam now said: 'She is made of bone and flesh from my bone and flesh; so, she can be called 'woman' for she was taken out of man."

That is why a man leaves his father and mother and is united to his wife and, in marriage, they become one flesh.

Today, everything we know (and we think we know) about love: the first encounter – the liking for and attraction towards each other – the courtship – the unbreakable companionship of elderlies and old couples (who, amazingly, look almost the same), it all started with two naked humans in a garden (or, shall we say 'a bower'?). According to pastor Comer, we are created to absorb the love of God into our bloodstream and then to share it with another human being. Once the man and woman are united, they are no longer two, but one. The whole idea is what God had joined together ('marriages are made in heaven', as the proverb goes), no one and no circumstance can separate. The joining material – the glue is 'LOVE'.

Comer's 'Loveology' is described as the 'Theology of Love'. It is an exploration of what the Bible has to say about the never-ending story of male and female.

Going by the Holy Bible, Comer concludes that God created man and woman as if they were inseparable conjoined twins and imbued in them love, romance and sexuality and bound them up in marriage (possibly there was no customary marriage in ancient pre-Bible era). In my treatment of 'love', I will make an attempt to look from several other angles including from those available from latest researches on the mind and the brain.

So, my 'LoveOlogy' will have a different outlook. You can note the difference! My 'LoveOlogy' has a capital 'O' between 'Love' and 'logy' which Comer's does not have.

A Special Note: Incidentally, in course of my internet search on 'logy's, I came across some most unexpected data. I discovered two reference materials with a 'logy' at the tail end.

1. ***Buy.ology***: *Truth and Lies About Why We Buy* by Martin Lindstrom, (Foreword by Paco Underhill), published by Crown Currency, 2010.
2. ***Click.ology:*** What Works in Online Shopping and How Your Business can use Consumer Psychology to Succeed.

Adultery is Sinful

Before I shift to my concepts, let me share with you a live case on how adulterous behaviour can bring family curses.

Tammy Comer is the wife of pastor John Mark Comer. Tammy and John Mark had been married for 20 years. The start of Tammy's health limitations came when her first son Jude was born. When Tammy was six, she was bitten by a tic and when she was eleven, she was hospitalised with Lyme disease. After Jude was born, the couple knew there was something grossly wrong with her body. She could hardly get out of bed to attend to her crying baby. She had always envisioned herself to be a very strong capable woman, so she was deeply disappointed at the limitations she was experiencing. Although she was diagnosed with post-Lyme polyneuropathy, after a few years she began having spasms in her eyes, face and mouth. She was also having bouts of shaking and lost substantial amount of vision.

For 15 years, Tammy lived with the progressive sickness. Then suddenly on 14th October 2020, her brother called to tell her that he had discovered something. He learned that their great-grandmother from Mexico City had lived with a man she never married. It was a case of infidelity. He was a diplomat working between Mexico and Cuba. They had eight children together but he had never mentioned that he had a wife whom he had put in a mental institution back home. When the man's wife came to know about her husband's misdeed, she blamed Tammy's great-grandmother and put a curse on her and her bloodline, declaring that every firstborn girl would suffer from a terrible illness, or have an early death. And, looking back on their family tree, it was discovered that every firstborn daughter on her father's side either died young or suffered from some severe illness. John Mark and Tammy could locate a godly man who had the power to break curses and he could manage to lift the curse and Tammy was totally cured for good. (Reference 15)

References

1. J. Panksepp, *Affective Neuroscience: The Foundation of Human and Animal Emotions*, Oxford: Oxford University Press, 2005.
2. Jason S. Wright and Jaak Panksepp, "An Evolutionary Framework to Understand Foraging, Wanting, and Drive", *Neuropsychoanalysis*, 2012, Vol. 14, No. 2, pp. 5–39.
3. "The seeking system" itmakessense.com.au
4. J.K. Kiecott-Glaser, L.D. Fisher, P. Ogrocki, J.C. Stout, C.E. Speicher, and R. Glaser, "Marital quality, marital disruption, and immune function", *Psychosomatic Medicine*, 1987, Vol. 49, Issue 1, pp. 13–34.
5. Janice K. Kiecolt-Glaser and Tamara L. Newton, "Marriage and health: his and her", *Psychological Bulletin*, Vol. 127, Issue 4, July 2001, p. 472.
6. Janice K. Kiecolt-Glaser and Stephanie J. Wilson, "Annual Review of Clinical Psychology", 18th May 2017, Vol. 13, pp. 421–443.
7. Janice K. Kiecolt-Glaser, Stephanie J. Wilson and Annelise Madison, "Marriage and Gut (Microbiome) Feelings: Tracing Novel Dyadic Pathways to Accelerated Aging", *Psychosomatic Medicine*, Oct. 2019, Vol. 8, No. 8, pp 704–710.
8. Regina Spektor – *Loveology* [Official Lyric Video – on YouTube].
9. *Loveology* – Regina Spektor with the National Symphony Orchestra, Live at The Kennedy Center (Video on YouTube)
10. Regina Spektor – *Loveology* live on Broadway, 2019-06-21 (Video on YouTube)
11. "Regina Spektor – Loveology" *GENIUS* (https://genius.com/Regina-spektor-loveology-lyrics)

12. "Regina Spektor" – *Vogue*
13. *Anti-folk* – Wikipedia.
14. John Mark Comer, *Loveology: God. Love. Marriage. Sex. And the Never-Ending Story of Male and Female*, New York: Zondervan (Harper Collins Christian Publishing), 2014.
15. "I had made peace with dying, but the thought of being crippled was harder", *woman alive*, 25th November, 2021.

CHAPTER 4

What Love Means

Love??

Before I proceed any further and delve deeper, let us try an understand what 'Love' is.

The word 'love' is very generic. A faithful Vaishnava says 'I love Lord Krishna', a faithful Muslim says 'I love Allah', a faithful Christian says: 'I love Jesus', a faithful Buddhist says: 'I love Buddha'. The same faithful person may tell his girlfriend or wife: 'I love you sweetheart'. The same faithful person may say at the breakfast table: 'I love coffee better than tea'. The word 'love' moves from the 'post-human' ('God' or 'God's apostle or 'Prophet') plane to 'human' and also the 'material' or 'object' plane. Its spectrum is broad.

That love's spectrum is really broad when we note the following seven types of love:

Love between a man and a woman
Love between the pet-owner and the pet
Love between a parent and a child
Love between a friend and a friend
Love between a guru and his disciple
Love between a teacher and a student
Love between a devotee and God

The next thing to note is that 'love' can be a 'noun' – it can also be a 'verb'. 'Love' as a 'noun' is an emotion – it is a feeling of affection. 'Love' as a 'verb' signifies 'action' as in the phrase 'falling in love' or 'falling out of love'. When 'love' is 'noun', you are in the passenger's seat. When love is 'verb', you are in the driver's seat – at the wheel. When 'love' is 'noun' you are the recipient, you are the taker – earning something. When 'love' is 'verb', you are the giver – spending or losing something.

To classify 'love' into different categories, you have to use adjectives: examples are – romantic love, erotic love, affectionate love, familiar love, playful love, parental love, obsessive love, enduring love, divine love, self-love, selfless love, and so on. In proposing this classification, I have taken the help of ancient Greek 'Theory of Love'. (Reference 1)

From pastor John Mark Comer, an exponent of the sacred text, 'Bible', I've learnt the three different connotations of the word 'love' as prevalent in the Hebrew language. (Reference 2)

The first connotation of 'love' in Hebrew is 'Raya' which means a 'friend' or a 'companion'.

The second connotation is 'Dod' which means 'intimate love' as expressed in a Jewish poem:

> *"Let him kiss me with the kisses of his mouth – for his love (Dod) is more delightful than wine".*

The third connotation is 'Ahava' – the deepest form of love – the love that goes down to the soul. It is very well-expressed in the following stanza of a Jewish poem:

> *"Place me like a seal over your heart,*
> *like a seal on your hand;*
> *for love ('ahava') is as strong as death,*
> *its jealousy unyielding as the grave,*
> *It burns like blazing fire,*
> *like a mighty flame.*
> *Many waters cannot quench love ('ahava')*
> *rivers cannot sweep it away*
> *If one were to give*
> *all the wealth of one's house for love ('ahava')*
> *it would be utterly scorned."*

'Ahava' is strong, solid, unbreakable. 'Dod' is weak – it can break, it can go, it can be swept away. 'Ahava' stands for 'commitment'.

Love & Invisible Synchronies?

Young Martha McClintock, while she was a student of psychology, had published a paper in 'Nature' (1971) which said that women, who begin living together in close proximity, experience their 'menstrual cycle' onsets becoming more synchronised together in time than when previously living apart. She had published her first study which had covered women living together in dormitories at Wellesley College in Massachusetts, USA. McClintock's 'menstrual synchrony' phenomenon, known as 'McClintock Effect' or 'Wellesley Effect' had hypothesized that body pheromone could cause such an effect. 'Pheromones' are substances which are secreted outside the body of an individual and received by a second individual, who may be attracted or distracted by its scent. However, other mechanisms have also been proposed, most prominently synchronizing with lunar phases. (References 3 & 4)

Although controversial, McClintock might have had a point as we find other such invisible synchronies, and/or forces or pulls of attraction, present amongst couples. Let me cite one example here. Taking the context of male-female partnerships, evolutionary theorists have suggested that when women are most fertile, they become more interested in 'manly' men with greater genetic fitness (that is, genes that promote health and physical attractiveness) – and, indeed, some research found support to this idea. (Reference 5). In other words, when women are most likely to conceive, they are thought to become more attuned to partners who would offer the most genetic benefits to their children. Nevertheless, I'm not too sure whether this is applicable when the lovers are attracted towards each other on the physical plane and not on the platonic plane like in my "Ginni Kunja" case study where the moonstruck couples had never thought of having kids. I don't suppose they were beyond plain and simple physical pulls.

I've, from my own observations, classified 'male-female partnership' which I call 'mateship' into the following categories. The very first one is, of course, 'Physical Mateship' based essentially on the body factor where both are physically attracted towards each other, My second one is the 'Energetic Mateship' where both have abundant energy for as much togetherness they want to enjoy. My third one is the 'Heart Mateship' where the relationship is essentially romantic. The fourth one is the 'Brain Mateship' where the cause of attraction is: mutual intellectuality. The fifth and the last one is 'Soul Mateship' where the binding factor is the spirit. Such mateships, I suppose, would bring 'microbial synchronies'.

Now, what do I mean by 'microbial synchrony' in the case of lovelorn couples? Couples influence each other's mental and physical health. One main root cause, which is invisible, is their near identical microbiomes. Recent studies have shown that the couple's intestinal microbial communities – or gut microbiotas and health behaviours are more similar to each other than those of unrelated partners, providing common pathways for shared disease risks. (References 6 & 7).

Organisms that dwell on the skin are known as commensal organisms. They settle on the skin through contact with air, clothes, and others, or through touch. We build immunity against them, which is why there is no manifestation of infections. Couples living together share these microbes and build immunity as they are in frequent contact with each other. A third person may be harmed by these microbes. Couples tend to harbour similar levels of microbial diversity. With couples, there is continuous contact on the same surfaces, which leads to similar microbes being found in them. While it is often said that couples deeply in love start to look alike over time, new research suggests their skin bacteria may do the same. (References 8 & 9)

Diversity in a person's microbiome – whether in the gut or on the skin, is healthy. By microbial diversity, I do not necessarily mean a balanced mix of all kinds of good bacteria. I mean a mixture of good and bad bacteria both. Good bacteria keep the bad ones in check. A lack of such diversity in the gut's microbial community has been linked to increased risks of certain conditions related to metabolism and immune function – including obesity, type 1 diabetes, and asthma. (Reference 10)

References

1. Mateo, "8 Different Types of Love According to the Ancient Greeks", *lonerwolf*, 28th January, 2023.
2. John Mark Comer: Loveology Video Bible Study Session 1 – YouTube.
3. M.K. McClintock, "Menstrual Synchrony and Suppression", *Nature*, 1971, Vol. 229, No. 5282, pp. 244–5.
4. Amy J. Harris and Virginia J. Vitzthum, "Darwin's Legacy: An Evolutionary View of Women's Reproductive and Sexual Functioning", *Journal of Sex Research*, 2013, Vol. 50. Issue 3-4, pp. 207–46.
5. S.M. Cantu *et al.*, "Fertile and selectivity flirty: Women's behaviour towards men changes across the ovulatory cycle", *Psychological Science*, 2014, Vol. 25, No. 2, pp. 431–438.
6. D. Rothschild *et al.*, "Environment dominates over host genetics in shaping gut microbiota", *Nature*, 2018, Vol. 555, pp. 210–5.
7. J.K. Kiecolt-Glaser and S. Wilson, "Lovesick: How couples' relationships influence health", *Annual Review of Clinical Psychology*, 2017, Vo. 13, pp. 421–43.
8. Indulekha Arakkal, "Couples share not just love, but bacteria too", *Deccan Chronicle*, 28th July 2017.
9. "Your partner could affect your microbiome, study says", *Medical News Today*, 22nd December 2022.
10. "Couples end up sharing the same bacteria", *news24/Life*, 31st July, 2017.

CHAPTER 5

The Molecule of Love

At the Site of a Wedding

Can 'love' be measured? Latest biomedical sciences say: "Yes! Because, there is a molecule of 'love'". Let us see what that molecule is.

I had introduced you to three moonstruck couples living in a house on Purna Das Road in South Kolkata. While I was a student, India Tobacco Company (presently ITC Ltd.) used to run an annual competition for married couples. The competition was called 'Made for Each Other' contest. I have no idea whether one of the several criteria that the contestant couples had to satisfy was the presence of 'True Love' between them. Now, I will take you to the beautiful countryside of Devon in England where a Christian wedding is in progress at Huntsham Court, a Victorian Manor House which has a church adjacent to it.

Dr Paul Zak (Reference 1), the father of the 'love molecule' 'Oxytocin' ('O'), had flown from California with all his accessories for drawing blood samples from the bride, the groom, their parents and other close kin who had together assembled to participate in the family's social event.

Blood samples were drawn before and after the ceremony and there was a clear indication of a rise in the level of 'O' in most of the cases, signifying the development of a well-bonded relationship in the people present.

'Oxytocin' ('O') is a small molecule (or, 'peptide'*) that serves as a neuro-transmitter sending signals within the brain from one neuron

---

* *'Peptides' are short chains of amino acids bound by peptide chains.*

to another. It also functions as a hormone carrying messages through the bloodstream to different organs, skin, muscles, and other tissues. In 1906, Sir Henry Dale (1875–1968), the 1936 Physiology/Medicine Nobel Laureate (Reference 2) first identified 'O' in the brain's pituitary gland. He combined the Greek words for 'quick' and 'childbirth' to name the neurochemical as 'Oxytocin'.

Your brain's 'hypothalamus' that controls functions like blood pressure, heart rate, body temperature and digestion makes 'O', but your posterior 'pituitary gland' located below the 'hypothalamus' stores and releases it into your bloodstream. (Reference 3)

Obstetricians and gynaecologists were familiar with the function of the molecule since it controlled the onset of labour and the flow of milk for breast-feeding. Medical scientists and researchers were completely in darkness as to whether the chemical had any other functions.

Gradually, over the years, it became known the 'O' was responsible for a well-bonded relationship-building between the mother and the child (for the bonding between the father and the child & its mother, the more aggressive & protective chemical 'Vasopressin' is responsible), between 'moonstruck' lovers and couples – before, during and after marriage, between two intimate friends, and amongst a well-knit work team in any context including business and industrial organisations. Paul Zak, being an industrial & business economist by training and practice had a lot of contribution to brand 'O', through his research in industry, as the 'Trust Molecule'. Without mutual trust and faith in each other between the team members, the team cannot give the best quantity and quality of output at the least cost. (References 4, 5 & 6).

One of the building blocks of LOVE is 'trust'. Unless you trust someone truly, how can you love him or her? A normal delivery child trusts her mother, most naturally, as while being pulled out of the delivery canal she got bathed in 'O'. (Whether a C-section child will have the same amount of trust for her mother is doubtful as she does not get bathed in 'O'). While being breast-fed, the child and the mother both earn 'O' which helps also in lactation (Whether an artificially fed infant will have the same level of 'O' is again doubtful).

'O' is essentially a chemical for strong inter-personal relationship. It is thus a 'must' for a well-bonded, sustained marital partnership. The tightening and loosening of the bond would reflect in the ups and downs in the level of 'O' in the bloodstream in both the partners if both are affected, otherwise, it could in either of them and vice versa.

For addiction to anything, 'O' is also responsible. If it is addiction to one's 'True Passion', then it is an ideal case and an excellent proposition, but if it is to a substance of abuse (like nicotine, marijuana or cannabis) or to an activity of abuse (such as overuse of sex), then it is too bad and certainly harmful. 'O' deprivation leads to anxiety and depression like it happens when the person you loved most has passed away, or your most beloved is physically located at a distance from you, as it happens now-a-days when a simple & plain Facebook friendship turns into courtship and then marriage. 'O' has many other colourful features. I will familiarise you with that rainbow slowly and gradually.

Love in the Rodent World

From the beautiful countryside of England's pretty Devonshire, let us move to the prairies of North America. Prairies are enormously vast stretches of grasslands where it is grass, grass and only grass. There are no trees or bushes which are the habitats for predating birds and animals. Prairies are thus a very safe place for a very special member of the rodent species to make their home. These are the 'Prairie Voles'. Their speciality is that they are monogamous and enjoy the same male-female partnership throughout their lives. This is in contrast with the 'Meadow Voles' who live in the meadows. A prairie is always semi-arid and usually denotes a natural landform. Meadows could be grassy patches in the woods, which are quite often cultivated. Promiscuity is very much present amongst the 'Meadow Voles' and they often change their partners to suit their tastes.

In a systematic study, meadow voles were found to be more affiliative and more interactive with strangers; whereas prairie voles exhibited partner preferences indicating that selective peer preferences are the norm in prairie voles, maintained in part by aggression toward unfamiliar individuals, as in mate partnerships. In contrast, social tolerance was an important feature of meadow vole peer affiliation. Prairie voles displayed less anxious behaviour than the meadow voles, possibly as they enjoyed a tight pair bonding. (Reference 7)

Larry Young, a researcher at Atlanta's Yerkes National Primate Research Center, has been studying voles for nearly two decades. (Reference 8) Young and his colleagues see the voles as the key to understanding some of humankind's most tender and mysterious impulses: why we care for our partners, being a main one amongst those.

Most notable prairie voles are monogamous forming bonds that last very long after mating, nearly permanent (often for the short life that these tiny creatures have). Male and female come together, male courts the female, by adopting alluring strategies, so that she becomes sexually highly charged and receptive. Then they mate for an unusually long time; and, remain bonded together even for hours, days and weeks after such mating. The males stick around to raise the resulting offspring if the females become pregnant. The female clearly expects such fatherly behaviour from the male and when the partner dies, voles experience grief just like humans.

Young teamed up with Sue Carter, an University of Illinois researcher and they started experimenting with the 'love molecule' 'Oxytocin' ('O'). When a female prairie vole received an 'O' injection in her brain, she huddled with her partner more and formed stronger bonds, 'Vasopressin' ('V'), the hormone related to 'territoriality', was found to promote pair-bonding in males. (References 9, 10 & 11)

These researchers concluded that if the chemicals responsible for maternal behaviour in females and territoriality in the males were released during the sexual act, they would foster this strong male-female partnership bond. Subsequent studies showed that unlike the bondless meadow voles, prairie voles have 'O' and 'V' receptors in areas of their brains associated with reward and addiction.

Have you not noticed that the word 'vole' is, after all, an anagram for 'love'?

Love between Pets & Their Owners

Love between pets and their owners is a well-known fact. I've been a pet-lover right from my childhood and, at my instance, my parents kept pets, especially dogs, throughout my school, college and university days in Calcutta. Even when I left for Britain for my graduate studies, we had a big Alsatian by the name of 'Leo' and I missed him while at the University in Glasgow. Once when I had come home on vacation and I did not find Leo around – on enquiry, my mom told me that Leo had passed away within two months after I'd left for abroad. Possibly, he was grief-struck not finding me around much though it had sniffed at every nook and corner of our big house trying to find me out.

I was so much sad that I decided not to keep any pet any more, but I was compelled to keep some birds as me and my team members started doing research on the behaviour of birds – to what extent they are loyal to their keepers. Loyalty comes out of a feeling of trust and I had not known about the 'trust molecule' 'Oxytocin' ('O') then. We had a few pigeons and a parrot as pets; and, most amazingly, even if we left the doors of their cages open they will come out, fly here and there for a little while and then get back into their little homes. Was it their 'territorial instinct' that was active or the 'O' released from their brain's 'Pituitary Glands', I'm not sure still.

My daughter Ishita got married to Anand Krishnan and the wedding ceremony took place in the spacious backyard of our house. After they left for the US, suddenly one fine morning we found a stray dog – a female one, entered into our backyard and came straight up on the balcony adjacent to the garden. Then, in course of the next few days, she entered into our living room. We tried to drive her out, but she just wouldn't leave. So, we started calling her 'Lucy' and she would readily respond to that name. She became old in a few years' time and had a massive heart attack on one stormy evening. The streets were so much water-logged that we had to pay extra money to a taxi and the driver's helper to take deceased Lucy to the canine graveyard in the outskirt of the city and bury her there. We had given away all our bird pets to our friends and, as I was hungry for a pet, one of my students brought for us a snow-white male puppy – a little English terrier. We named her 'Joy' and started taking good care of him. He got used to go out of the house for his toilets but suddenly one evening once he went out, he never came back. Possibly, he was stolen as there was a sudden power cut for an hour or so. We looked for him over the next few days in the neighbourhood, but in vain.

All these memories about our pets came as flashbacks as I read a headline in the Times of India, Kolkata edition of 4th September 2023, which read as: "Loyal strays guard elderly Behala couple, accompany them to hospitals, shops and bank." (Reference 12) I read the amazing case study through in one go. Badal & Eva Barua, a couple in their 70's, residing in the Behala area of Kolkata go out of their house every day for buying provisions, medicine & other stuff. Sometimes, they go to their bank, or to a hospital for check-up – Eva on an old wheelchair and Badal pushing her. The most uniquely interesting part of the case study is that in front of them, three dogs trotted and stopped to keep pace with the elderly couple. For two years now, the dogs have been accompanying them to the bank, hospital, drug stores, and grocery shops. When Badal leaves Eva on the wheelchair and goes in to get something, the dogs patiently wait and guard Eva. Their son has abandoned the parents, but with the dogs around, they make a complete family and the absence of a loving & caring son is never felt. Eva had a brain stroke in 2021 that partially confined her to the wheelchair. Recently, she had a head injury from a fall and while Badal took her to the "Outpatients' Dept." in the local hospital, the dogs guarded her wheelchair as they went in leaving it outside. The dogs will growl if you went near the wheelchair, an ambulance driver reported.

These three dogs who are Badal & Eva's care-givers are not pets – they are just local street dogs, strays. They reminded me of 'Lucy' who was a local stray and how she became our pet. I recalled, whenever any outside visitor – a student or a research scholar would come to visit me, she will lie down at my feet guarding me and if anyone would try to touch my feet to get my blessings, she will charge and bite – what a great protector of her master she was!! My eyes get wet when I recall those happy days of my life with my pets! Even with Joy, whenever

I would come back after some work outside home and ring the door bell, when the door was opened, he will jump on me and greet me back home, as if she was missing me all the while I was away. The great Cambridge parapsychology scholar Prof. Rupert Sheldrake (born 1942) has developed his 'Theory of Morphic Resonance' based on such inexplicable phenomena (References 13, 14 & 15).

I suggest, you also read "AC rooms, gym, handlers' accommodation: ER's canine squad set for lifestyle upgrade" (Reference 16). This press release reports that a lifestyle change is in order for the Eastern Railway sniffer dog squad. The Railway Authorities have invited bids for two plush kennels as part of a pilot project to upgrade the homes of its canine squad – with AC rooms, a modern gym, and a sprawling courtyard. The kennels will also be equipped to house handlers day and night, like USA's K9 squads who have resident handlers to develop 'Oxytocin'-based bonding. Very interesting indeed!!

References

1. Paul J. Zak, *The Moral Molecule: How Trust Works*, New York: PLUME (The Penguin Group), 2012.
2. *Sir Henry Dale* – Wikipedia.
3. "Oxytocin" – *Cleveland Clinic.*
4. Paul Z. Zak, "The neurobiology of trust", *Scientific American*, June 2008, pp. 88–95.
5. Paul J. Zak, R. Kurzban and W.T. Matzner, "The neurobiology of trust", *Annals of the New York Academy of Sciences*, 2004, Vol. 1032, pp. 522–27.
6. Paul J. Zak, R. Kurzban and W.T. Matzner, "Oxytocin is associated with human trustworthiness", *Hormones and Behaviour*, 2005, Vol. 48, pp. 522–27.
7. S. Lee Nicole *et al.*, "Affiliation, Aggression, and Selectivity of Peer Relationships in Meadow and Prairie Voles", *Frontiers of Behavioural Neurosciences*, Vol. 13, 19th March 2019.
8. Abigail Tucker, "What Can Rodents Tell Us About Why Humans Love?" *Smithsonian Magazine*, February, 2014.

9. Alex Dessay, "The biology of 'love': Lessons from prairie voles", *Open Access Government*, 14th February 2020.
10. Steven Phelps *et al*, "Monogamous Prairie Voles Reveal the Neurobiology of Love", *Scientific American*, 1st February 2023.
11. Sophie Fessi, PhD, "It's the Power of Love – in Voles", *Dana Foundation*, 9th February 2021.
12. Debayan Tewari, "Loyal strays guard elderly Behala couple, accompany them to hosp, shops and bank", *Times of India*, Kolkata ed. 4th September 2023, p. 4.
13, "*Rupert Sheldrake*" – Wikipedia.
14. Rupert Sheldrake, *Morphic Resonance: The Nature of Formative Causation*, New York: Park Street Press, 2009.
15. Rupert Sheldrake. *Dogs That Know When Their Owners Are Coming Home*, London: Arrow Books, 2011.
16. Ajanta Chakraborty, "AC Rooms, gym, handlers' accommodation, ER's canine squad set for lifestyle upgrade", *Times of India*, Kolkata, 4th September 2023, p. 2.

CHAPTER 6

Love Agents that You Cannot See

Invisible Love

AD is a middle-aged sitar player. He lives in Howrah, adjacent to the Kolkata metro city with his family in his ancestral home. He and his wife came to me, nearly two decades ago, for consultation regarding their only son who is brain retarded since birth. They attended one of my workshops on parenting of retarded kids and have kept in touch ever since.

AD had his training in sitar from one of the most distinguished and favourite disciples of Pt. Ravi Shankar, but because of his family problem, he does not go much for stage concerts outside Kolkata and restricts himself to teaching students at home as well as a few in other parts of the country and overseas, on-line.

During the Covid pandemic, he had to restrict his teaching to the on-line mode only but since many of his school-going students did not have digital back-up, his income dwindled. His income from other assignments like playing in dramas, Bengali movies and local functions also had stopped. He was running his family by whatever little savings he had and also from the rent by letting out a large portion of his ancestral house which badly needed proper maintenance and renovation.

Suddenly, one day, he rang me up and what he told me I just couldn't believe!!

He said: "Sir, I was so depressed because of the economic problems that I decided to put an end to my life. So, I locked myself into my music room and when I was just about to consume an overdose of sleeping pills, I could hear the whisper of my most favourite sitar which was as if in tears and saying – we are partners, you and I are inseparable……we cannot exist one without the other …..what shall I do, where shall I go if you kill yourself?" AD said: "I immediately threw away the balance pills and rushed to embrace my favourite instrument whom I had given the name 'Dil Bahar'. It had been gifted to me by my Guru when he was in his deathbed waiting for his end suffering from cirrhosis of liver ......he was as alcoholic as everyone knows!"

AD continued: "Can you tell me Sir what had happened that I suddenly reversed my decision from 'dying' to 'living'?"

It was quite late in the night so I did not prolong our conversation. I rang him up the next day and told him that your favourite sitar 'Dil Bahar' carried your learned Guru's microbes and as you being his Gurukul disciple had shared his microbes, 'Dil Bahar's surface microbes found you compatible as their new host. You and your instrument had vibed very well. It was an 'Oxytocin'-based bonding. Now, if you had ended your life without handing over 'Dil Bahar' to your most favourite disciple, the instrument's musical quality would have been totally lost so the instrument's microbes felt insecure and sent you their tensed feelings through vibrations, which you could feel and that changed your mind!"

AD exclaimed: "That is fantastic Sir! I consulted my medical doctor friend who is a renowned physician, but he couldn't explain! He only scolded me and told me only stupid fools end their lives impulsively out of frustration!"

The chair at my work station carries my microbes....the laptop which I'm using to type out this piece carries my microbes. I share my microbes with everything I use, I touch. Whenever somebody touches my feet and I touch her/his head to give blessings, the two of us have exchange of microbes. The same thing happens when I hug someone.

Love involves exchange of microbes from one to another if there is a bonded relationship between the two; otherwise not!! That love is not visible!! (References 1, 2, 3, 4, 5 & 6)

The Scent of Love

I remember having watched a fabulous movie, some months ago, where Al Pacino acted in the role of a cranky old retired army lieutenant colonel who had lost both his eyes in the battlefield. His eyesight having gone, his power of smell emerged to compensate the loss. He used to predict the nature of women from their body scents, natural as well as artificial obtained from perfumes and body deodorants. Al Pacino got both the Academy and the Golden Globe Awards for Best Actor in a Leading Role in 1993. (Reference 7)

The magic scent of love is not some special perfume that the body emits spontaneously, but it is the aromatic effluence of the immune system of human physiology. Grand old Charles Darwin had a few thought waves on this issue during his time. He came to believe that natural selection designed animals to produce only two types of body odour – one is totally 'defensive' like in the case of a skunk to evoke an 'away' response; while the other was meant for demarcation of one's own territory and for attracting mates into that territory; example of the latter is the musk deer. That mammals like cats, dogs, tigers, lions, bears, wolves and hyenas engage in evaluative sniffing during courtship provides clue that scent is the chemical equivalent of a peacock's plumage or the cuckoo's song which essentially are nature's gift for attracting suitors. (Reference 8)

Subsequently, several animal pheromones were identified, but none for human beings. 19th century's leading scientists noted that the primates' social olfactory (that is, related to the power of smell) abilities got almost diminished compared to those of other mammals. Monkeys, apes, and humans represented, they observed, the ascending steps from arboreal sniffers to sight-oriented walkers.

Recent discoveries, however, disclaim the earlier notion that our little dependence on smelling power is a wrong understanding. The most concentrated scent glands of the human body are located in the hands and on the face, apart from a third location – besides the ears; and these occur around all the body's openings including eyelids, ears, nostrils, lips, and nipples. The secretion from these glands kills harmful microorganisms and contain fats to keep the skin supple and waterproof. Human sweat, urine, breath, saliva, breast milk, skin oils, and sexual secretions all contain scent-communicating chemical compounds.

Apocrine glands develop in the hairy areas of the body like the scalp, armpits and groin. These glands produce viscous, lipid-rich sweat, which is also comprised of proteins, sugars, and ammonia. These are generally regarded as scent glands involved in the production of 'pheromones' (contributing to 'body odour'). Most interestingly, they are functional only after puberty, when we begin searching for mates. (References 9 & 10). Women have a strong favourable reaction to the smell of apocrine glandular secretion when they are most likely to conceive. They get attracted towards those men whose body scents are different from their own. Hence, any given man's scent could be pleasingly alluring to one woman, yet an offensive turnoff to another. (References 11 & 12)

Smell acts directly on the most ancient part of the brain – the 'limbic system' – the department dealing with instincts, emotions, and unconscious, spontaneous perceptions. In this part of the brain, our motivations and desires are formed.

A set of our genes determine what smell we emit from our body. Because of each person's unique gene ownership, each of us have a distinctive body scent, which is made up of thousands of scent molecules that we exude from every part of our skin. Use of scented soaps, deodorants, body oils, body sprays, talcum powder and flavoured shampoos destroy the natural body scent which results in the loss of a primitive instinctive power – the power to attract a compatible partner who will be attached to an individual's body scent and would like to develop a well-bonded partnership. Today, with all the artificial stuff that we use change our natural body scent, although grossly we are close, subtly we are very much distant from each other. This is one of the hidden reasons for the gradual deterioration in the tightness in most of the marital relationships today.

True love is literally present in our vicinity in the air. We only have to take advantage of it, grasp it by giving up the habit of using fragrant toiletries and cosmetics. Up to the use of the right brand of toothpaste for bad breath management is okay. Beyond that leave it to Mother Nature for love-making!!

The Love Hug

An Australian (who used the pseudonym 'Juan Mann') flew back home from London to Sydney and was too heart-broken to find that there was no one to greet him. He had a conviction that human warmth was something that we needed most to feel cared for and happy, he made a cardboard cut-out sign saying 'Free Hugs', stood at one of the busiest intersections in Sydney with this display. Initially, the pedestrians took note of it but avoided contact; within a short while, one person broke the ice to accept Juan's hugs – soon it was followed by others and eventually it went viral to turn into a movement. Juan Mann became famous to get invited to the Oprah Winfrey Show. 'Love Hug' produces 'Oxytocin' ('O'). (Reference 13)

Have you heard of the 'Hugging Saint' Amma? Mata Amritanandamayi (known as 'Amma') is an Indian Hindu spiritual leader and guru, who is revered as the 'Hugging Saint' by her devotees & followers. Born to a family of lower-caste Malayali fishermen in Kerala in 1953, she is the chancellor of multi-campus research university 'Amrita Vishwa Vidyapeetham'. She has authored many books, including "Compassion: the Only Way to Peace" & "The Awakening of Universal Motherhood". As a part of her daily chores, Amritanandamayi collected food scraps from neighbours for her family's cows and goats, through which she was exposed to the intense poverty and suffering of the people in her neighbourhood. She would bring these people food and clothing from her own home. She used be scolded and punished by the elders in her family for her noble act. This did not dissuade her from how she had been serving people. In addition to helping people with food and clothes, she started embracing them spontaneously from the core of her heart to comfort them and provide some solace to the suffering hundreds. To quote her own words: "I don't see if it is a man or a woman. I don't see anyone different from my own self. A continuous stream of love flows from me to all of creation. This is my inborn nature. The duty of a doctor to treat patients. In the same way, my duty is to console those who are suffering." (References 14 & 15). Eventually, at the behest of the spiritual seekers who used to follow her, the 'Mata Amritanandamayi Math' ('MAM'), a worldwide foundation, was set up. In 1987, at the request of her devotees, she began to conduct programmes in countries throughout the world.

Her way of giving 'darshana' is hugging people. She says: "People used to come and tell me their troubles. They would cry and I would wipe their tears. When they fell weeping into my lap, I used to hug them. Then the next person too wanted it. And so the habit picked up." The 'Hugging Saint" has embraced more than around 35 million people throughout the world for over 30 years. (References 16 & 17). She believes the hugging gesture can help to awaken dormant spiritual energy within her followers. Does helping to release 'Oxytocin' ('O') from brain's 'Pituitary Glands' help to awaken the spiritual energy that is dormant within us? By 'spiritual energy' does she mean 'energy' bathed in compassion-warmth-understanding-and-trust? Does 'Amma's hugging represent the love that a loving mother pours out to her children? The hugging gesture possibly sends a message through the ribs, to the vagus nerve which is rich in 'Oxytocin' ('O') receptors. This innervates the gut [as the vagus nerve represents the 'Gut-Brain Axis' ('GBA')] and causes people to relax and feel safe. (Reference 18)

We certainly have a lesson to learn as most of us in today's competitive & combative environment, deprive our spouses and, as parents deprive our kids of all ages, of the spiritual energy of the 'Hugging Effect' due to pre-occupation with our success-oriented materialistic pursuits which haunt us even in our dreams.

Different Love Chemicals

Let me take you into the time machine and let us ride to move fast backward to the year 1519. This was the year of the first visit of the Spanish explorer Hernan Cortes to Mexico. Cortes found, much to his liking there, in particular the Aztec princess Dona Marina. His infatuation for her was reinforced because the princess introduced Cortes to a drink made from the pods of a tree which the Aztecs called 'chocolatl' or 'food for the gods'. The concoction was also laced with dried chili peppers as Donna Marina said would stimulate amorous adventures. (Reference 19)

Cortes must have been impressed by the effects because, on his return to Spain, he presented Emperor Charles V with a sample of cocoa, as we call the substance today. Within a few years, the Europeans were indulging in chocolate and singing its praises. However, the nuns were forbidden to partake of chocolate's pleasures because of the potential consequences.

Chocolate, it was found, contains 'Phenylethylamine' ('PEA') – an amphetamine-like substance that has been labelled the 'chemical of love'. Thus, there is a love-chocolate connection!! People in love have been found to have higher level of 'PEA' in their brain as surmised from the fact that their urine is richer in a metabolite of this compound. In other words, lovelorn people's urine quality is different from that of those who are not in love.

'Sauerkraut' is finely cut raw cabbage that has been fermented by various lactic acid bacteria. It has a long shelf life and can be taken as a pickle in your diet. 'Sauerkraut' has a high level of 'PEA'. So, if you want to be more attractive to your partner, take a generous help of 'Sauerkraut' at dinner time or have some chocolate or drink some cocoa after dinner, before going to bed. (Reference 20)

Passionate love is when sexual drive is involved. Researchers scanned people's brains in an fMRI scanner while they looked at photographs of either strangers or people they were in love with. In the latter case, the 'Caudate Nucleus' was activated in the brain, it was observed. This brain area has receptors for 'Dopamine' ('D') – the molecule that causes feelings of exhilaration, gives people extra energy (as if the flow of energy appears suddenly out of the blue), focuses their attention, and makes them hungry for rewards. (Reference 21). Once you get the taste of 'D', you want it more and more; it is so addictive. (Reference 22)

'PEA' and 'D' together provide enough energy and reason to a person to stay up all night and talk to the person to whom she/he is attracted. 'D' can be obtained from protein-rich foods: for vegetarians – from dairy products, soybean, and legumes (like lentils, gram, beans) – for non-vegetarians – from eggs, turkey and beef. (Reference 23)

The third molecule in both companionship and passionate love is 'Oxytocin' ('O'). (Reference 24) Unlike 'PEA' and 'D', 'O' is released in close non-romantic relationships like in family, friendships, and other types of love (like between the pets and their owners). 'O' is the molecule responsible for close psychological connection rather than a physical one. Hugging, care-giving to a patient, breast-feeding, nursing a baby, and orgasm – all release 'O'. It produces 'bonding' regardless of the type of relationship. 'O' helps in feeling for and understanding others.

'Serotonin' ('S') is another important neurotransmitter that matters in the regulation of mood, sleep, and a few other brain processes. People who are madly in love and obsessed & compulsive in passionate love show patterns similar to the patients of 'Obsessive Compulsive Disorder' ('OCD') who have problems with 'S'. In a study in Italy, the blood test confirmed that those passionately in love and those with 'OCD' showed similar 'S' patterns – that is 40 percent less than the group that was neither in love, nor had OCD.

References

1. Sharon Gil *et al.*, "Commensal Bacteria Play a Role in Mating Preferences of Drosophila Melanogaster," *Proceedings of the National Academy of Sciences of the United States of America*, Vol. 107, No. 46, 16th November 2010, pp. 20051–56.
2. Sharon Gil *et al.*, "Symbiotic Bacteria Are Responsible for Diet-Induced Mating Preference in Drosophila Melanogaster, Providing Support for the Hologenome Concept of Evolution", *Gut Microbes*, Vol. 2, No. 3, June 2011, pp. 190–92.
3. S.E. Erdman and T. Poutahidis, "Chapter 5 – Microbes and Oxytocin, Benefits for Host Physiology and Behaviour", *International Review of Neurobiology*, Vol. 131, 2016, pp. 91–126.
4. Scott C. Anderson, "What Do Microbes Have to Do With Your Love Life?", *Psychology Today*, 21st April 2019.
5. "Do My Microbes Love You? How Your Bacteria Affect Your Love Life?" *Copan*, 14th February 2020.
6. Susan E. Erdman, "Oxytocin and the microbiome", *Current Opinion in Endocrine and Metabolic Research*, Vol. 19, August 2021, pp. 8–14.

7. *"Scent of a Woman"*, A Martin Brest directed movie released in USA on 23rd December 1992, based on Giovanni Arpino's 1969 book in Italian language "II buio e il miele".
8. Bryant Furlow, "The Smell of Love: Why do some people smell better to you? A look at how human odour influences sexual attraction", *Psychology Today*, 1st March 1996.
9. Lindsay B. Baker, "Physiology of sweat gland function: The roles of sweating and sweat composition in human health", *Temperature: Medical Physiology and Beyond*, 17th July, 2019.
10. *Apocrine sweat gland* – Wikipedia.
11. Matthew Solan, "You don't say? The smell of love", *Harvard Health Publishing*, 1st February 2023.
12. Anna Gracheva, "The Smell of Love", *L'Official*, 5th December 2020.
13. Paul J. Zak, *The Moral Molecule: How Trust Works*, New York: Plume (The Penguin Group), 2013, p. 47.
14. *Mata Amritanandamayi*, Wikipedia.
15. "The Humanitarian Initiatives of Sri Mata Amritanandamayi Devi (Mata Amritanandamayi Math)" (PDF) – *embracing the world*, p. 7.
16. Carol Kuruvilla, "This Week in Pictures: Faith in Practice Around the World", *The Huffington Post*, November 9–15, 15th November 2014. Updated 6th December 2017.
17. Rediff.com: The Rediff Interview/Mata Amritanandamayi, *lm.rediff.com*, 2nd August, 2002.
18. Paul J. Zak, *The Moral Molecule: How Trust Works*, New York: Plume (The Penguin Group), 2013, p. 48.
19. Joe Schwartz, "The 'Chemical of Love'", *McGill Office for Science and Society: Separating Sense from Nonsense*; 13th February 2020.
20. *Sauerkraut* – Wikipedia.
21. Mark Leary, "PEA, Oxytocin, and Other Chemicals of Passionate Love", *Wondrium Daily*, 25th November 2020.
22. Daniel Z. Lieberman and Michael E. Long, *The Molecules of More: How a Single Chemical in Your Brain Drives Love, Sex, and Creativity....and Will Determine the Face of the Human Race*, Dallas, Texas: Ben Bella Books, 2019.
23. Erica Julson, "10 Best Ways to Increase Dopamine Levels Naturally", *Healthline*, 10th July 2023.
24. Paul J. Zak, *The Moral Molecule: How Trust Works,* New York: Plume (The Penguin Group), 2012.

CHAPTER 7

Exchange of Gaze & Other Factors: For Evaluation of Love Status

Love Gaze

Looking directly into the eyes of others, which is described as 'gazing', is important in almost every aspect of our lives that involves interacting with people. It is almost instinctive. Systematic studies have reported that those who are gaze-exchangers they are usually more sincere, honest, confident and conscientious; and, gaze-avoiders are generally the opposite, although they may include people who are shy and too introverted as well as those who avoid social contacts like patients suffering from 'Autism Spectrum Disorder' ('ASD').

In love-related relationship, expressing honesty and sincerity is a critical factor to develop a long-lasting bonding. When it comes to love, the eyes have a lot to say for themselves. "While meeting the gaze of a potential love interest may send your heart aflutter; it also stimulates a host of activity in your brain. Research in the Journal of General Psychology reveals that a shared gaze causes us to see a stranger as closer and more similar to us. And, in the game of love, similarity is often the first box that gets ticked when determining compatibility." (Reference 1)

In the context of love, exchange of positive eye contact or 'gaze' is thus an important factor. Joan Kellerman, PhD, who is Professor of Psychology at the University of Massachusetts, Dartmouth is well-known for some pioneering investigations on 'love gaze'. One of Kellerman's specialities is in the area of 'Obsessive Compulsive Disorder' ('OCD'). Possibly, she became curious to find out if there is any link between 'OCD' and 'Obsessive Love' ('OL'). You must be wondering what is 'Obsessive Love' ('OL'). 'OL' is, in my perception, a condition when someone is so madly in love with another person that it becomes a passionate obsession.

Kellerman and her co-researchers took 48 pairs of unacquainted undergraduate students of opposite sex. Then, they put them in 4 combinations of 'gazing' for 2 minutes at the others' hands or eyes. In a 5th condition, the students were asked to count the others' eye blinks. Students who were gazing at their partner's eyes and whose partners were reciprocating (that is, gazing back), reported significantly higher feelings of affection than the students in any other condition. In another study, with 36 pairs of unacquainted, opposite sex undergraduate students who engaged in mutual 'gaze', increased significantly their feelings of passionate love, and liking for the partner. (Reference 2)

The pupils in our eyes are constantly changing. They get enlarged (commonly described as 'dilated') in darker conditions to allow more light to enter the eye. And, they get smaller (commonly described as 'constricted') in brighter conditions to minimize the amount of light to enter. Dilated pupils are perceived as attractive. In fact, the pull is so strong that in the famous study by Kellerman and her co-researchers, complete strangers who were paired up to gaze directly at each other for 2 minutes found feelings of 'passionate love' were stirred. (Reference 2). Clearly, the eyes have quite some pulling power.

The eyes still have an important role to play for those who are in love even after years of being together. Harvard researcher Zick Robin revealed that couples who were together after several years and still deeply in love, maintained direct eye contact while talking to each other 75 percent of the time compared to the average of 30 to 60 percent. (Reference 3)

In the context of 'Love Gaze', I'm tempted to share with you the lyric of the famous song written by Burt Bacharach & Hal David and sung by different artistes including Dusty Springfield, Diana Krall & Trijntje Oosterhuis (Reference 4):

"The look of love is in your eyes – A look your smile cannot disguise
The look of love – It's saying so much more than just words could ever say

And what my heart has heard, well, it takes my breath away
I can hardly wait to hold you, feel my arms around you
How long I have waited, waited just to love you
Now that I have found you
You've got that look of love
It's on your face – the look that time can't erase."

Similarity > Love

In course of my research into 'Love' and its different aspects, while I was studying what Islam talks about love (Reference 5), I bumped into two most impressive stories narrated by the 13th century Sufi Mystic Rumi (Jalal al-Din Muhammad Rumi, 1207–1273) in his creation 'Masnavi' (References 6 & 7), which I feel tempted to share with you while talking about 'Love'. I feel these two stories are relevant as they talk about 'Love Gaze' which I have just discussed.

The 'Masnavi' (also written 'Mathnawi' or 'Mathnavi', is an extensive poem written by Rumi. It is one of the most influential works of Sufism, ascribed to be like a "Quran in Persian". Some Muslims regard the 'Masnavi' as one of the most important documents of Islamic literature, falling behind only the Quran. It has been viewed by many commentators as the greatest mystical poem in world literature. It is a spiritual text that teaches Sufis how to reach their goal: BEING TRULY IN LOVE WITH GOD.

Rumi's first story is about a very wise and well-known Greek physician who asked his disciples for some specific medicine for himself. His disciples were shocked.

They said: "Oh, Sir! The medicine that you have asked for is for the treatment of madness, but you are the sanest and wisest person that we know. Why are you asking for it?"

The master replied: "On my way to this place from my home, I met a mad person. As he saw me, he looked into my eyes with a look of love and smiled at me. Now, I am afraid, he must have found some SIMILARITY between me and himself. Otherwise, why should he engage his gaze and smile at me? It seemed he really enjoyed looking at me."

So, the lesson Rumi had wanted to convey was that 'Similarity breeds love'.

Although, his second story is not about humans, but about birds, Rumi's message is the same. The second story relates to another wise man saw a raven who had formed a bond with a stork. They were so full of affection and love for each other that they were inseparable. They perched together, and flew together. The wise man could not understand how the birds of two different feathers have been flocking together. He watched them from close and discovered that both had only one leg.

It is a soul-touching story. If you want to know more about how males and females having disabilities fall in love and get married, please read Marisa DeBellis's "A Group Home Exclusively for Married Couples with Developmental Disabilities: A Natural Next Step". (Reference 8).

Can Love be Measured?

Can you take a ruler, a measuring tape, a thermometer, or a sphygmomanometer and measure the amount of love one has for the partner?

In 1958, psychologist Harry Harlow suggested that "so far as love or affection is concerned, psychologists have failed in their mission. The little we know about love does not transcend simple observations, and the little we write about it has been written by poets and novelists." (Reference 9)

Researchers have proposed a number of different theories to understand the nature of love. (Reference 10). Helen Fisher is the most prominent amongst them. I will share her ideas on love separately later on. Many have even attempted to devise ways to measure the instinctive emotion of love. However, social psychologist Zick Rubin of Harvard was one of the first to develop an empirical instrument (not a physical or a chemical one) designed to measure love. (Reference 11)

Rubin, based on his observations, has concluded that 'love' is made up of three components: (i) passion (attachment): the need to be close to the other person; (physical contact and acceptance/approval are its constituents); (ii) caring: valuing the other person's happiness and needs as much as your own; and, (iii) intimacy: sharing private and personal thoughts, ideas, feelings, needs, desires with the other person.

Is there a difference between 'liking' and 'loving'? (Reference 12) Yes, there is. 'Loving', as I said, according to Rubin is a mix of attachment, caring, and intimacy – which may be present in different proportions in different love-relationships or even at different times between the two partners. 'Liking', on the other hand, is a cocktail of closeness, admiration, warmth, and respect.

Rubin developed two sets of questions: one to measure 'liking' and the other for 'loving', and administered those first on 198 undergraduate students and conducted a, what is called 'factor analysis' with the answers. Based on the results of the 'factor analysis' which was meant for 'screening', Rubin identified 13 questions for 'liking' and another set of 13 for 'loving' that he firmed up as reliable measure of these two basic emotional activities which are cornerstones of human existence.

I'm sharing with you some examples which are somewhat similar to some of the questions used in Rubin's 'liking' and 'loving' scales. (Reference 13)

Liking Measurement

1. I feel that .... is a very stable person.
2. I have confidence in ....'s opinions.
3. I think that .... can adjust well with anyone and any situation.
4. .... is one of the most likeable persons I know.

Loving Measurement

1. I feel strong feelings of attachment towards................
2. I like it when ....confides in me.
3. I would do almost anything for.................
4. I do not take...........'s faults, lapses and shortcomings seriously.

How to score: For each item, you have to rate your response on a scale from '1' (not true) to '9' (definitely true).

It is important to remember that Rubin's concept of 'loving' does not apply just to romantic love. It can apply to love that develops in many inter-personal relationships including those between members of the same family, or kins and friends.

References

1. "Eye contact and love – what's the science behind it?" *Optix.*
2. J. Kellerman, J. Lewis and J.D. Laird, "Looking and loving: The effects of mutual gaze on feelings of romantic love", *Journal of Research on Personality,* Vol. 23, No. 2, 1989, pp. 145–161.
3. Kendra Cherry, "Rubin's Scale of Liking and Loving", *verywellmind,* 10th April, 2022.
4. The Look of Love lyrics © *Colgems-emi-MusicInc.*
5. "Human Love", *Al-Islam.org*
6. *Rumi* – Wikipedia.
7. *Masnavi* – Wikipedia.
8. Marissa DeBellis, "A Group Home for Married Couples with Developmental Disabilities: A Natural Next Step", *Touro Law, Jacob D. Fuchsberg Law Center,* July 2012, Vol. 28, No. 2.
9. H.F. Harlow, "The nature of love", *American Psychologist,* 1958, Vol. 13, No. 12, pp. 673–685.
10. N.D. Kapusta, K.S. Jankowski, V. Wolf *et al.*, "Measuring the capacity to love: Development of the CTL Inventory", *Frontiers of Psychology,* 2018, Vol. 9, p. 1115.
11. Zick Rubin, "Measurement of Romantic Love", *Journal of Personality and Social Psychology,* 1970, Vol. 16, pp. 265–273.
12. Cherry, Kendra, "Rubin's Scales of Liking and Loving", *very well mind,* 10th April, 2022.
13. "Rubin's Love and Liking Scale pdf".

CHAPTER 8

Love-Heart Link

Heart: The Fountainhead of Love

Ancient Egyptians and Greeks used to regard the heart as the source of all our love and affection. You may feel the happy and warm vibrations of your heart when you think of your loved one. Or, in the case of someone for whom love becomes a madness or an unstoppable obsession, the heart may skip a beat or begin to race fast. The Greek philosopher Aristotle was the first to think that man's mind was in his heart. (Reference 1)

Your heart is a very special biological pump unlike the usual mechanical (hydraulic) pump. It had cost a great deal of intellectual energy and genius to design world's first replaceable artificial heart which was transplanted for the first time in medical history by Dr Denton Cooley who had performed surgery on Satyajit Ray and R.D. Burman, whose names we are very much familiar with. Dr Cooley's name always remains fresh in my memory as he used to play music throughout the long duration of his complicated cardiac surgery procedures. (References 2 & 3)

The New York cardiologist and author Dr Sandeep Jauhar has written a book titled *Heart: A History* exploring the connection between the fist-sized organ and the 'heart of love'. To quote him: "The metaphorical heart is the way we thought of the heart before science came along. The heart was the seed of the soul. It was where our emotions resided – emotions like love and courage. And what I have observed in my two decades now as a cardiologist is that the heart that is associated with love, that 'metaphorical heart', directly impacts our biological heart. People who have healthy, loving relationships have better heart health." (Reference 4)

As a matter of fact, the warm feeling of love ramps up our 'ParaSympathetic Nervous System' ('PSNS'), helping us to rest, relax and digest conveniently. Stress is reduced and feelings of anxiety and insecurity are improved. Blood vessels tend to dilate a little bit more, and blood pressure tends to drop when one interacts with the loved one and it can really be felt by those concerned. Research has shown that men and women who were happily married had less risk of a cardio-vascular problem than single men and women. Thus, happy wedlock was found to be a strong safeguard against heart problems. A loving relationship has a positive impact on the heart by encouraging healthy behaviour that reduces the risk of heart disease. Of course, I must tell you that loving relationship must be supplemented by regular light exercise (freehand stretching-bending, brisk walking, slow jogging or yoga), and giving up smoking and consumption of alcohol.

Finally, I must point out that impact of a failed love or lack of love has a reverse effect on the heart. People who are in loveless or in difficult relationships with their partners, spouses or children, or who are unhappy at work and in life, tend to suffer from heart-related ailments.

Love: Good for Your Heart Health

The New York Times of 10th January 2022 published a report which would interest us (Reference 5). The report narrated the story of a 57-year-old man, David Bennett Sr. with life-threatening heart disease had received a heart from a genetically modified pig – a ground-breaking procedure followed by Dr. Bartley Griffith, the director of the cardiac transplant programme at the University of Maryland Medical Centre. The pig's heart inside Mr Bennett Sr's rib-cage was working normally showing normal pulse rate and blood pressure. Mr Bennett decided to gamble on the experimental treatment because he would have died without a new heart. He had exhausted other treatments and was too sick to qualify for a human donor heart. The patient lived for two months with a strong functioning heart showing no obvious signs of rejection. (Reference 6). The whole medical community was abuzz with speculations as to why did the patient die and several reasons were cited, seminars and symposia were held, papers were published in general and specialised medical journals but there was hardly any mention anywhere in any forum whether after the pig heart transplantation, the patient had got back his love-related emotions although biomechanically the functions were satisfactory of the transplanted heart.

The human heart is a highly emotive organ. We express our romantic emotions – our desire, satisfaction, falling in and out of love, heartbreak, betrayal and disappointment through images of the heart. We use a variety of expressions such as; heart-felt, heart-throb, to the heart's content, heartbreak, hungry heart, heart of gold, and so on. But, how is it that the beating organ inside our chest become linked to the feelings about emotions arising out of relationships. Literature – both prose and poetry are rampant with various manifestations of love-heart link. Patients connected with the artificial heart-lung machine while they await their heart transplants can experience the difference from how the emotion of love used to affect them when the functions of their hearts were normal.

Just one example I will share. Heartbreak is both metaphorical and physical. 'Metaphorical' when Juliet cries mistakenly believing that Romeo is dead: "O, break my heart!!". And 'physical' when heartbreak was formally recognised in the 1990s as an acute cardiac syndrome called 'Takotsubo Syndrome' (informally known as the 'Heartbreak Syndrome'). (Reference 7)

Why love is good for your heart? Let me share a short list. (i) Spending time with your loved ones lowers blood pressure. (ii) When you meet a person you love a lot, your heart gets an automatic workout. (iii) Hugs are good for the heart. (iv) Laughter resulting from a love-linked interaction makes your blood flow freely. (v) Love-linked messages lower your cholesterol when you go through them. (vi) Having a successful love life reduces the risk of heart attack. (vii) Holding hands calms nerves. (viii) A happy married life is a preventive for heart disease. (ix) Married people recover better from a heart attack than those who are single. (Reference 8)

Christopher Suhar, MD, a cardiologist and director of Scripps Center for Integrative Medicine says:

> *"I think love in your life is paramount to living a healthy lifestyle. The goal is gaining peace through love, which decreases stress and anxiety in your life and benefits your heart." (Reference 9)*

Love: The Best Care-giver

I was most curious to know what the great Indian cardiac surgeon Dr Devi Shetty, MB BS, MS, FRCS thinks about the love-heart link and Google made me bump into a smart video where he is addressing the students at the Indian Institute of Management-Bangalore. He was sharing his experience about a project which his son, an alumnus of the Stanford Business School in USA and his friends undertook in one of Dr Shetty's multiple hospitals. According to him the project was on how learning can save lives – how you can train people a little bit and that can make a huge difference between life and death. However, I would highlight it as a case study on how love can be the best care-giver in the post-operative stage.

When patients undergo a heart surgery, they stay in the care of the hospital for five days. During this period, the patient's spouse generally stays with the patient but not allowed to touch the patient, or do anything for the patient like dressing the wounds or administering medicine. The patient is totally under the intensive care of the doctors and nurses. The spouse plays the role of a silent spectator.

Exactly four days after the heart operation, the spouse (generally the wife) is called. She is given a plastic bag with all the tablets and told to go home with the husband and take total care of him. This is what happens all over the world. However, with such an abrupt instruction, she is lost as much as her husband is. They don't know what to do. There was total intensive care by trained and experienced staff at the hospital; and now, at home, there is nothing.

Dr Shetty gave the project to the young MBAs on how to educate the spouse for effective care-giving soon after the operation. Dr Shetty explained to the youngsters that care-giving with affection and compassion comes naturally when our loved ones are suffering. It is an inherent skill – some possess it less and some others, more; but it is with everyone. But after a critical heart surgery, what would effective care-giving include, the fresh MBAs had to interact with all concerned, make a list of do's and don'ts and educate a set of spouses. (Reference 10)

The few things the students found were essential included:

1. Reading/checking the blood pressure using a BP measuring apparatus
2. Dressing the wound properly.
3. What all medicine are to be administered and what are the likely side-effects.
4. Importance of taking the medicine on time as prescribed by the hospital.
5. Simple physiotherapy and body movements.
6. Maintaining input-output chart: what the patient drinks and how much urine he passes.

Once the patients' spouses were educated on the above, the readmission rate following a discharge came down by 30 percent – because when the patient went home there was someone to take care of him with love and empathy. Why the spouses learnt so fast during their very short 5 days' stay in the hospital because of their genuine loving relationship with the patients and as they wanted them to recover and restore normalcy or near-normalcy as soon as possible.

This live case study from a world-renowned cardiac surgeon reminded me of an experimental study I had done with the reputed gynaecologist & obstetrician Dr Gouri Kumra MB BS DGO MD on premature twins about a year ago where I recommended the infant's mother to remain in the intensive care and pick up care-giving tips in addition to the music medicine that I had applied. This case study has been documented in my recent book on 'Bio-musicology'. (Reference 11)

The Heart's Little Brain

Did you know that your heart has a 'little brain'? Any organ or system in the body where there are brain cells (called 'neurons') present, qualifies to be regarded as a 'brain'. The cranial tissue located between our ears – the 'head brain' has 8,500 to 10,000 million neurons, the 'gut' or the 'Enteric Nervous System' has 100 to 600 million neurons (it is thus called the 'Second Brain') whereas the heart's 'little brain' or the 'Intrinsic Cardiac Nervous System' ('ICNS') is composed of approximately 40,000 neurons. Dr. J. Andrew Armour of the HeartMath Institute, USA showed in 1991 that the heart brain, like the brain proper, has an intricate network of several types of neurons, neurotransmitters, proteins, and support cells. It can act independently to learn, remember, feel and sense. (References 12 & 13)

The connection between the heart and the brain goes back to 1884 when the father of 'Psychology', William James (1842–1910) famously described this scenario. To quote him: "Imagine you are walking through the woods and you come across a grizzly bear. Your heart begins to race. You feel afraid, and you run." The concept suggests that the physical reaction (a racing heart) and the emotional experience (fear) are inter-connected. The heart receives input from the environment (external and/or internal) and it adjusts to maintain its outputs like heart rate and blood pressure accordingly. The heart-based neurons are thought to play a crucial role in heart-health, helping to fine-tune heart rhythm and perhaps protecting people against certain kinds of heart disease. (References 14 & 15)

The heart's neurons are responsible for keeping the organ healthy. They are sensitive enough to respond to any stimulus that is carried from the cranial 'head brain' via the 'Vagus Nerve' ('VN') which is the main connector starting from the 'head brain' and ending in the 'gut brain' and, most amazingly, connected with every organ like the lungs and the liver on its long route. (Reference 16)

Signals from the 'heart brain' reach the medulla (in the 'hindbrain'), the hypothalamus, thalamus & amygdala (in the 'midbrain') and the cerebral cortex (in the 'forebrain'). (Reference 17)

One of the 'key' discoveries HeartMath Institute (HMI) researchers made about the 'heart brain' (which they also call the 'intelligent heart') is really most fascinating. They found that intentionally experiencing emotions can change the information that the heart sends to the brain. It means that if you can deliberately/intentionally nurture a positive feeling in your mind, such as love, care, compassion, empathy, or fellow-feeling, it can benefit you in many ways. For example, in one HMI study, hundreds of participants were asked to intentionally feel positive emotions. The result was that their heart rhythms became smoother and more stable. Smooth and stable heart rhythms are signs of 'COHERENCE' – a psychophysiological state in which our mental perception, intuitive awareness and performance in a range of activities improve. (Reference 2) 'COHERENCE' is the state when the heart, mind, and emotions are totally in alignment, energetically; and, they cooperate with each other. This calmer yet focused state improves: (i) learning; (ii) making more intelligent & better choices; and, (iii) openness of the mind – provides an expanded view of options.

The heart has an electromagnetic energy field 5,000 times greater than that of our head brain. This energy reaches about 3 feet (91.44 cm) outside the physical body and can be detected in another person sitting nearby via an electrocardiogram (ECG). (Reference 18)

A true lover radiates positive energy when she/he meets her/his most beloved person. And, if is a reciprocal event, then there is 'Mutual Coherence'. And, if such 'Mutual Coherence' continues (as it may happen in a very successful marriage), then, there is: reduction in stress, increase in adaptability to change, psycho-social well-being, higher cognitive capacity, improvement in performance, development of resilience and better problem-solving skill, emotional stability, mental clarity, intuitiveness and creativity, onset of regenerative/anti-ageing process.

For any individual, since childhood, it has become a normal habit for the heart to respond and feel in a specific way on receiving a stimulus from the environment – external as well as internal. That habit has to be changed. Just like the cranial brain can be re-trained through 'neuro-plasticity', so can be the heart. It is possible to train the heart using positive emotions so that the brain more consistently releases chemicals that support healing and well-being.

"You've Got the Love"

In the song "You've Got the Love", I have a fine example of how the depressed singer gives her intermittent doses of reassurance that she has God's love to see her through. The message is addressed to the 'little brain' in the heart and not to the 'cranial brain' in the head. From the 'heart' level, it travels to the 'head' level.

The song goes like this:

"Sometimes I feel like throwing my hands up in the air
But you've got the love I need to see me through.
Sometimes it seems that the going is just too rough
And things go wrong no matter what I do.
Now and then it seems that life is just too much
But you've got the love I need to see me through.

When food is gone you are my daily meal
When friends are gone, I know my saviour's love is real.
You know it's real.

'Cause you've got the love
You've got the love
You've got the love
You've got the love
You've got the love
You've got the love.

Time after time I think, "Oh, Lord, what's the use?
Time after time I think it's just no good
'Cause sooner or later in life, the things you love you lose
But you've got the love I need to see me through.

You've got the love
You've got the love
You've got the love
You've got the love
You've got the love
You've got the love

You've got the love
You've got the love
You've got the love
You've got the love
You've got the love
You've got the love.

Sometimes I feel like throwing my hands up in the air
'Cause I know I can count on you
Sometimes I feel like saying, "Lord, I just don't care"
But you've got the love I need to see through.

(Songwriters: Anthony B. Stephens/Jamie Principle/Anthony Harris/ John P. Bellamy Jr.)

References

1. Sandee LaMotte, "How love sparks better heart health", *CNN health*, 14th February 2019.
2. *Denton Cooley* – Wikipedia.
3. Lawrence K. Altman, "Dr Denton Cooley: Whose Pioneering Heart Surgery Let Off a 40-Year Medical Feud, Dies at 96.", *The New York Times*, 18th March 2016.
4. Sandeep Jauhar, *Heart: A History*, New York: Penguin Viking, 2018.
5. Roni Caryn Rabin, "In a First, Man Receives a Heart from a Genetically Altered Pig". *The New York Times*, 10th January 2022.

6. Deborah Kotz and Bill Seiler, "Patient Survived for Two Months After First-of-Its Kind Transplant at the University of Maryland Medical Center", *University of Maryland Medical System*, 22nd June 2022.
7. Claire Hansen, "At the heart of romance: why a vital organ is linked to love", *ANU Reporter*, 14th February 2023.
8. Jaimie Dalessio Clayton, "7 Reasons Love is Good for Your Heart", *Everyday Health*, 23rd January 2012.
9. "How Love Affects Your Heart", *Scripps*, 8th February 2022.
10. Devi Shetty, "Labour of Love/Future of Learning/IIM-Bangalore: 7th December 2020, YouTube.
11. Siddhartha Ganguli, *Music is Magic/Music is Medicine*, Noida: Allied Publishers Pvt. Ltd., 2023.
12. J. Andrew Armour *et al.*, "The Little Brain in the Heart", *HeartMath Institute*
13. Sara Childre (HeartMath Institute), "The Little Brain in the Heart", *Providencetherapybc.com*
14. "Researchers Map and Explore the Heart's 'Little Brain'" *mbf Bioscience*, 20th October 2021.
15. Laura Saunders, "A new 3-D map illuminates the 'little brain' within the heart", *Science News*, 2nd June 2020.
16. Karuna Meda, "Little Brain" *Thomas Jefferson University*, 19th April 2022.
17. Ali M. Alshami, "Pain: Is It All in the Brain or the Heart?" *Current Pain Headache Reporter*, 14th November 2019, Vol. 23, No. 12, p. 88.
18. Jessica I. Morales, "The Heart's Electromagnetic Field is Your Superpower: Training heart-brain coherence", *Psychology Today*, 29th November 2020.

CHAPTER 9

Brain in Love

Your Brain in Love

Dr Sandra Langeslag, a behavioural neuroscientist at the University of Missouri who has been researching on the distractive properties of love says: "In one of my studies, we asked people how often they think of their beloved when they are awake. And the average was 65 percent of the time, with the highest being around 90 percent." (References 1, 2, 3 & 4)

People who are in love are first shown a picture of their beloved and then of their friend or even a stranger. They are studied with the ERP (Event-related Potential) method. There are two brainwaves with ERP components that indicate attention (namely, 'immediate attention' and 'sustained attention'). These components are usually longer when people see the pictures of their loved ones, than when they see their friends' or strangers' photos. Langeslag also found that when attention is directed to someone's beloved, it slowed down task performance.

There are three areas of the brain that are connected with 'love'. These are:

- 'Ventral Tegmental Area' ('VTA') – which releases 'Dopamine'; 'Nucleus Accumbens' ('NA') – which contains many 'Oxytocin' receptors; and, 'Ventral Pallidum' ('VP'), containing many 'Vasopression' receptors. 'Dopamine' is responsible for allowing you to feel pleasure, satisfaction and motivation. (Reference 5). 'Oxytocin' plays roles in behaviour that include understanding, empathy, trust, social bonding, reproduction, childbirth and the period immediately following childbirth till the end of infancy. (Reference 6). 'Vasopressin' is responsible for protective, grooming, locomotor and social behaviour, apart from numerous biological processes. (Reference 7).

- 'VTA' starts the show. 'NA' links the pleasurable feelings of romantic love to our sensory system. It is responsible for how we connect a smell, a colour, or a song to a loving feeling we have for a person. 'VP' is mainly involved in processing signals of motivation and reward, and cementing certain actions associated with these rewarding feelings in our mind. As far as 'Dopamine' is concerned, there are different receptors that respond to falling in love, staying in love, and breaking up. People who have a greater amount of 'Oxytocin' receptors in 'NA', have a higher likelihood of forming lifelong pair bonds.

People's breathing aligns when they are involved in a romantic relationship and sleeping together in the same bed synchronises the heart rhythms. Loving bonds are a cognitive strategy for sharing risks. Sexual bonds are of one kind and friendship bonds are of another. However, they both involve sharing of risk with each other.

Knowledge of the biology of love – knowing the names of the molecules and the brain areas that are involved frees us from some of the mysteries that used to veil the emotion of 'love', prior to the days of neuroscientific findings.

Your Brain in Romantic & Erotic Love

Richard Scwartz and Jacqueline Olds are both professors at the Harvard Medical School. They have been happily married for nearly four decades. Jacqueline Olds's father, James, had discovered the 'Ventral Tegmental Area' ('VTA') inside the human brain when she was just seven years old. I'm not sure whether her Dad's discovery left a lasting impression on her growing mind that prompted her to go for medicine with further specialisation in psychiatry.

The 'VTA' is a part of the 'reward circuit' which is considered to be a primitive neural network, thus evolutionarily old. It links with the 'Nucleus Accumbens' ('NA'). Some other structures that contribute to the reward circuit are: the Amygdala, the Hippocampus, and the Pre-Frontal Cortex. These areas are exceptionally sensitive to (and reinforcing of) behaviour that induces pleasure such as sex, food consumption, and drug use. When the brain's reward circuit is active, the bodily symptoms are: racing hearts, sweaty palms, flushed cheeks, feelings of passion as well as anxiety.

The primitive areas of the brain are involved in romantic and erotic love. These areas light up on brain scans when talking about a loved one. These areas can stay lit up for a long time for some couples, says Jacqueline Olds who is a Harvard Medical School associate professor of psychiatry at Boston's Massachusetts General Hospital.

In addition to the positive feelings that romance brings, love also deactivates the neural pathway responsible for negative emotions, such as fear and social judgment (what others will think, how others will view ….. etc.). These positive and negative feelings involve two neural pathways. The one linked with positive emotions connects the Pre-Frontal Cortex to the Nucleus Accumbens; while the other, which is linked with negative emotions, connects the Nucleus Accumbens to the Amygdala. When we are engaged in romantic love, the neural machinery responsible for making critical assessment of other people, including assessments of those with whom we are romantically involved, shuts down. "That's the neural basis for the ancient wisdom 'LOVE IS BLIND'", said Professor Schwartz.

Love begins as a 'stressor' as during the first two to three years after falling in love, there are ups and downs of positive (neuro-transmitter: 'Serotonin') and negative emotions (steroid hormone: 'Cortisol') because of the uncertainty. Once the feeling of love settles down and becomes lasting, the levels of 'Serotonin' and 'Cortisol' return to normal. Then, love becomes a buffer against stress. Brain areas associated with reward and pleasure are still activated, but the constant craving and desire that are inherent in romantic love often lessens. From passionate love, there is a change-over to compassionate love – love that is deep but not explosive as the one that had been experienced during the early stages of romance.

Most amazingly, being madly in love is still possible after decades of marriage. For those whose long-term marriage has transitioned from passionate, romantic love to a more compassionate, routine type of love, Professor Olds indicated that it is possible to rekindle the flame that characterised the relationship during the early days. "We call it the rustiness phenomenon – couples get out of the habit of sex, of being incredibly lost in love, and often for good reasons: work, children, a sick parent. But that kind of love can be reignited." Sexual activity, for example, can increase 'Oxytocin' levels and activate the brain's reward circuit making couples desire each other more. (Reference 8)

Brain-imaging Studies of People in Love

Stony Brook University ('SBU') Dept. of Psychology scientists had been doing some neuro-imaging studies of long-term married couples still in love and couples who had recently fallen in love. (Reference 9). While studying partners who are closely bonded and deeply in love, similar brain activities were found in individuals who yearn for a deceased loved one or experience cocaine-induced high, thus linking 'attachment bonds' with 'addiction-related' properties. Sexual frequency was positively associated with activity of the posterior 'hippocampus' ('hippocampus' is thought to be the centre of emotion, memory, and the autonomic nervous system), in an area found in studies of hunger and craving, as well as obsession and early-stage love. Similar observations were made by other researchers also. (Reference 10)

Another interesting 'SBU' finding has been regarding the love of the Easterners and the Westerners, if any. There used to be an impression that Easterners (those from collectivistic cultures such as China) seem to regard 'love' differently from Westerners (those from individualistic cultures such as the United States). A group of researchers from Stony Brook University and Albert Einstein College of Medicine (both in the US), and Southwest University and the Chinese Academy of Sciences (both in China) conducted a neuro-imaging study using the fMRI technique. The study found that the patterns of brain response were extremely similar for the Chinese and the Americans. For people intensely in love in both the cultures, viewing images of the beloved elicited brain activations in the midbrain-Dopamine-rich reward and motivation system (a system closely related to drug addiction). (Reference 11)

The researchers also followed up on the Chinese participants 18 months after they had been in the scanner to investigate whether brain activation during the 'madly in love' stage of the relationship predicted relationship satisfaction as the relationship developed over time. It was found that there was greater relationship satisfaction 18 months later. (Reference 11)

The brain-imaging studies of individuals who were still 'in love' with their rejecter supplies further evidence that the passion of 'romantic love' is a goal-oriented motivation state rather than a specific emotion, the researchers concluded; thereby meaning that a 'goal' is fixed to win over an individual with 'love' but when the 'goal' is not reached, there is 'rejection'. In such cases, brain-imaging studies showed some similarities between romantic rejection and cocaine craving. The findings are concluded with the hypothesis that 'romantic love' is a specific form of 'addiction'. Feelings and behaviours related to romantic rejection are difficult to control. Romantic rejection is a major cause of depression and, in extreme cases, suicide. (Reference 12)

Mughal Emperor Shah Jahan's Brain in Love – Part 1

Shah Jahan was the dearly loved son of Jahangir and Nur Jahan and the grandson of Akbar the great, who also kept his grandson free from all the worries and gave him all the royalties of the world. (Reference 13)

14-year-old Prince Khurram (Shah Jahan's boyhood name) was once taking a walk by the lanes of Meena Bazaar in Agra in the year 1607. He then saw a beautiful girl who was selling and assembling some silk items and even some glass beads. The beauty of the girl enchanted him and he started to talk to the girl a bit. Soon, he came to know that the girl he had seen in the market, her name was Arjumand Bano Begum and she was a relative of his mother Nur Jahan.

Prince Khurram rushed to his father Jahangir immediately and notified that he wanted to marry that pretty girl. Love towards his son, made Emperor Jahangir allow to marry the girl. However, they were too young then and hence, their wedding was postponed for few years and they were married in 1612.

As per Shah Jahan, the wife was a lucky charm for him. So, after a few years from his marriage, Shah Jahan captivated the throne of Mughal Empire winning over his four brothers and became a rebel emperor of the great throne in the year 1628. He also awarded his wife Arjumand Bano Begum with the lovely title of 'Mumtaz Mahal' which means 'the jewel of the palace'.

The emperor had several other wives as per the culture of that era but he had a special bond and love for Mumtaz Mahal – this was all because she was very beautiful, witty, and intelligent. The queen helped the emperor in taking political, strategic, and administrative decisions. She was really his 'better half'. His love for her was so deep that he never left her alone even for a second. The emperor was falling in love with her more and more with every passing second and day. The Badshah and the Begum were inseparable. The Begum was content to have lots of children with her husband; and, she died giving birth to their 14th child. (Reference 14)

When the queen died during childbirth, Shah Jahan was totally lost and announced two long years of mourning, which was unprecedented. Later, when he could collect himself, he thought of the promise he had made to his deceased wife that when she dies, he would make the tomb of her grave so big and amazing that the world will lose a breath looking at its magnificent beauty. Taj Mahal took twenty-two years to get completely furnished and ready to be showcased to the world. Twenty-two thousand workers from India and Persia worked day and night to construct the Taj.

Emperor Shah Jahan and his beloved Mumtaz made the people of the world believe that love is a pious type of feeling and, if you love someone, it has to be pure and true love as had existed between the royal couple.

To quote the English poet Sir Edwin Arnold: "Not a piece of architecture, as other buildings use, but the proud passion of an emperor's love wrought in living stones." (Reference 15)

Mughal Emperor Shah Jahan's Brain in Love – Part 2

I am holding your hand to get exposed to the invisible happenings inside your brain when you are in love. You are getting to know the brain chemicals (namely, the 'neuro-transmitters' and the 'neuro-modulators') that get released when you meet, or even think about or visualise someone you love. But let me tickle you with a question that suddenly popped up on my mind's screen. The question is: was the idea, the concept of Taj Mahal an outcome of the organic cocktails in the great Mughal Emperor Shah Jahan's brain? The Mughal Badshah Shah Jahan (1592–1666) built the Taj Mahal in the 1600s for his beloved wife, Mumtaz Mahal, who died during childbirth. (Reference 16)

Shah Jahan's other wives were: Qandahari Mahal, Akbarbadi Mahal, Lilavati Bai of Kharwah, and Fatehpuri Mahal. But Mumtaz was his consort and most favourite wife and he was so overwhelmed with 'True Love' for her that he wanted a very special memorial for her around and over her tomb. His love was so strong that the memorial, Taj Mahal, an ivory-white marble mausoleum situated on the right bank of the river Yamuna in Agra, Uttar Pradesh, India is still regarded as one of the modern Seven Wonders of the World. It has also been a protected UNESCO World Heritage Site since 1983. It is still one of the most impressive architectural constructions in human history. (Reference 17)

The Taj Mahal is an architectural and structural wonder, but the organic chemicals that got activated inside Shah Jahan's brain are no longer considered unique – those are present in everyone's brain, waiting to be stimulated and nurtured when the brain is in love. (Reference 18)

Once Taj Mahal was built and Shah Jahan was looking at it with awe and admiration, did he have the interplay of the same neuro-transmitters and hormones in his brain and body? Possibly, yes!

He would have got a rush of the reward chemical 'Dopamine' in the 'Ventral Tegmental Area' ('VTA') and its associated neural structures of his brain. He got a ping at his 'Hippocampus' – the memory area in the tissue between his two ears as he was retrieving the love-linked memories of the most passionate moments he had spent with his beloved Queen. He would have got a release of 'Serotonin' – the 'good mood' molecules and also of 'Oxytocin' – the 'love-empathy-understanding-trust' chemical. He had a rush of the male sex hormone 'Testosterone' in his body parts reliving the physical experience that he used to have with his beloved. He also had, in his arteries and veins, high levels of 'Adrenalin' and 'Norepinephrine' which excitement generates. This was possible due to the working of the 'Hypothalamus' of his brain. 'Norepinephrine' (also known as 'Noradrenaline') gave a butterfly feeling in his stomach. He must have also had an arousal.

Please note that your neurochemicals, neuromodulators and hormones that are prominent in your love life, are also released when you are passionately in love with what-you-do, you become CREATIVE, as it happened when Emperor Shah Jahan conceived of the idea of the Taj Mahal and got it built. He and his beloved have become mingled with dust inside their tombs, but his creation still remains not only as a physical landmark but as a prominent milestone in the history of mankind. Why don't you think of making some special contribution, maybe a very small one, for the progress of the mankind – for the sake of your most beloved person? Think about it, after reading this piece.

References

1. Macpherson Frankie, "This is your brain on love: the beautiful neuro-science behind all romance", *BBC Science Focus*, 12th February 2021.
2. Sandra J.E. Langeslag and Michelle E. Sanchez, "Down-regulation of love feelings after a romantic break-up: Self-report and electrophysiological data", *Journal of Experimental Psychology: General*, Vol. 147, No. 5, pp. 720-733, (APA PsycNet)
3. Sandra Langeslag, "Is it love or infatuation? This relationship questionnaire will help you tell" *(yahoo!)*, 17th February 2023.
4. Dan Reus, "Disrupting Love with Sandra Langeslag", *Entrepreneur Quarterly*.
5. *Dopamine* – Wikipedia.
6. *Oxytocin* – Wikipedia.

7. *Vasopressin* – Wikipedia.
8. Scott Edwards, "Love and the Brain", *Harvard Medical School*, Spring 2015.
9. "Love Can Last: SBU Imaging Study Shows Brain Activity of Those in Love Long-Term Similar to Those Newly in Love", *Stony Brook University News*, 7th January 2011.
10. K. Daniel O'Leary; Bianca P. Acevedo and Debra Mashek, "Is Long-term Love More Than a Rare Phenomenon? If So, What Are Its Correlates?" *Social Psychological and Personality Science*, 5th August 2011.
11. "SBU Researchers and Colleagues Find That In The Brain, Early Stage Intense Passionate Love Seems To Be Universal", *Stony Brook University News*, 28th May 2010.
12. "Anguish of Romantic Rejection May Be Linked to Stimulation Of Areas of Brain Related To Motivation, Reward and Addiction", *Stony Brook University News*, 21st July 2010.
13. "Love Story of Mumtaz & Shah Jahan", *Taj Mahal Tour*, 9th April, 2018.
14. Geeta Pandey, "Taj Mahal: Was India's 'monument to love' built out of guilt?" *BBC News*, 25th June 2014.
15. *Mumtaz Mahal* – Wikipedia.
16. *Shah Jahan* – Wikipedia.
17. Rosie Lesso, "Why Is the Taj Mahal a World Wonder?" *THE * COLLECTOR*, 21st November 2022.
18. Deutsche Welle, "In love? Here's what's happening in your brain", *Hindustan Times*, 20th July 2023.

CHAPTER 10

Love-Hate Seesaw

Love-Hate: Opposite Poles

'Love' and 'Hate' are two opposite poles.

To quote Martin Luther King, Jr., civil rights leader, "Returning hate for hate multiplies hate, adding deeper darkness to a night already devoid of stars. Darkness cannot drive out darkness; only light can do that. Hate multiplies hate, violence multiplies violence, and toughness multiplies toughness in a descending spiral of destruction." (Reference 1)

Bipolar behaviour is typical of natural phenomena: light and darkness, day and night, sunshine and rains, summer and winter, windy and windless. We, as creatures of Mother Nature are no exceptions to such bipolar occurrences. One such phenomenon is the love-hate interpersonal relationship – it's very common when emotions are intense – between a parent and a child, between two friends, between two siblings, even between a husband and a wife. (Reference 2)

In a family, there may be complete estrangement between an adult offspring and one or both the parents because of: poor bonding in infancy, depressive symptoms of parents, borderline or narcissistic pathology in the adult child, and/or parental alienation in childhood. Parents who follow 'divide & rule' policy and alienate their children from the other parent frequently suffer from 'Borderline Personality Disorder' or 'Narcissistic Personality Disorder'. (Reference 3). Research from Yale University suggests love-hate relationship may be the result of poor self-esteem. (Reference 4)

One of the developmental tasks for humans is to BALANCE the primary or basic 'love' and 'hate' drives to develop tolerances towards a loved object. Primary or basic 'love' (both 'Smart' and 'Short-lived/Short' varieties, according to my classification) releases the neuro-chemical 'Dopamine' and the male sex hormone 'Testosterone' whereas 'hate' releases either of the two negative hormones – 'Adrenalin' (if the mood is 'aggressive') or 'Cortisol (if the mood is 'depressive'). A BALANCE between the two will help to develop a feeling tolerance towards the object of love. Or, otherwise, such a BALANCE is auto-generated if the love is of 'Sustained' variety with the release of 'Oxytocin', where it is taken for granted that there cannot be only light or only day, or only sunshine or only happiness – the positive and negative sides both must coexist.

To quote Martin Luther King Jr. again: "Hatred paralyzes life; love releases it; hatred confuses life, love harmonises it; hatred darkens life, love illuminates." (Reference 5)

A love-hate relationship may develop when people have completely lost the 'intimacy' within a loving relationship, yet still retain some passion for, or perhaps some commitment to each other, before degenerating into a love-hate relationship leading to a total separation.

Love-hate relationships exist in every culture; in some culture, it may be more whereas in some other cultures, it is somewhat less, but not absent altogether. In Eastern cultures, it is not so much expressed as it is in the West. For instance, in Japan, there is a character found which is described as 'tsundere' who frequently switches between dishonouring and insulting her/his love interest and acting love-struck from time to time, eventually becoming very sober, tolerant and kind. (Reference 2)

When we love someone, we want them to thrive. When we hate someone, we are most likely to wish they would suffer, or at least change their outlook, their attitude, their values, their conduct, their behaviour. Can 'love' and 'hate' co-exist? Yes, when your love is not reciprocated. And, when you have to give up your autonomy and personal freedom for the person you love (in romantic love, in friendship love, in parental love). Your own preferences and priorities may suffer unless you meet both demands – yours and theirs, half-way and make a compromise. Thirdly, when you become exposed to the person you love, with your idiosyncrasies and hidden agendas.

Fourthly, when the other person does not open up and maybe tries to manipulate you.

When love blends with hate, this is a case of ambivalence. Ambivalence is the state of having mixed feelings or contradictory ideas about something or someone. Ambivalence is usually short-lived, but it lasts longer whenever the two emotions or desires generally compete with each other. You are in love with two people, but it's now time to choose who to be in a relationship with. Or, you hate your spouse as much as you love her/him and have some difficult decisions to make. (Reference 6)

Thin Line between Love and Hate

I am tempted to share the lyric of a popular song by The Persuaders. The song is titled "Thin Line between Love and Hate"

"It's a thin line between love and hate
It's a thin line between love and hate

It's 5 O'clock in the morning, I'm just getting in; I knock on the door
A voice sweet and low says (Who is it?) She opened up the door and let me in
Never once did she say, where have you been? She says (are you hungry?)
"Are you hungry, honey? Did you eat yet? Let me hang up your coat.

The woman tells me, pass me your hat; All the time she smilin' never once raises her voice
It's 5 O'clock in the morning; And, I don't give it a second thought

It's a thin line between love and hate; Don't think you can keep breaking your woman's heart
It's a thin line between love and hate; And still sit back and enjoy it
It's a thin line between love and hate; Yes, it is a thin line between love and hate
She's gonna fool you one day!

The sweetest woman in the world; Could be the meanest woman in the world
If you make her that way; You keep on 'hurtin' her, she keeps being quiet
She might be holding something inside; That really hurts you one day.

Here I am laying in the hospital; Bandaged from feet to head; In the state of shock
Just that much from being dead; I didn't think my woman could do something like this to me
I didn't think the girl, had the nerve, here I am;
I guess action speaks louder than words!

It's a thin line between love and hate; Don't think you can keep treatin' your woman bad,
It's a thin line between love and hate; And she won't ever get mad
It's a thin line between love and hate; Yes, it is
She's gonna fool you one day
It's a thin line between love and hate
Every smilin' face ain't a happy one".

(*Songwriters:* Jackie Members, Richard Poindexter; Robert Poindexter; Source: LyricFind)

Dr Eric Berne's Ego-States

Every individual, while growing up from infancy to adulthood, develops in his (no gender bias) 'psyche' three distinctly different – what Dr Eric Berne had called, 'ego-states'. Eric Berne, MD (1910–1970), was a practising Canadian psychiatrist who used to record his patient case studies and observations on them, at different stages of his treatment, meticulously. He created the theory of 'Transactional Analysis' ('TA') as a way of explaining human behaviour. His TA theory was based on the ideas of two giant psychotherapists, Sigmund Freud and Carl Jung, but was distinctly different. (References 7 & 8)

I'm explaining what the concept of 'ego-states' is in my own way, which may be a little different from Dr Berne's. When a child is borne, he possesses only one 'ego-state'. Let us call it (C). If the child did not suffer from any stress while staying inside the womb or during early infancy, (C) represents an innocent, playful, fun-and-game loving personality which is hungry for love from its parents and care-givers making it an 'Obedient Child' ('OC'). If it had been subjected to stress inside the womb or even after being taken out of it (due to factors like premature birth, affected by infection in the place of birth, injury during delivery, or even due to the painful experience of circumcision), then the 'freeze-fight-flight' switch is triggered inside its brain, making it a 'Rebellious Child' (RC). OC is quiet, adaptive, non-reactive, respectful towards authority, takes commands, follows instructions, advices & suggestions without any hassle. 'RC' is just the opposite – negative in all these respects, most reactive, beyond any control.

While the infant is growing up, the mirror neurons inside its brain are very active and it copies the parental behaviour. So, inside the growing child's psyche a 'Parent' (P) ego-state develops. Again, (P) are of two types: 'Autocratic' or 'Critical Parent' (CP) (dictatorial, authoritarian, dominating, fault-finding, blaming, disciplining) and 'Benevolent' or 'Nurturing Parent' (NP) (loving, affectionate, kind-hearted, forgiving, prepared to listen). (OC) adjusts well with both (CP) and (NP) whereas (RC) has trouble with both. So, between (NP) and (OC), there is loving relationship whereas between (CP) and both (OC) and (RC), there is hateful relationship. However, between two (P)s, there is good love-based relations, as much as there is between two (C)s.

Now, you must appreciate that both the (P) and (C) ego-states are full of emotions – logical, analytical, intelligent thinking is missing. But, as the child grows in age, the cognitive powers of his brain start to develop so a mature 'Adult' (A) 'ego-state' develops. Most interestingly, an (A) can be appreciated by and vibes well with another (A) only. An (A) does not adjust at all with either a (CP) or (NP) or an (OC) or (RC).

Now in a loving relationship, both the partners have all the three 'ego-states'. So, when they are vibing well and there is no conflict, then 'Love' exists and just the opposite happens when there is a feeling of

'Hate' between them. What is the lesson then? The lovers should be conscious about the pre-dominance of their ego-states under different circumstances and try to adjust so that 'Love' prevails and 'Hate' is avoided.

Love-Hate Seesaw

Many of the pairs in love tend to see-saw through extreme emotions which are bipolar by nature: 'love' at one end, and 'hate' at the other. The stable graph of feelings is missing quite often. What kinds of opposite emotions are those? Let us see from the experience that I had gathered in my own 'Happiness' clinics that used to run for more than three decades.

Sometimes, you love your partner most because he is dynamic, focused in life, always very helpful and cooperative, very attentive towards your needs. But, at other times, you hate him because you feel his ego raises its stupid (you think so) head in the company of your parents and kin. He behaves very rudely and proudly, with a lot of vanity. (You do not understand that he does not want to share you with others – emotionally – he wants you to love him with all your heart & soul!!)

In a love-hate relationship, you love and hate each other with passion. When you both argue, it would be intense and can lead to name-calling and threats of breaking up. You find each other highly attractive at the moment of love and highly repulsive at the moment of hate. It becomes clearly visible from your body language and tonal quality in both the situations. However, whenever the heat comes down, you both make up. You just forget that you were at each other's throats just a little while ago. Interestingly, the cycle of making up and breaking up goes on.

It was going fine with your partner. All of a sudden, you get exposed to some negatives in him which repel you, but you have invested so much time, effort and energy to develop intimacy that you take it up as a challenge, and instead of calling it a day, continue with the see-saw love-and-hate swings. The see-saw ride develops into a regular habit.

Not unlikely that you start comparing your relationship with that of others whom you know closely, compare notes with them, and get frustrated that your relationship is not 100 percent in your favour as you find in those of others. You start criticising your partner for his lapses and start finding faults with him. You both start playing the blame game, and the natural outcome is the love-and-hate see-sawing.

Both of you are extremely emotional. And, both of you carry extra emotional baggage. And, emotions are wavy in nature, so the living with the emotional ups-and-downs is natural for you, and you have to accept it as inborn nature cannot be changed easily.

A few things that you dislike are very much liked by your partner; like he smokes, he drinks alcohol, he occasionally flirts with other women at parties and get-togethers. Still, when you're both together, both of you are brimming with love like two houses on fire. Although your hatred for his bad habits is not overtly expressed, you carry the hate feeling inside your mind which affects your health at times.

You talk more about what you don't like in your partner than what you like in him, although there is an undercurrent of love flowing beneath the surface. This sometimes causes see-saw movement between love and hate.

A healthy relationship is where both of you can be true to yourselves – loving each other without boundaries and borders. You accept each other without any reservations. Otherwise, both of you get preoccupied with thoughts as to how you can be acceptable as flawless to each other.

To make a flat love-love relationship possible, you must be able to: (References 9 and 10)

- Subdue your ego
- Endeavour to be compatible
- Bend your personality to adjust with each other
- Resolve conflicts
- Control issues
- Give up deception, hypocrisy and envy
- Keep your brain cool.

References

1. "The Reverend Dr. Martin Luther King, Jr.: 'Hate cannot drive out hate; only love can do that'." *Death Penalty Information Center*, 20th January 2020.
2. *Love-hate relationship* – Wikipedia.
3. A.J.L. Baker, "Patterns of Parental Alienation Syndrome: A Qualitative Study of Adults Who Were Alienated from a Parent as a Child", *The American Journal of Family Therapy*, 2006, Vol. 34, No. 1, pp. 63-78.
4. "The mystery behind love-hate relationship" *ScienceBlog.com*, 8th June 2006.
5. Jamie Kravitz, "37 Best Martin Luther King Jr. Quotes That are More Relevant Than Ever", *Woman's Day*, 13th January 2023.
6. Berit Brogaard, "It's a Thin Line between Love and Hate: Why we hate the people we love", *Psychology Today*, 27th March, 2018.
7. *Eric Berne* – Wikipedia.
8. Eric Berne, *Games People Play*, New York: Grove Press, 1964.
9. Sanjana Lagudu, "10 Signs You are in A Love-Hate Relationship", *Mom Junction*, 17th July 2023.
10. Aastha Pahadia, "11 Signs of Love-Hate Relationship: Understand Your Emotions", *Pinkvilla*, 14th September 2023.

CHAPTER 11

A Theory of Love

The Triangular Theory of Love

I am not going to talk about a 'love triangle' where two men are chasing one woman or two women are chasing one man. I'm going to talk about the 'Triangular Theory of Love' which had been proposed by Robert Sternberg, a professor at Yale University. This theory describes different types of love in terms of three components: 'passion', 'intimacy', and 'commitment' – which form three corners of a triangle. 'Passion' involves physical attraction; 'Intimacy' involves sharing of thoughts, ideas, emotions and feelings; and, 'Commitment' is sticking with the same person over time. (Reference 1)

However, even if the third component 'commitment' does not materialise due to some reason or the other, if only the other two components are strong then a 'bridge' is built, which does not break even if it is not used for a long time. The 'love', which develops once deeply, may go to sleep but it may again wake up under changed circumstances. I will prove it to you by sharing the plots of two popular American movies: 'Sunrise' & 'Sunset'. (References 2 & 3).

On June 16, 1994, Jesse, an American man meets Celine, an European young woman on a train from Budapest, and they strike up a conversation. Jesse is going to Vienna to catch a flight to the United States, whereas Celine is returning to university in Paris after visiting her grandmother. In course of their train journey, they develop a 'liking' for each other. When they reach Vienna, Jesse asks Celine to disembark with him so that they can spend some more happy time together, as 10 to 20 years down the road, she might not be happy with her partner and might wonder how her life would have been different if she had picked someone else. It would give them some more time to ascertain if they are suited for each other. Lacking enough money to rent a hotel room for the night, they decide to roam around in Vienna until Jesse's flight the next morning.

After visiting a few landmarks in Vienna and having a few hours together without any third person intruding, they started feeling a 'romantic connection'. As they continue to roam around the city, they begin to talk more openly with each other. Celine tells Jesse that her boyfriend broke up with her six months ago although she 'loved' him too much. Jesse reveals that he had initially come to Europe to spend time with his girlfriend who was studying in Madrid, Spain, but they broke up soon after he was there.

Eventually, they admit their 'attraction' for each other and strong 'passion' made them go to a beautiful park and be physically close to each other. The emotional 'intimacy' was followed by physical 'intimacy'. They celebrated the moment with a bottle of wine that they had purchased locally. The next day, when Celine's train is about to leave for Paris, the couple decide not to exchange any contact information, but instead makes a 'commitment' to meet at the same place after six months. This 'commitment' could not be kept from both sides. Thus, in Robert Sternberg's 'Triangular Theory of Love', we have only two components: 'passion' & 'intimacy'. The third component 'commitment' is missing.

Nine years after meeting Celine in Vienna, Jesse has written a best-selling novel 'This Time' based on their time together in Vienna. During a book tour of Europe, he does a reading at a Paris bookstore where he meets Celine again by chance. Required to leave for the airport in an hour, Jesse and Celine use the time to roam Paris. Their conversation soon becomes deeply personal (arising due to the past 'intimacy' factor) and they lament their failure to meet again in Vienna or exchange contact details.

They reveal how their lives had changed in the nine years apart. Jesse is married and has a son, while Celine has become an environmental activist and is in relationship with a photojournalist. They each express dissatisfaction with their lives as they walk around Paris, and their old romantic feelings are slowly rekindled. Jesse says his novel was inspired by the hope of seeing Celine again; and, she says that listening to his book reading at the Paris bookstore has caused her painful memories.

Celine and Jesse arrive at her apartment, even after continuous insistence that Jesse should not miss his flight. Jesse persuades Celine to play a love song on her guitar. Then, Jesse plays 'Just in Time' on Celine's stereo. Celine dances as he watches; the pair acknowledging that Jesse will miss his flight. Euphoric feeling of 'love' does not make Jesse feel that he is really going to miss something.

The Empathy Effect

Empathy is the capacity to feel what another person is experiencing – something good or bad, something pleasurable or painful. (Reference 4)

The English word 'empathy' is derived from the Greek word '*empatheia*'. Peculiarly, while in ancient Greek language, it meant 'physical affection' or 'passion' representing 'love' which is our concern, in modern Greek, the same word, depending upon the context, may mean: prejudice, malevolence, malice or hatred. What a contrast!! In 1903, the German aesthetic term representing 'empathy' was added to German psychological theory & practice; and, in 1909, the German word was translated into English as 'empathy'.

Most interestingly, ever since its introduction into English, 'empathy' has acquired a wide range (sometimes conflicting) of definitions which encompass a broad range including: caring for other people and having a desire to help them – purely out of love without any selfish motive or any expectation or not out of dutifulness; discerning what the other person is thinking or feeling; and, experiencing emotions that match another person's emotions. (References 5 & 6)

Empathy may be related to some bodily feeling (that is, 'Physical Empathy'). It may be related to emotions, feelings, beliefs or convictions (that is, 'Affective Empathy'). It may be related to some cognitive perception or understanding or interpretation of something (that is, 'Cognitive Empathy'). It may be related to a proposed action or to an action already taken (that is, 'Action Empathy').

Is there any difference between 'sympathy' and 'empathy'? Yes, of course! 'Sympathy' is more of a feeling of pity for the other person, conveying the 'I'm OK, you're not OK' mind-set. It is indirectly a feeling of relief in not having the same problem. 'Empathy' involves supporting a person in tough times. A typical example of empathetic communication is: "Oh! My God! I know exactly how you feel! I feel as if it has happened to me!" – or "I can literally feel your pain!" or, "Don't worry! I'm with you!" Contrarily, "Nothing has happened to you – it is all in your imagination – things are going fine!" – or – "There is no reason for you to break down – nothing is wrong!" – or "Increase your resilience – the power to cope with the odds!" all sound like unwanted sermons to the affected person who is hungry for empathy. Such messages make the sufferer feel that 'he does not understand me – there is a distinct gap between us, which unless bridged, will affect our relationship adversely". It takes time, energy & skill to build bridges. For inter-personal bridge-building, 'empathy' is the building material, the bonding agent, the glue, the adhesive!! (Reference 7) Sympathy creates separation whereas empathy creates synchronization and fosters connection.

Mirror neurons in the brain is a relatively recent discovery. These brain cells can make us empathize in two possible ways. In one case, the mirror neurons can simulate or mimic the observed action. (Reference 8) More than two decades ago, while observing monkey's brains, a group of Italian researchers noticed that certain cells activated on both occasions – once when a monkey performed an action and when that monkey watched another monkey performing the same action. "Mirror neurons" were discovered. Since that time, mirror neurons have been hailed as a cornerstone of human empathy, language and a few other vital processes. These neurons are in the 'Pre-Frontal Cortex' ('PFC') areas of the brain. These are 'motor command neurons' which get activated when we indulge in some movements or motor actions. A subset of these mirror neurons also fire, when we watch another person taking some motor action. It is simple unconscious mimicry. To describe using common phrases: 'Empathy' signifies "getting into the other person's shoes"; and, "walking a mile in another person's shoes".

The 'Insular Cortex' ('IC') fires cells and we experience a painful sensation. The agony is possibly explained in the 'Anterior Cingulate' ('AC'). The same brain area would be activated in me when I see somebody else is feeling the pain physically and not me. I may not feel it physically but it will certainly be felt by me emotionally. That is what 'empathy' is. Mirror neuron dysfunction may be involved in 'autism'. Empathy makes us social – socially acceptable. Autistic persons are just the opposite – they are not social; they avoid social contacts & relationships.

How do you know that you are an empathetic person? The main factors include: (i) Effective Listening: you're a very good listener – you never interrupt the speaker – you go on listening most patiently with sustained positive eye contact; (ii) Trustworthiness: people often open up to you and share their personal problems & feelings; (iii) Counselling Ability: other people come to you for advice; (iv) Caring Attitude: you care deeply about people you love; and, (v) Conflict-free Relationships. (Reference 9)

A team of researchers at the Mt. Sinai School of Medicine in New York had shown that the 'Anterior Insular Cortex' ('AIC') area of the brain is the activity centre for human empathy. The study was published in the September 2012 issue of the journal *Brain*. (Reference 10)

Functional MRI research indicates that the 'Inferior Frontal Gyrus' ('IFG') area of the brain plays a critical role in the experience of empathy. This area helps to recognise others' emotions through facial expressions. (Reference 11)

To get a clearer idea about the brain and its 'Empathy Circuit' you can watch Josh Kornbluth's video "Citizen Brain: The Empathy Circuit" (Reference 12). However, to get a very clear idea about what 'empathy' is, I would follow the unparalleled Mother Teresa, who was canonised by the Catholic Church as Saint Teresa of Calcutta. (Reference 13).

Love: A Strength or A Weakness?

'Love' is a 'strength' within the 'virtue' category of humanity as it manifests in caring relationships with others. 'Love' is an inter-personal 'strength' and most relevant in one-to-one relationships. Nevertheless, if you fall for the wrong person, 'love' is a weakness. 'Love' must not be misconstrued as 'lust' which is certainly a critical weakness whereas 'True/Genuine Love' is a towering strength.

Most interestingly, 'love' is strange. It can make the weakest person strong and a strongest person weak. That is the reason why 'devils' do not love. I recently had a chance-viewing of a German film "Meine Tueflische Gute Freundin" which had a very unusual storyline. (References 14 & 15).

"Actually, 14-year-old Lilith looks like a normal teenager. However, she is the daughter of the devil, who has his headquarters in a high-rise building in Frankfurt am Mainhas. Lilith actually feels that her life is hell because her strict father hardly gives her any freedom; He also believes that she is too young to work as a devil. She would like to be really evil, but she is only allowed to do that on the Internet and under the supervision of her private teacher. Because she's bored, she wants to go out into the world and show what she's made of. So, she negotiates a deal with her father and is allowed to go to Earth for a week. If she manages to seduce a good person to become evil within this very week, she can stay there. Otherwise, she has to go back to the hellish boredom and take a job in her father's accounting department."

"In the tranquil town of Birkenbrunn, Lilith's father chooses the kind-hearted Greta Birnstein as a victim. Lilith moves into an accommodation with Greta's warm-hearted family. Greta is the eldest daughter of the Birnstein family and, in Lilith's opinion, a strange girl. Lilith begins her mission first. However, Greta is a more difficult case than expected because she doesn't have a shred of malice in her personality. Lilith also faces another problem at school in the form of her classmate Samuel, with whom Lilith falls in love (devils are not allowed to love). Time is running out – Lilith must finally deliver results. Her father wants to come to the school festival to examine his daughter's evil work and the chaos she has caused. After a friendship develops between Lilith and Greta (Reference 15), she is in danger because she is finally no longer able to be evil."

"Friendship makes everything possible: through a less-than-good stage performance, a few nasty pranks and a portion of nail polish, with which she even outwits the devil, Greta manages to get Lilith to stay with her." (Reference 16)

In any relationship, it is not fair to play a 'win-lose' game. Do not calculate what you're giving and what you're getting. Then you're selfish in a way. 'True love' should not be a trading relationship. You'll be happier if you follow the route of giving more and expecting less. Then you're compassionate, you're forgiving, you're tolerant, patient & perseverant. All these make you happy and if you are happy, it means, according to the research of the University of Wisconsin neuroscientist Prof. Richard Davidson, you are active on the Right Half of your Cerebral Cortex, if you're a right-handed person. (References 17)

References

1. Catherine A. Sanderson, "The Different Types of Love", *Wondrium Daily*, 8th October 2022.
2. *Sunrise* – Wikipedia.
3. *Sunset* – Wikipedia.
4. "Empathy" – *Psychology Today*.
5. *Empathy* – Wikipedia.
6. Kendra Cherry, "What Is Empathy?" *verywellmind*, 22nd February 2023.
7. "The Difference Between Empathy and Sympathy" (By Psychiatric Medical Care Communication Team), *PMC (Psychiatric Medical Care)*
8. Jason Marsh, "Do Mirror Neurons Give Us Empathy?" *Greater Good Magazine*, 29th March 2012.
9. Kendra Cherry, "What Is Empathy?" *verywellmind*, Updated on 22nd February 2023.
10. "Researchers Identify Area of the Brain That Processes Empathy", *Mount Sinai School of Medicine*, New York.
11. A.E. Hills, "Inability to empathize: Brain lesions that disrupt sharing and understanding another's emotions", *Brain*, 2014, Vol. 137, No. 4, pp. 981–997.
12. Josh Kornbluth, "Citizen Brain: The Empathy Circuit" – video on You Tube.

13. *Mother Teresa* – Wikipedia.
14. The German movie "Meine Teuflische Gute Freundin" (My devilishly good friend), 2018, directed by Marco Petry.
15. *My devilishly good friend*, Wikipedia.
16. "The Neuroscience of Well-being" – video presentation by Prof. Richard Davidson of the University of Wisconsin, Madison, USA.
17. Richard Davidson & Sharon Begley, *The Emotional Life of Your Brain*, London: Hodder & Stoughton, 2012.

CHAPTER 12

Love Deities

The Roman Deity of Love

Venus is a Roman goddess, who represents love, beauty, desire, sex, fertility, prosperity and victory. Roman mythology claims that she was the ancestor of the Roman people through her son Aeneas, who survived the fall of Troy and fled to Italy. Her Greek counterpart was Aphrodite although in the later classical tradition of the West, Venus became one of the most widely referred deities of Greco-Roman mythology as the embodiment of love and sexuality. (Reference 1)

Venus's male counterparts Vulcan and Mars are both active and fiery. Venus absorbs and tempers the male essence, uniting the opposites of male and female in mutual affection. She is essentially assimilative and benign, and embraces several otherwise quite disparate functions. She can give military victory, sexual success, good future and prosperity. The Latin name 'Venus' means: love and charm; the old Indic equivalent 'vanas' means 'desire'.

The bondage of 'love' is quite a literal statement of the agency of Venus. The late Republican polymath and grammarian Varro explained in a passage of his "De Lingua Latina" which describes how heat and moisture are embodied, respectively, in the male and female reproductive forces:

> *"....and fire in male, which the semen is in the other case, and water is female because the embryo develops from her moisture, and the force that brings, that 'binding' is Venus – 'Love'." (Reference 2)*

Venus is identified with water – an aspect of the water principle. To generate life, the watery matrix of the womb requires the virile warmth of fire. To sustain life, water and fire must be balanced, excess of either one, or their mutual antagonism, are unproductive, or destructive.

In some Latin mythology, Cupid was the son of Venus and Mars, the god of war. At other times, or in parallel myths and theologies, Venus was understood to be the consort of Vulcan or as the mother of the 'second Cupid', fathered by Mercury.

I am sharing with you some section of the beautiful song by the English singer Dee D. Jackson:

"I'm Venus, the goddess of love. Come and touch me
And see for yourself. Look at me and be really sure
I'm Venus, I'm Venus! The goddess of love.

An angel from heaven. Come down on me
He gave me his time. But I gave him me.
I knew who he was but Oh! he didn't know
What he could do.
He changed all of me. I'm what you see in front of me.

....

His magic surrounds me. It's touching my soul.
I don't want to leave him. But I got to go.
I feel it is so hard, but Oh! I know it is true.
I've got to get through I'm what you see
That woman is you in front of me.

I'm Venus the goddess of love. Come and touch me.
And see for yourself. Look at me and be really sure
I'm Venus, I'm Venus. The goddess of love." (Reference 3)

The Greek Deities of Love

Heriod was an ancient Greek poet (active between 750 to 650 BC), generally regarded as the very first written poet in the Western tradition. Ancient authors credited Heriod and Homer with establishing Greek religious customs. Modern scholars refer to Heriod as a major source of Greek mythology. Heriod's masterpiece 'Theogony' concerns the origins of the world ('cosmogony') and of the gods ('theogony') beginning with, amongst others, god Uranus (Heaven) and goddess Gaia (Earth). (Reference 4)

Uranus, the son of Gaia was the sky god and the first ruler. Gaia created him without any help from anyone. He then became the husband of Gaia and together they had many offspring. Uranus was a bad father and husband. He imprisoned some of his own children by pushing them into the hidden places of the earth, Gaia's womb. This enraged Gaia and she plotted against Uranus. (Reference 5).

She urged her children to punish their father. She fashioned a sickle to be used to punish Uranus and gave it to Cronus, the youngest of her sons who agreed to cooperate with her. When Uranus came to lie with Gaia, Cronus reached out and castrated his father, casting the severed genitals into the sea. Cronus then assumed supreme command to rule the cosmos.

According to Heriod's epic poem 'Theogony', Aphrodite – the Greek goddess of beauty, grace, love, desire, sexual pleasure, fertility and procreation emerged from the sea from the foam and bubbles formed by the severed genitals of Uranus, as if the sperms that came out from his semen fertilised the ova of the sea. She is described as exceedingly beautiful and youthful. She lived together with other gods and goddesses on Mount Olympus.

She was married to Hephaestus, god of the forge and craftsmanship, though she often took other lovers including her husband's more handsome brother Ares, the god of war. Aphrodite and Venus are regarded as the same. She was worshipped throughout the ancient Greek world. Aphrodite won the young Trojan prince Paris over by promising him the most beautiful woman in the world as his bride. After Paris chose in Aphrodite's favour in a beauty contest with her fellow goddesses Hera and Athena, she kept her promise and caused Helen of Sparta, the most beautiful woman in the world, to fall in love with Paris. But when the two lovers ran off, Helen's husband Menelaus raised an army and sailed to Troy to retrieve his wife, thus sparking the Trojan war.

Aphrodite, it was believed, had the power of LOVE, in all its positive and negative connotations. Her attributes included her enchanted magic girdle and a mirror which she could use with anyone to induce desire and romantic love. Her favourite animals included birds such as the dove or swallow. (Reference 6)

In classical mythology, 'Cupid' (meaning 'passionate desire') is the god of desire, erotic love, attraction, and affection. He is often portrayed as the son of the love goddess 'Venus' (alias 'Aphrodite') and the god of war 'Mars' (alias 'Ares'). He is also known as 'Amor'. The Roman 'Cupid' was equivalent to the Greek god 'Eros' (Reference 7)

Portrayed as a chubby boy, the bow and arrow that Cupid carries represents his source of power. A person, or even a deity, who is shot by Cupid's arrow is filled with uncontrollable desire. In the Middle Ages, under Christian influence he often had a dual nature as 'Heavenly' and 'Earthly' love. In contemporary popular culture, Cupid is shown drawing his bow to inspire romantic love, often as an icon on "Valentine's Day".

Cupid is winged, allegedly because lovers are flighty and likely to change their minds, and boyish because love is irrational.

To quote William Shakespeare in "A Midsummer Night's Dream":

"Love looks not with the eyes, but with the mind
And therefore is winged Cupid painted blind.
Nor hath love's mind of any judgement taste;
Wings and no eyes figure unheedy haste.
And, therefore, is love said to be a child
Because in choice he is so oft beguiled." (Reference 8)

Cupid's powers are similar, though not identical, to 'Kamadeva', the Hindu god of human love. (Reference 9)

The Hindu Deities of Love

There is a trinity of Hindu gods. 'Brahma' is the creator, 'Vishnu' – the preserver, and 'Shiva' (alias 'Maheswara') – the destroyer. (Reference 10). This concept represents an individual's life cycle. We are born, we develop and grow, then we fade out, our life comes to an end in death. The mythological analogy is really remarkable – easy to visualise for common people with less than ordinary and ordinary minds.

Lord Brahma, the god of creation has supernatural powers. He could create offspring from his mind by his thoughts. 'Kamadeva' (alias 'Kama') is one of the mind-born sons of Lord Brahma. In Sanskrit, it is expressed as 'manas putra' or 'manoja' or 'manasija'. It is said that after Brahma created all the 'prajapatis' (who are agents of creation) and a maiden named 'Sandhya', an extremely handsome young man emerges from his mind. This young man asks Brahma what is the purpose of his birth – why has he been brought to life. Brahma names him 'Kama' and asks him to spread love in the world by shooting flower-arrows. The creator of the myth possibly had as the purpose of this plot to turn the lecherous lustful pre-humans into affectionate compassionate humans; that is the idea behind Kama's flower-arrows. (Reference 11)

Mischievous young Kama decides to use his first arrow on his creator Lord Brahma himself who became attracted towards his own creation 'Sandhya' and becomes desirous to be in love with her. Lord Dharma, the god of justice (Reference 12) becomes worried at the attitude & behaviour of Brahma and calls Lord Shiva who becomes amused and laughs at both Brahma and Kama. He helps Brahma to restore his good sense. Brahma, being outraged, curses Kama to be burnt to ashes in future. However, on Kama pleading to his creator, Brahma assures him that he will be reborn.

Sandhya had died after Brahma desired for her as she could not stand his lustful vibrations. However, Lord Vishnu the preserver brought her back to life as 'Rati' and presented her to Kamadeva. Goddess Rati becomes the consort and chief assistant of Kama and comes to be regarded as the goddess of love for the Hindus. She is the female counterpart representing sexual pleasure. Besides Rati, Kama's another main assistant is 'Vasanta' – the god of the spring season who was also created by Lord Brahma. Kama also leads the celestial nymphs, the 'apsaras' who are often sent by Indra, the king of heaven, to disturb the penance of the sages to prevent them from achieving divine powers through high discipline and meditation.

Indra and the heavenly gods were suffering at the hands of the demon Tarakasur who could not be defeated by any god except the male child of Lord Shiva who was yet unborn. The gods made a strategy to motivate Shiva to have a son with Parvati but Shiva was so engaged in deep meditation that he was not conscious of the presence of exquisitely pretty Parvati who was desirous of coming in close contact the highly masculine Shiva. Indra assigned Kamadeva the job of disturbing Shiva and break his concentrated meditation. Kama awakens Lord Shiva with his invincible flower arrow but the destroyer god, instead of getting influenced to pay attention to Parvati, gets outraged and opens his mysterious third eye to turn Kama instantaneously into ashes. Eventually, however, Shiva and Parvati's marriage results in a son, Kartikeya, who goes on to defeat Tarakasura. Kama was reborn as the eldest son of Krishna and his chief consort, Rukmini and came to be known as 'Pradyumna'.

Kamadeva, the wielder of the creative power of the universe, is decked with ornaments and his bow is made of sugarcane and his arrows are decorated with five kinds of fragrant flowers – white lotus, blue lotus, flowers from the Ashoka tree, mango tree flowers, and jasmine. His companions are: a cuckoo, a parrot, humming bees, and gentle breeze. He represents the spring season, and his festival is 'Holi' – the festival of colours. The Ashoka tree is said to be the symbol of love and is dedicated to Kamadeva.

Deities of Love in Krishnaism

Radha-Krishna is the combined form of Hindu deity Krishna with his chief consort and shakti Radha. This divine pair is regarded as the feminine as well as the masculine realities of God. (Reference 13)

The three main potencies of God are: spiritual bliss, eternality, and existential consciousness. Radha is an embodiment of the feeling of love towards Krishna, the outcome of which is spiritual bliss which is related to the domain of 'Anandamaya Kosha' in the 'Pancha Kosha' model of Taittiriya Upanishad. (References 14 & 15). Radha personifies devotional service in loving servitude.

The popular Gita Govinda written by Jayadeva in the 12th century CE depicted Radha and Krishna as a couple. Each and every god has its partner – a 'Shakti' without whom it is powerless. The special feature in this case is that Radha & Krishna are inseparable. (References 16 & 17)

For any creation, the male and female principle is most basic. Female is the 'shakti' and male is the 'shaktiman'. Even if an individual is creating something, it is the female & male energy and consciousness in her or him that are responsible for the act. That principle is beautifully represented by the Radha-Krishna model. Chaitanya Mahaprabhu is the combined avatar of Radha and Krishna. Krishna wanted to know how Radha feels for Krishna. So, Krishna came as Chaitanya Mahaprabhu to understand Radha's mood. (References 18 & 19)

In Jayadeva's Gita Govinda, Krishna speaks to Radha: (Reference 20)

> *"O woman with desire, place on this patch of flower-strewn flow your lotus foot,*
> *And let your foot through beauty win,*
> *To me who am the Lord of All,*
> *O be attached, now always yours,*
> *O follow me, my little Radha!"*

There are many lessons that can be taken from the Radha-Krishna model even in the modern world. I'm sharing only the 'key' five of them (Reference 21).

1. **Devotion:** Once you've developed bonding with someone never be calculative as to what you're giving and what you're getting.
2. **Patience:** If you are impatient by nature, bonding of love with someone is an opportunity for you to cultivate & culture patience. You must handle situations with a balanced and calm mind and not impulsively, as impatient persons do. Development of understanding for and with the person you love is what is called for.
3. **Strength:** Love, for you, must not be a weakness – instead, it should give you strength.

4. **Connectivity:** Inculcate a very deep connection with the person you love. Learn from the Radha-Krishna model. It was proven when Lord Krishna had gone into the Yamuna River to kill the poisonous serpent, Kaliya Naag. Radha Rani was the only one who was ready to end her life for him. Work to make your bonding so deep and profound.
5. **Sacrifice:** Another word for 'True Love' is 'sacrifice'. You have to give more, without being asked, than what you are getting. You must ignore the weaknesses, lapses and shortcomings of the person you love. Be controlled in using your brain's 'Error Detection Circuit' which is always ready to detect deviations from expectations and what is right.

Outside Hinduism, Radha and Krishna are mentioned in the scriptures and commentaries of Sikhism and Jainism. Guru Gobind Singh, in his 'Dasam Grantha', describes Radha: "Radhika went out in the light of the white soft moon, wearing a white robe to meet her Lord. It was white everywhere and hidden in it, she appeared like the light itself in search of Him." (Reference 22)

Egyptian Deity of Love

All the love deities that I have talked about already were in both genders. I decided to study Egyptian deities as Egyptian civilisation is one of the most ancient ones; (Reference 23) and, there I was surprised to find only one female deity of love. Possibly ancient Egypt had a matriarchal society. I'm not too sure as I was not a student of mythology like the now-famous Devdutt Pattanaik. (Reference 24)

'Hathor' was a major goddess in ancient Egyptian religion. She was a versatile goddess, who played a wide variety of roles. Like the Hindu gods and goddesses were stationed in the heaven, Hathor was a sky deity. Moreover, she was the mother or consort of the sky god 'Horus' and the sun god 'Ra' – both of whom were connected with kingship. She was the symbolic mother of the Pharaohs, the earthly representatives of the sky gods.

Hathor's positive side represented LOVE, sexuality, maternal care, joy, music and dance. Interestingly, she acted as the consort of several male deities, and the mother of their sons.

[You may remember that I had classified human consciousness into: 'pre-human' (forest-dwelling hunter-gatherer stage when there was no social bonded relationships like families – people were fulfilling the primary biological objectives of 'survival & replication'); 'human' (where a secondary objective of 'bonded relationship-building' was added to the primary one); and, 'post-human' (where the consciousness transcended the mundane levels of 'survival, replication, and bonded relationship-building' and it followed 'attachment with detachment')] Being exposed to the profile of goddess 'Hathor', I'm inclined to conclude that the ancient Egyptians might still had been in the 'pre-human' consciousness stage.

'Hathor' represented the Egyptian concept of femininity. (References 25, 26 & 27). She crossed the boundaries between two worlds – the earth and the sky, helping deceased souls in the transition to the afterlife.

Her common form was that of a woman wearing a headdress of cow horns and a sun disc placed between the two cow horns. Cows are venerated in many cultures, including in ancient Egypt as symbols of gentle motherhood and nourishment, because they care for their calves and provide humans with milk. A cow's head with inward-curving horns surrounded by stars is often used in Egyptian artwork and sculpture symbolising that such motherly creatures came from the sky (Hindu>Heaven), to offer care and serve the members of the mankind. Goddess 'Hathor' thus symbolises loving and caring womanhood and not the sex-crazy, man-hunting aggressive females. So, I suppose, the ancient Egyptians believed in motherly, womanly, caring females as girlfriends, wives and mothers. Hathor was thought as the cow who birthed the sun god and placed him between the horns to provide vigilant protection. She was said to give birth to the sun god every dawn. In some creation myths, it is mentioned that she helped to create the world itself. She mated with the god 'Khonsu' to enable creation.

'Hathor' was called the 'mistress of love' as an extension of her sexual aspect. Over the years in ancient Egypt, she became one of Egypt's most important deities. More temples were dedicated to her than to any other goddess. However, after the end of the New Kingdom, 'Hathor' was increasingly overshadowed by 'Isis', but she continued to be venerated until the extinction of the ancient Egyptian religion in the early centuries AD.

References

1. *Venus (mythology)* – Wikipedia.
2. Stephen Hinds, "Venus, Varro and the votes: toward the limits of etymologizing interpretation", *Dictynna*, 3/2006, Varia.
3. "Venus The Goddess of Love", *The Genius, genius.com*
4. *Heriod* – Wikipedia
5. *Uranus (mythology)* – Wikipedia.
6. Avi Kapech, "Olympian Goddess Aphrodite", *Mythopedia*, 10th April 2023.
7. *Cupid* – Wikipedia.
8. Shakespeare: *A Midsummer Night's Dream* 1.1, pp. 234-239.
9. Roshan Dalal, *Hinduism: An Alphabetical Guide*, London: Penguin Books, 2014. (Entry: "Kama")
10. 'Three Hindu Gods' – Khan Academy.
11. *Kamadeva* – Wikipedia
12. *Yama (Hinduism)* – Wikipedia.
13. *Radha Krishna* – Wikipedia.
14. *Pancha Kosha* – Vikaspedia
15. *What is Pancha Kosha? – Definition from Yogapedia* – Yogapedia
16. *Gita Govinda* – Wikipedia.
17. Barbara Stoler Miller, *The Gitagovinda of Jayadeva: Love Song of the Dark Lord*, New Delhi: Motilal Banarasidas, 2022.
18. ISKCON Desire Tree.
19. "Caitanya Mahaprabhu Is Radha And Krishna Combined" – *HARE KRISHNA.*

20. Archer, "The Gita Govinda", 2004.
21. "5 love lessons to take from Radha Krishna" – *E Times (Entertainment Times)*, 17th February 2022.
22. M.S. Ranadhawa, Kangra Valley Painting, Publications Division, Ministry of Information & Broadcasting, Govt. of India, 2017.
23. *Ancient Egypt* – Wikipedia.
24. *Devdutt Pattanaik* – Wikipedia.
25. *Hathor – Egyptian goddess* – Britannica.
26. *Hathor* – Wikipedia.
27. "Hathor – Egyptian goddess of love" – *Pinterest.*

CHAPTER 13

Learning from Helen Fisher

Helen Fisher on 'Love'

Helen Elizabeth Fisher (born 1945) is the foremost scholar on the 'Biology of Love & Attraction' in the world today. A biological anthropologist, she is a senior research fellow at the Kinsey Institute, Indiana University, and a member of the Centre for Human Evolutionary Studies in the Department of Anthropology at Rutgers University. Prior to her engagement to Rutgers University, she was a research associate at the American Museum of Natural History in New York City.

Fisher earned a BA in Anthropology and Psychology from New York University in 1968; an MA in Physical & Cultural Anthropology, Linguistics, and Archaeology from the University of Colorado at Boulder in 1972, and a PhD in Physical Anthropology: Human Evolution, Primatology, Human Sexual Behaviour & Reproductive Strategies from the University of Colorado in Boulder in 1975.

Fisher says that when she began researching for her dissertation, she considered one thing that all humans have in common – the urge to procreate, as I've been telling all the while that our Basic Biological Imperatives comprise: survival & replication. (Reference 1)

In her book, "Why We Love: The Nature & Chemistry of Romantic Love", Fisher proposed that humans have evolved, through their entire evolutionary history in its various stages, three (3) brain systems for reproduction, the means for which is 'mating'.

These are: (i) 'lust': the sex drive or libido – the urge to have physical union; (ii) 'attraction': romantic love which involves courtship and regular 'dating'; and, (iii) 'attachment': deep feeling of long-lasting union with a partner of choice. (References 2 & 3)

Love can start with any of these feelings. Nevertheless, young boys and girls go on dates, try out sex driven by 'lust', and if that releases the 'feel good' chemical 'Dopamine' ('D') from the brain's reward circuit, becomes hungry for more 'D' release and has sex again. Although it may provide one or both the partners with physical pleasure, it may not lead to the next two subsequent phases – 'attraction' and 'attachment'. As long as the urge for 'D' reigns supreme in the brain, the next two phases, especially the one related to 'attachment' may never come. To lead to the stage of 'attachment', the brain's 'Pituitary Glands' must get stimulated to release the love-compassion-trust-empathy-bonding molecule 'Oxytocin' ('O') which I have already introduced to you.

As a matter of fact, I was surprised to know that Dr Paul Zak, the father of the love molecule 'O' was introduced to this amazing neuro-chemical by Dr Helen Fisher in the year 2000, when both of them met at a conference on economics and law at the Gruter Institute for Law and Behavioural Research at a ski resort in the Sierra Nevada, USA. (Reference 4)

The Tikal Temple of Love in Guatemala and Brain State in Love

I'm indeed indebted to Helen Fisher as what I came to know from one of her TED talks (Reference 5), I had never known before. It is about a temple that stands in the jungles of Guatemala in South America. The temple, known as Tikal Temple I, is one of the major structures at Tikal, one of the largest cities and archaeological sites of the pre-Columbian Maya civilisation in Mesoamerica. It is also known as the Temple of the Great Jaguar because of the existence of a lintel that represents a king sitting upon a jaguar there. The temple has a stepped pyramidal structure made of limestone. It's dated approximately 732 AD. (Reference 6)

It was built by the grandest sun-king of the grandest civilisation of the Americas, the Mayas. His name was Jasaw Chan Kawiil. Nearly six feet tall, he lived into his 80's and he was buried beneath this monument. Mayan hieroglyphic inscriptions proclaim that he was deeply in love with his wife. So, he built a temple in her honour and memory facing his. And, every spring and autumn (about 20th March & 22nd September), exactly at the equinox, when the day and night are of approximately equal length, the sun rises behind his temple and perfectly bathes her temple with his shadow. And, as the sun sets behind her temple in the afternoon, it perfectly bathes his temple with her shadow. Even after 1300 years, the spirits of this lover couple still touch and kiss each other from their tombs.

As a matter of fact, love is universal. Anthropologists have found the existence of love in 170 human societies. They have not found a single society which did not have it. (Reference 5)

Helen Fisher and her co-researchers had put 37 people who were madly in love into a fMRI brain scanner, and observed that feelings, thoughts and acts of love stimulated the 'Ventral Tegmental Area' ('VTA') where 'Dopamine' ('D') is made and released. 'VTA' is a part of the midbrain and controls diverse behavioural repertoire, including motivation, reward processing, aversion, stress modulation, drug addiction, learning and memory. 'VTA' sends dopaminergic neural projections to both the limbic and cortical areas. (Reference 7)

When you're in love, your brain enters the 'FLOW' state, which means that you're totally in tune with your partner – your 'self' has vanished. The 'FLOW' state in relationships makes it easier to reach the high point of happiness where you progress in harmony. Both of you enjoy being involved in an activity that may be morally wrong and you are strong enough to face any adversity. (References 8 & 9)

Helen Fisher and her co-researchers have found activities in three different areas of the brains of people in love. The first area is the 'VTA' which I've already talked about. 'VTA' gets involved in 'Romantic Love' which is a drive – a basic mating drive; but it is different from 'sex drive' which drives you to go for the sexual act indiscriminately. 'Romantic Love' is when you've set your eyes on only one person as the target of your love. 'Sex Drive' causes wastage of mating energy whereas 'Romantic Love' conserves it to start and continue relationship with a single individual that you wish to mate with. (Reference 5)

These researchers have noticed activity in a second brain region also – and that is, in the 'Nucleus Accumbens' ('NAc') which is a region in the basal forebrain rostral or front part located below the 'Corpus Striatum', which has the most important role in reward & reinforcement circuit of the brain. 'NAc', referred to as the pleasure centre, plays a role in motivation and cognitive processing of aversion. (Reference 5)

The third brain region involved is the one associated with deep attachment with another individual, which is 'Ventral Striatum' ('VS') – formed by the fusion of 'Caudate Nucleus' and 'Putamen'. It is also known as the 'Nucleus Accumbens Septi' ('NAcS'). (Reference 5)

Instead of using 'Psychology', perhaps it will be easier to use 'Biology' to define and describe 'love' in not too distant a future when one should be able to evaluate the right proportions of the neuro-transmitters 'Dopamine' & 'Serotonin' and also of the sex hormones 'Testosterone' & 'Estrogen' which combine to create the strong biological pull.

Strangely enough, I get an echo of how one would feel with the right mix of these bio-chemicals in the bloodstream, from the following verse, when someone is departing from the person she/he loves:

"Fire runs through my body with the pain of loving you.
Pain runs through my body with the fires of my love to you.
Sickness wanders my body with my love for you,
Pain like a boil about to burst with my love for you,
Consumed by fire with my love for you.
I remember what you said to me
I am thinking of your love for me
I am torn by your love for me
Pain and more pain........
Where are you going with my love?
I am told you will go from here
I am told you will leave me here
My body is numb with grief

Remember what I said, my love,
Goodbye my love, goodbye!"

This, told by an anonymous Kwakuitl Indian of Southern Alaska to a missionary in 1896, captures the excruciating pain of lost love. (Reference 10)

Fast, Slow and Sustained Love

Helen Fisher's 'lust', 'attraction' and 'attachment' can be renamed as 'fast love', 'slow love' and 'sustained love' in the same way as I have been categorising happiness. Like my 'Smart Happiness', 'lustful love' is transitory as it releases the pleasure chemical 'Dopamine' ('D') from our brain's 'Reward Circuit'. Like my 'Short-lived' or 'Short Happiness', 'attraction' in the love sequence cherishes the experience of the 'lustful love' which prompts one to experience it again – that is the onset of 'attraction'. Like my 'Sustained Happiness', 'attachment' in the love sequence means long-lasting liking for each other – which releases the bonding chemical 'Oxytocin' ('O') from the brain's 'Pituitary Glands'.

Dr Fisher has been studying the phenomenon of 'love' most systematically in a very focused way. When you relate what she says to what you've experienced or you find others experiencing, you find how true and realistic her observations are. She says, shutting down of various brain systems takes place when you're madly in love. You mobilise all the energy you have during such madness. The oldest part of the brain gets activated – the brain region associated with craving, with obsession, with motivation. Cognitive regions in the 'Prefrontal Cortex' ('PfC'), which have evolved recently, begin to shut down. The brain regions associated with the evaluation of 'good' and 'bad', 'profit' and 'loss'-based decision-making, problem-solving and planning become inactive. You become blind, deaf and dumb.

So, Dr Fisher's advice to those who are seeking love-ful partnership, will be to spend a good deal of time with the chosen person so that the early-stage intense feelings subside and you begin to see what you've actually got. She recommends two to three years of 'Slow Love' before you feel you're heading for the ultimate stage of 'Sustained Love'.

During the 'Fast Love' stage, you are driven by the sex hormone 'Testosterone' and the neurotransmitter 'Dopamine'. In order to transcend into 'Slow Love' and subsequently into 'Sustained Love', you have to use genuine 'novelty' and 'humour'. Situations must be created to experience 'novelty' and enjoy 'humour' together. When both the partners have the same brain chemicals 'Dopamine', 'Serotonin', 'Oxytocin' and 'Endorphin' released inside their brains at the same time, a neuro-synchrony will develop which would act as a reinforcement for the 'attachment' to make it stronger and deeper. Such practices will activate the brain regions associated with: (i) empathy; (ii) control of own emerging emotions; and, (iii) positive illusion. The third point needs a little elucidation. If you develop the spontaneous (not artificial or fake) habit of saying at least 3 to 5 good things to your partner every day, it will reduce the flow of bad cholesterol in her/his bloodstream, reduce the level of the stress chemical 'cortisol' and will boost the immune system. (Reference 11)

Stages of Love-Making

Helen Fisher has studied, most extensively & thoroughly, the love-linked relationship process through her own researches as well as by surveying the relevant literature on love-making in different cultures. (Reference 12)

According to Fisher, the Stage 1 is "Attention-seeking":

> *When one has set the goal of developing a relationship with another person, he/she tries to draw attention of the other person with the help of various 'body signals' and different 'displays'.*

The 'body signals' may include: smiling, gazing, body shifting, body swaying, preening, stretching, moving softly in own territory, twisting curls, looking up coyly, giggling, touching brows, flickering tongues, licking upper lips, blushing, hiding the face. These 'body signals' are all 'gestures' when both the persons are sitting face to face across the table, or sitting side by side on a bench or sofa, or a dining table. If both the persons are standing & have clear territorial demarcation, then the gestural body signals may be combined with a few postural ones. However, the 'inter-personal distance' will not be very close at this stage of the encounter.

'Displays' are also very much used to draw attention at this stage. For 'displays', one may use his or her inherited personal physical resources like the height, beautifully proportioned body, the breasts & buttocks (for women), the personal brain resources like smart/quick/sharp intelligence, imagination or visualisation power, the art of communication & story-telling. Acquired personal resources are: gym-built athletic body, the dress, shoes, accessories, jewelleries, tattoo, hairstyle, hairdo, watches-spectacles-mobile phones, tablet or laptop, umbrella, motor bike, automobile (I leave it to you to add on to this list, which is certainly not complete). While getting introduced to each other, one may also enquire about or share qualifications and experience which are amongst personal acquired resources.

The hidden or implied message is: "I'm here", "I'm important", "I'm available for friendship".

According to Helen Fisher, "Stage 2" is "Recognition" (thereby meaning "Attention Given/Attention Received"). This stage involves exchange of gaze or 'eyes meeting eyes', exchange of smile, slight body shift (coming closer). And then, starting to talk – getting introduced to each other. This stage usually is the onset of romance.

Helen Fisher's "Stage 3" is "Grooming Talk" – meaningless conversation – voices become higher, softer, mellower, more sing-songey, affectionate. "Grooming Talk" starts with ice-breakers, like "Rain has marred the festival mood. Don't you think so? Could you go out much?" What you say matters less than how you say. "Hello!" is potent with romantic intent whereas "Hi!" is matter-of-fact, rarely leading to an intimate relationship. The conversation may be accompanied with flirting laughter.

"Stage 4" is the "Touch Stage". It may involve: leaning forward, extending one arm towards the other to touch his/her fingers, moving one's foot closer, stroking one's own arm as if to stroke to the other's. Then, it progresses by touching each one on the shoulder, the forearm, the wrist, or some other socially available body part.

Fisher's "Stage 5" is "Body Synchrony" where both the bodies move in perfect rhythm as a mirror image of each other. In the western culture, dancing would feature in "Stage 5" where 'Body Synchrony" is automatically featured, encompassing rhythmic gestures and tandem body movements.

Physical Love and Romantic Love

Having received some tips from Helen Fisher, I'm adding some of my own perceived inputs on 'Love in Humans'.

The urge for 'romantic love' arises at the chest level – from the heart and from the respiratory process as pulse and respiratory rate both increase to romantic excitement. And, the urge for 'sexual' or 'physical love' (or 'lust') arises from the genitalia level. In terms of the subtle energy centres or 'chakras', the former arises from the 'Anahata' or the 'Heart Chakra' and the latter from the 'Muladhar' and 'Swadhisthan Chakras'.

Helen Fisher, in the Chapter 2 ('Animal Magnetism: Love among the Animals') of her book 'Why We Love: The Nature and Chemistry of Romantic Love' has shared authentic data on how 'romantic love' is not a rarity in the animal world. (Reference 13). 'Romantic Love', evolutionarily, is a step ahead of the grassroot level 'physical level' where 'lust' is the main driving force, good enough for fulfilment of the need for 'replication'. When the birds and animals look for the best partner mating with whom will lead to the birth of the best quality offspring, then the question of 'romance' arises.

The attraction animals feel for particular mates is linked with elevated levels of 'Dopamine' ('D') and 'Norepinephrine' (also called 'Noradrenaline') ('N') in the brain. Elevated levels of 'D' in the brain produces extremely focused attention, as well as unwavering motivation and goal-oriented behaviours. These are characteristics of 'romantic love'. (Reference 14) Lovers intensely focus on the beloved, often to the exclusion of everything and all people around them. They concentrate so much on the positive qualities that they easily overlook the lapses. They also regard the beloved as novel and unique.

'D' has been associated with learning of novel stimuli. (Reference 15). Ecstasy is another outstanding trait of love. This too, appears to be associated with 'D', 'D' is also associated with increased energy level, hyperactivity, sleeplessness, loss of appetite, a fast-beating heart and accelerated breathing. Sometimes, there could also be development of mania, anxiety, or fear. (Reference 16).

'Romantic love' involves courtship which meant concentration of all time, attention, energy, and effort on one individual only instead of frittering away these personal resources on many in a polygamous situation. In the evolution of mankind, it is certainly a step forward from their animal ancestors. Long-term attachment and the urge to set up a nest and a family is the stage where most of us are placed now. Desire for long-term nesting was the outcome of a motivation our ancestors had to rear their young ones together over a much longer maturation period than our immediate ancestors, the apes.

After a few thousand years, the circuit of 'romantic love' has got embedded in our brains. This has now become a fundamental human drive, like the craving for food and water. It is a biological need to find, court and win a particular mating partner – a requirement which remains unfulfilled in arranged or negotiated marriages prevalent in certain cultures in the East and in a few in the West too. However, once the hive which used to be filled with the honey of love becomes dry and withered, the negative consequences like depression, adultery, estrangement, separation, divorce, even suicide and homicide crop up in all societies around the world. It is interesting to note that humans are unable to feel romantic love for more than one partner at a time.

'Romantic Love' may also vary in degrees. The weakest 'Romantic Love' is 'infatuation'. When the strength of love increases during the courtship, the love takes a 'Passionate' form leading to the strongest level of 'Obsessive Love'. However, some psychology scholars have grouped 'romantic love' into only two categories: 'reciprocated love' and 'unrequited love'.

In any case, 'love' consists of a kaleidoscope of feelings, which vary from person to person, and stage to stage of togetherness. These include:

passion, compassion, ecstasy, desire, suspicion, doubt, fear, anxiety, jealousy, awkwardness, and embarrassment; although a limited few may feel like Violetta in Verdi's tragic opera "La Traviata" who said: "Let's live for pleasure alone, since love, like flowers, swiftly fades". (Reference 17)

Scientists have been at a loss to find out why males have preference for females irrespective of their oestrous cycles or sexual conditions. The oestrous cycle is a set of recurring physiological changes induced by reproductive hormones in mammalian females. (Reference 6). Investigation is certainly called for to find out whether such preferences depend on the characteristics of the microbiome. Is it the looks, health, age, shape, size and other physical characteristics, or the pheromones or body scents, or the microbial attraction – nobody has gone into that study, as yet.

Love at first sight: could it be pre-destined from one of the previous births or is it a case of morphic resonance (according to Prof. Rupert Sheldrake's hypothesis)? (Reference 18)

Animals, big and small, are biologically driven to prefer, pursue, and possess specific mating partners: there is an underlying chemistry to animal attraction. And, this chemistry must be the precursor of human 'romantic love'. Two brain chemicals are involved – 'Dopamine' ('D') and 'Norepinephrine' ('N') (also known as 'Noradrenaline'). A rise in the level of 'D' makes the person move towards the goal – the person she/he loves. 'D' plays the role of the motivational chemical here. And, 'N' may contribute to the magnetism – the attractive power of the individual, as it increases arousal and alertness, and focuses attention (References 19 & 20)

Romance and the Brain

Love-stricken men and women become dependent on the romantic relationship. Dependency and craving are symptoms of 'addictions' – all of the major addictions are associated with elevated levels of 'D'. 'Romantic Love' is thus an addiction. When a reward is delayed, 'D'-producing cells in the brain increase their work, pumping out more of

'D' to energize the brain, focus attention and drive the pursuer to strive even harder to acquire a reward. And, as 'D' increases in the brain, it often drives up levels of 'Testosterone' ('T') – the hormone of sexual desire.

High levels of 'Norepinephrine' ('N') produces exhilaration, excessive energy, sleeplessness, and loss of appetite. 'N' is also associated with increased memory for new and novel stimuli. (Reference 21). A third chemical may also be involved and, that is: 'Serotonin' ('S'). Lovers' obsession with the thoughts of their beloved may be associated with low levels of 'S'. As levels of 'D' and 'N' climb, the level of 'S' may go down. This is the reason why a lover's romantic ecstasy actually intensifies the compulsion to daydream, fantasize, muse, ponder, obsess about a romantic partner. (Reference 22)

These three chemicals, 'D', 'N' and 'S' vary in their concentration and combinations as the relationship waxes and wanes. These chemicals form the backbone of obsessive, passionate 'romantic love'.

The 'Caudate Nucleus' and other parts of the brain's 'Reward System' are very primitive. Naturally, they ought to be, because every creature is hungry for 'rewards' although the nature of 'rewards' do vary. 'Rewards' are essential for any creature to satisfy its 'Survival & Replication' need. The 'Reward System' structures are located in the hind brain – the 'Reptilian Complex'.

Those who are in longer relationship than just a few months would show activity in the 'Anterior Cingulate Cortex' ('ACC') and also in the 'Insular Cortex'. 'ACC' is involved in certain high-level functions such as: 'attention allocation', 'reward anticipation', 'decision-making', 'ethics' and 'morality', 'impulse control (e.g. performance monitoring and error detection)' and emotion. (Reference 23). The 'Insular Cortex' ('IC') is a portion of the cerebral cortex folded deep within the 'lateral sulcus' (the fissure separating the temporal lobe from the parietal and frontal lobes) within each hemisphere of the brain. 'IC' plays a role in diverse functions which include compassion, empathy, taste, perception, motor control, self-awareness, cognitive functioning and inter-personal relations which are relevant in the context of 'romantic love'. (Reference 24) 'IC' collects data from the body regarding external touch and temperature as well as internal pain and activities of the stomach, gut, and other viscera. With this brain part, we register 'butterflies' in the stomach, a pounding heart and our many bodily reactions.

A 'DRIVE' is a neural state that energizes and directs behaviour to acquire a particular biological need to survive or reproduce. We have lots of 'Drives' which lie on a continuum. Is 'Romantic Love' a 'Drive'? Let us examine.

'Drives' are of two types. At one end of the continuum, are 'Drives' which can be redirected or even quelled with time and effort. These are: sex drive, hunger, parental (especially, maternal) instinct. At the other end of the continuum are 'Drives' that cannot be extinguished until satisfied. Examples are: thirst, need for warmth. 'Falling in and being in love' is in between the two extreme ends. All the 'Drives' are, incidentally, associated with elevated levels of 'Dopamine'.

There are regions in the brain's 'Pre-Frontal Cortex' ('PFC') with which we monitor rewards. Several parts of the PFC have direct connections to the 'Caudate Nucleus' ('CN') – the 'motor of the mind' from which the passion of love emanates. The passion is then fuelled by 'Dopamine'. All along the process of falling and being in love, the PFC monitors the pursuit, assessing the gains and losses and registering one's progress towards the goal: emotional, physical – even spiritual reunion with the beloved.

More about 'Romantic Love'

Love is "as sweet and musical/As bright Apollo's lute strung with his hair/Makes heaven drowsy with the harmony". Shakespeare must have had 'romantic love' in mind, when he had written it!! In fact, this is one of the best descriptions of 'romantic love' that I've come across so far. But, in whatever poetic, metaphorical way you describe 'romantic love', nobody can dispute the fact that 'romantic love' is intertwined with two other mating 'drives': 'lust' – the craving for sexual gratification and 'attachment' – the feelings of calm security, and union with a long-term partner.

'Mating' is a game that is played universally, and it is indeed a grassroot affair. It makes use of the intertwined 'drives' to motivate us to mix with an array of potential sexual partners, choose one of them to dote upon, then remain emotionally engaged to him or her at least long enough to rear a child together.

The mating 'drive' or 'lust', as an urge, is very different from 'romantic love'. It is associated primarily with the male sex hormone 'Testosterone' ('T') in both men and women. Men and women who have higher circulating levels of 'T' tend to engage in more sexual activity. Male libido peaks in the early twenties, when levels of 'T' are highest. Many women feel more sexual drive around ovulation, when levels of 'T' increase. Levels of 'T' are inherited. Levels fluctuate according to the day, the week, the year, and the life cycle. Moreover, the existing level of 'T', 'Estrogen' ('E') and other bodily ingredients as well as social circumstances, and a host of other factors – all play a role in when, where, and how often we feel 'lust'. 'T' is the main role player here. 'Dopamine' ('D') can trigger the release of 'T'. Novel experiences drive up levels of 'D' in the brain.

'Romantic love' is linked with 'Dopamine' and perhaps 'Norepinephrine' and 'Serotonin'. And, the 'attachment' 'drive' is linked with the neurotransmitter-hormones 'Oxytocin' and 'Vasopressin'.

'Lust' evolved to motivate individuals to seek sexual union. 'Romantic love' emerged to drive men and women to focus their mating attention on a preferred individual, thereby saving on precious courtship time and energy. And, 'attachment' developed to enable our ancestors to live with this preferred mate at least long enough to rear a single child through infancy, at least, together.

All three of these different brain networks – 'lust', 'romantic love' and 'attachment' are multi-purpose systems. Although the basic purpose is 'reproduction', together they serve to make friends and keep friends, provide pleasure-fun-and-thrill, tone muscles, and make the mind light – at least temporarily. 'Romantic love' can be responsible for a sustained loving partnership or drive you to like and fall in love with a new person and initiate separation. And, feelings of 'attachment' enable us to express genuine affection for children, family, and friends and, of course, for the beloved partner.

Love changes over time. It becomes deeper, calmer, less turbulent. There are new feelings of security, comfort, and regulated union with the partner. This is the 'attachment' phase. 'Oxytocin' ('O') and 'Vasopressin' ('V') are the chemicals for 'attachment'. 'O' is released in all female mammals (including women) during the birthing and the breast-feeding processes.

There is an inverse relationship between 'lust' and 'attachment'. High levels of 'lust' – releasing 'T' can reduce 'attachment'. Men with high baseline levels of 'T' marry less frequently, have more adulterous affairs, commit more spousal abuse, and divorce more often. Single men tend to have higher levels of 'T' than married men. The reverse does also happen. As a man becomes more and more attached to his family, 'T' level declines.

References

1. *Helen Fisher* – Wikipedia.
2. Helen Fisher, *Why We Love: The Nature and Chemistry of Romantic Love*, New York: Owl Books, Henry Holt & Co., 2004.
3. Helen Fisher, "The science behind maintaining a happy long-term relationship", *Big Think*, 11th February, 2016.
4. Paul J. Zak, *The Moral Molecule: How Trust Works*, New York: Plume (The Penguin Group), 2013, p. 22.
5. Helen Fisher, "The brain in love", TED Talk February 2008.
6. *Tikal Temple I* – Wikipedia.
7. Jing Cai and Qingchun Tong, "Anatomy and Function of Ventral Tegmental Area Glutamate Neurons", *Frontal Neural Circuits*, 2022, Vol 16, Published online on 20th May 2022.
8. "The Flow State in Relationships", Exploring Your Mind. *<ploringyourmind.com*
9. Mihalyi Csikszentmihalyi, *Flow: The Psychology of Optimal Experience*, New York: Harper Perennial Modern Classics, 2008.
10. 'Powerful Love Poem (1896)', Sujen Man Maharjan, 4th August 2010.

11. Helen Fisher – "The Science of Love" – An Interview from "The Wall".
12. Helen Fisher, *Anatomy of Love: A Natural History of Mating, Marriage, and Why We Stray*, New York: WW Norton, 2016.
13. Helen Fisher, *Why We Love: The Nature and Chemistry of Romantic Love*, New York: St. Martin's Griffin, 2004.
14. T.W. Robbins and B.J. Everitt, "Neuro-behavioural mechanisms of reward and motivation", *Current Opinion in Neurobiology*, 1996, Vol. 6, pp. 228–68.
15. W. Schultz, "Multiple reward signals in the brain", *Nature Review Neuroscience*, 2000, Vol. I, (December), pp. 199–207.
16. A.L. Kruk and C.J. Pycock, *Neurotransmitters and Drugs*, 1991, New York: Chapman and Hall.
16. *La Traviata* – Wikipedia.
17. *Oestrous Cycle* – Wikipedia.
18. Rupert Sheldrake: "Morphic Resonance and Morphic Fields – an Introduction" *(sheldrake.org/research)*
19. Ethan S. Bromberg-Martin, Masayuki Matsumoto and Okihide Hikosaka, "Dopamine in motivational control: rewarding, aversive, and alerting", *Neuron*, Vol. 68, No. 5, 9th December 2010, pp. 815–834.
20. "Norepinephrine (Noradrenaline)" – Cleveland Clinic *(my.clevelandclinic.org)*
21. M.G. Griffin and G.T. Taylor, "Norepinephrine modulation of social memory: Evidence for a time-dependent functional recovery of behaviour", *Behavioural Neuroscience*, 1995, Vol. 109, No. 3, pp. 466–73.
22. Helen Fisher, *Anatomy of Love: A Natural History of Mating, Marriage and Why We Stray*, New York: W.W. Norton, 2017.
23. *Anterior cingulate cortex* – Wikipedia.
24. *Insular cortex* – Wikipedia.

CHAPTER 14

Love: Symphony and Harmony

Love: A Symphony

Love is a symphony of feelings with many notes and chords. The brain network of 'romantic love' combines with many more brain systems with circuits for other basic 'drives', as well as with many emotions, feelings, and many audio-visual and other sensory memories. All these add a beautiful glow to romance.

The six basic emotions of joy, anger, fear, sadness, disgust and surprise are all there involved as ingredients of 'romantic love' which has not yet attained a mature state. To give you an example, just when you're about to phone your lover you've a fear, a negative anticipation that she might be getting ready to accompany her parents to meet the family where the talk of her marriage is going on. However, your fear disappears when she picks up the phone and says she is getting ready to go to a movie with her varsity friends.

'Romantic love' is also linked with a host of higher cognitive emotions like: respect, admiration, loyalty, gratitude, sympathy, apprehension, and a sense of fairness. The entire landscape of the body develops according to the emotions felt by the lovers.

About 50 percent of our temperament is inherited; the rest is moulded by our upbringing and environment. But, 'romantic love' is a common emotion shared by every human being everywhere in the world.

The ancient Greeks had described various kinds of love (References 1 & 2).

'Eros': which is passionate, erotic, sexual, joyful, high-energy love. It is a combination of 'lust' and 'romantic love'.

'Mania': obsessive, jealous, irrational, possessive, dependent.

'Ludus': playful, casual, not serious, uncommitted, detached, mild lust coupled with fun & frivolity.

'Storge': affectionate, friendly, brotherly-sisterly kind of love; it is a form of 'attachment'.

'Agape': gentle, unselfish, dutiful, altruistic, 'spiritual'.

'Pragma': love based on compatibility and common sense; love based on calculation of 'gains' & 'losses', 'gives' & 'takes'.

Psychologist Robert Sternberg (References 3 & 4) has suggested the following types of 'love':

'Infatuation': composed of passion only.

'Romantic love': passion plus intimacy.

'Consummate love': passion, intimacy, commitment.

'Companionate love': intimacy & commitment – no passion.

'Empty love': only commitment.

'Liking': based on intimacy.

'Fatuous love': full of passion and commitment, lacking intimacy.

Love: Body Harmony

Masaccio (1401–1428) was a Florentine artist who is regarded as the first great Italian painter of the Quattrocento period of the Italian Renaissance. "Expulsion from the Garden of Eden" is a fresco by Masaccio which portrays a nude Adam and Eve as they are expelled from the Garden of Eden. The nudity of the couple shows the elegant slenderness of their bodies, beautifully proportioned, which must have been the principal cause of their mutual attraction. This, I would like to describe as 'love' based on 'body harmony' – amazingly orchestrated symmetrical body parts. (References 5 & 6)

Animals, animal researchers say, look for well-proportioned mates. One important invisible factor that guides most of us, humans, generally for choosing partners is well-proportioned body. Bodily symmetry can help to trigger 'romantic love', as the, ancient Greeks theorized. Almost

2,500 years ago, Aristotle maintained that there were some universal standards of physical beauty. One was balanced bodily proportions, including symmetry. He proposed a 'golden mean' or moderation between extremes. It has been noted that even two-month-old infants gaze longer at more symmetrical faces. (Reference 7)

Most unexpectedly, creatures with balanced, well-proportioned ears, eyes, teeth and jaws, with symmetrical elbows, knees, and breasts, have been able to repel bacteria, viruses, and other minute predators as opposed to those having some bodily irregularities. By displaying symmetry, animals and humans advertise their superior genetic ability to combat diseases and produced balanced offspring. (References 8 & 9). Our human attraction to symmetrical suitors is a primitive animal mechanism designed to guide us to select genetically sturdy mating partners. (Reference 10)

When a woman has an orgasm with a well-proportioned man, her orgasmic contractions suck up more of his sperms. (Reference 11) These sexual responses occur because as the woman looks at her symmetrical lover, the 'Ventral Tegmental Area' ('VTA') in her brain produces 'Dopamine' ('D') – which (in a series of interactions) triggers 'Testosterone' ('T') and enhances the sexual reaction.

Women's hands and ears are more symmetrical during monthly ovulation – a time when it is reproductively important to attract a man. Women's breasts become more symmetrical during ovulation too. (References 12 & 13)

Love and Aesthetics of the Body

Polyclitus, was the first Greek sculptor, active in the 5th century BCE, to theorize the aesthetics of the body and the nude. He wrote a treaty of ideal proportions called the 'Canon'. His canon is based on a fundamental rule: the balance and the ratio of proportion between the different parts of the body. Thus, beauty is based on the harmony between the different parts of the body and its whole. In other words, each part of the body must measure a certain size in relation to the total height of the body. A foot should measure a certain percentage of the whole body, as well as the head or the finger. This becomes a new representation of beauty on a strict mathematical and aesthetic law.

It goes like this:

> The head enters 7 times in the height of the body.
>
> The legs and the torso have the same height, measuring the same size/dimensions – 3 times that of the head.
>
> The knee-down-to-the-foot length is 2 times (twice) the height of the head, as is the width of the shoulders. This is the same as the height of the torso.
>
> The pelvis is 2/3rd of the height of the torso while the thighs are 2/3rds of the legs.

A century after Polyclitus, Lysippus revisited the canon. In his system, the body measures 8 times the height of the head against 7 in the canon of Polyclitus. Later on, Leonardo da Vinci used the logic of the canon of proportions to create the Vitruvian Man. He also applied the 'golden ratio' to capture his own canon of ideal, divine proportions. But whether it is Lysippus or Leonardo da Vinci, the principle remains the same: harmony between the parts and the whole. Man has a universal beauty, whose origin is, at the same time, divine, mathematical, and perfect. (Reference 14)

Women, whose waist circumference was about 70 percent of the circumference of their hips, are found to be most attractive according to some research studies. (References 15 & 16). The researcher D. Singh theorizes that male attraction to a specific female waist-to-hip ratio is a natural preference for healthy, fertile partners. This attraction takes place at the unconscious level of the male's mind, although sub-consciously or consciously he may be attracted by other factors such as: the family background, educational level, homemaking skill, musical-artistic-dancing-or-dramatic talents, communication skill, income generating potential and so on – which is not my purview here.

A study of the waist-to-hip ratio of 286 ancient sculptures from several African tribes as well as from ancient India, Egypt, Greece and Rome (Reference 17) revealed that all favoured a ratio that was smaller for women than for men. In a study of 330 artworks of Europe, Asia, the Americas, and Africa, some of which date back 32,000 years, scientists found that most women were depicted with a waist-to-hip ratio of almost the same value. In reality, most interestingly, even if this ratio is a little different, it adjusts itself during ovulation to come closer to 70 percent.

Women of odd shapes, such as egg-shaped, pear-shaped, or stick-shaped and all other differently shaped women have propensity to suffer from chronic diseases like diabetes, hypertension, heart disease, certain types of cancers, and problems with circulation. They are also prone to various personality disorders.

Men unquestionably find good-looking women aesthetically pleasing to look at. They also like to impress friends and colleagues with their dazzling lady companions – whether girlfriends or trophy wives. In fact, people, in general, tend to regard beautiful women (and good-looking men) as warm, smart, friendly, polite, sexy, and socially acceptable. Women prefer to have relationship with tall men, perhaps because they, due to their height, are more conspicuous than others and represent stronger bodily prowess.

To quote a relevant piece from the Old Testament:

"My love is shining and ruddy
He is the tallest in a crowd of ten thousand men,
His arms are like rods of gold
His legs are pillars of marble."

References

1. J.A. Lee, *Colours of Love*, Toronto: New Press, 1973.
2. J.A. Lee, "Love-styles" In: *The Physiology of Love*, ed R.J. Sternberg and M.L. Barnes, New Haven": Yale University Press, 1988.
3. R.J. Sternberg, *Beyond IQ: A Triarchic Theory of Human Intelligence*, New York: Cambridge University Press, 1985.
4. R.J. Sternberg, "A triangular theory of love", *Psychological Review*, 1986, Vol. 91, No. 2. pp. 119–35.

5. *Masaccio* – Wikipedia.
6. *Expulsion from the Garden of Eden* – Wikipedia.
7. J.H. Langlois *et al.*, "Infant preferences for attractive faces; Rudiments of a stereotype", *Developmental Psychology*, 1987, Vol. 23, pp. 363–69.
8. W.D. Hamilton and M. Zuk, "Heritable true fitness and bright birds: A note for parasites?" *Science*, 1982, Vol. 218, pp. 284–287.
9. R. Thornhill and S.W. Gangestad, "Human facial beauty", *Human Nature*, 1993, Vol. 4, No. 3, pp. 237–69.
10. S.W. Gangestad, R. Thornhill and R.A. Yeo, "Facial attractiveness, developmental stability and fluctuating asymmetry", *Ethology and Socio-biology*, 1994, Vol. 15, pp. 73–85.
11. R. Thornhill, S.W. Gangestad and R. Comer, "Human female orgasm and mate fluctuating asymmetry", *Animal Behaviour*, 1995, Vol. 50, pp. 1601–15.
12. J.T. Manning and D. Scutt, "Symmetry and ovulation in women", *Human Reproduction*, 1996, Vol. 11, pp. 2477–80.
13. J.T. Manning *et al.*, "Asymmetry and menstrual cycle in women", *Ethology and Socio-biology*, 1996, Vol. 17, pp. 129–43.
14. "The Canon of Proportions in Ancient Greek Sculpture: Searching for a Divine Odeal" *Artsper Magazine*, 4th July 2022.
15. D. Singh, "Adaptive significance of waist-to-hip ratio and female physical attractiveness", *Journal of Personality and Social Psychology*, 1993, Vol. 65, pp. 293–307.
16. D. Singh, "Female mate value at a glance: Relationship of waist-to-hip ratio to health, fecundity, and attractiveness", 2002, *Neuroendocrinology Letters 23 (suppl. 4)* pp. 81–91.
17. B.J. Ellis, "The Evolution of Sexual Attraction: Evaluative Mechanisms in Women"; In: *The Adapted Mind: Evolutionary Psychology and the Generation of Culture*, ed. J.H. Barkow, L. Cosmides and J. Tooby. New York: Oxford University Press, 1992.

CHAPTER 15

Love Pie

Love Pie – A Proposition

Let us conceive 'love' in the form of a 'pie chart' (Reference 1), divided into four quadrants. Now, let us assume that the 'pie' is broken into two equal halves of 180 degrees each, like the two hemispheres of the brain.

The right half (180 degrees) represents all your 'Inherited Personal Wealth' which again is divided into two quadrants: one representing the 'Inherited Personal Resources' having three portions: 'Body', 'Heart' and 'Head'; and, the other: 'Inherited Personal Assets' having three portions: 'Fixed', 'Movable' and 'Liquid'.

The left half (180 degrees) represents 'Acquired Personal Wealth' which again is divided into two quadrants: 'Acquired Personal Resources' ('Body', 'Heart' and 'Head'); and, 'Acquired Personal Assets' ('Fixed', 'Movable' and 'Liquid').

Let us go into the detail of the quadrants in the two halves now.

In the 'Inherited Personal Resources',

the 'Body' component will include: your height (tall, medium, or short), constitution or stature (fat, athletic, or thin), strength (strong, moderate, or weak), physical energy level (high, medium, or low), health (good, medium, poor);

the 'Heart' component will include: your emotional state (strong, moderate, or weak / positive, mixed, negative), compassion & empathy level (high, medium, low), friendliness (high, moderate, low), helpfulness & co-operation (high, moderate, low);

the 'Head' component will include: your intelligence level in general (high, moderate, low), your imagination-visualisation power (high, medium, poor), your decision-making & problem-solving skill (high, medium, low), your creativity level (high, moderate, low); your resilience (high, moderate, low).

In the 'Acquired Personal Resources',

the 'Body' component will include: your 'strength', 'energy level' and 'health status' at the time of evaluation.

the 'Heart' component will include the changes that might have come about over the years in the same aspects as under the 'Inherited Personal Resources'; and,

the 'Head' component will include the changes, if any, in the same aspects as under 'Inherited' plus your academic & professional qualifications obtained, the knowledge and the experience gained.

In the 'Acquired Personal Assets', the status of 'Fixed', 'Movable' & 'Liquid' Assets already acquired by the time of evaluation will be considered.

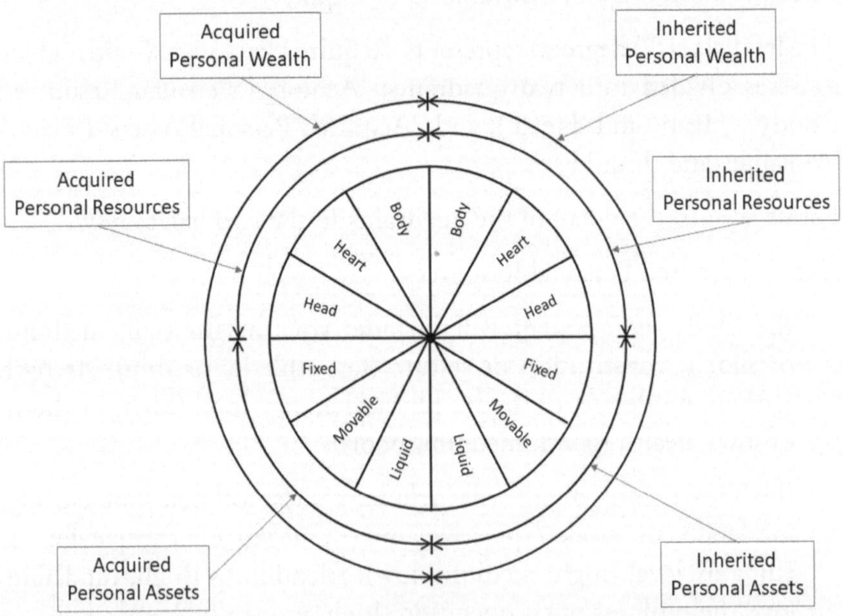

The Love Pie

Your power to attract will depend on the 'value system' of your potential love partner – which would be based on her/his 'attachment style' developed as a sum of her/his genetic propensities and influencing environmental factors (past & present). Too much attraction for physical factors will be regarded as signs of 'lust' ('kam' in Sanskrit/ Hindi) whereas too much attraction for 'wealth' – any one or more of the assets will be regarded as signs of 'greed' ('lobh' in Sanskrit'/'lalas' in Hindi).

Now, let us not forget what the female partner is interested in: is she interested in the short-term or the long-term: her own pleasure/comfort/ convenience & happiness or the pleasure/comfort/convenience/ happiness of her offspring?

For young lovers, their parents' outlook also is very important to consider.

Love Pie – Elaboration

The question that now pops up on my mind is that: all resource mobilisation, asset maintenance & building, converting resources and assets into value-added capital – is it for the self-development and personal growth of the individual who plays those roles and takes such actions, or is it to use those as displays and promotional materials to attract and remain attractive to the opposite sex in short-, intermediate/ middle- and long-terms?

Charles Darwin also had such enquiries, as peacock's gorgeous feathered tail, robin's sweet songs, and the presence of a whole host of decorative features in the bodies of all kinds of creatures including insects, birds, and animals used to attract his attention during his voyages. (Reference 2)

In most recent times, Geoffrey Miller (Reference 3) has taken up this issue as one of his focused studies and has been trying to throw some light. Miller (born 1965) is an American evolutionary psychologist, author, and associate professor of psychology at the University of New Mexico. He is known for his research on sexual selection in human evolution. (References 4 & 5). In 2015, in collaboration with writer

Tucker Max, Miller launched "The Mating Grounds", a podcast and blog offering advice about men's sexual strategies.

Miller's 2003 book. "The Mating Mind: How Sexual Choice Shaped the Evolution of Human Nature" (Reference 6) proposes that human 'mate choices', courtship behaviour, behaviour genetics, psychometrics, and life cycle patterns support the survival value of traits related to sexual selection such as art, morality, language, and creativity. According to Miller, the adaptive design features of these traits suggest that they evolved through mutual mate choice by both sexes to advertise intelligence, creativity, moral character, and heritable fitness.

Miller also cites the 'Fisherian runaway', a model created by Ronald Fisher to explain phenomena such as the peacock's plumage as forming through a positive feedback loop for sexual selection, as well as the 'handicap principle'. (Reference 7)

In his 2009 book, "Spent: Sex, Evolution and the Secrets of Consumerism", (Reference 6) Miller used 'Darwinism' to gain an understanding of 'consumerism' and how 'marketing' has exploited our inherited instincts to display social status for reproductive advantage. He argues that the modern marketing-dominated culture, is an aberration of the genetic legacy of 2 million years of living in small tribal groups, where social status has been a critical force in reproduction. Miller's thesis is that marketing persuades people – particularly the young – that the most effective way to display that status is through consumption choices, rather than conveying such traits as intelligence and personality through more natural means of communication, such as simple conversation. The belief that premium products are bought to display wealth, status, and taste, and they miss the deeper mental traits that people are actually wired to display – traits such as kindness, intelligence, and creativity – which limits the success of marketing. (Reference 8)

Love Pie – Justification

All resource mobilisation, converting the resources into capital are generally for self-development and/or for use as displays and advertising strategies to attract members of the opposite sex. Geoffrey Miller proposes that human beings have evolved extravagant traits to impress potential mating partners. (References 9 & 10). These human endeavours are all meant to win the mating game. Miller describes us as 'mating machines'.

As men and women, we play twin roles – on the one hand that of 'producers' and, on the other, 'choosers' of displays. The 'display chooser' role involves discrimination between courtship signals – preferring some while not preferring the others. Is there a 'display choice mechanism' in the brain? Is there a 'pleasure meter' in the brain? Of course, it is our brain's 'reward circuit' – the activation of which releases the 'pleasure' molecule 'Dopamine' ('D'). But, where from the 'drive' for choosing a particular one or a set of displays come?

It will not be a bad idea to look at the Upanishadic 'Pancha Kosha' model. (References 11 & 12) In this model, the outermost kosha is 'Annamaya' which represents everything materialistic that is responsible for pleasure satisfaction, comfort and convenience including the basics – food, clothes and shelter. The next sheath is 'Pranamaya Kosha' which represents everything physical, related to the 'Body' – health, fitness, body proportions, sex drive/libido. The next one is the 'Monomaya Kosha' which represents, in one word, the 'Heart' – social and emotional part of the person's nature. The next one – 'Vijnanamaya Kosha' is related to the 'Head' – intelligence, cognitive powers. And, the last one – 'Anandamaya Kosha' is all creativity – discovery, innovation, creation, composition, pioneering, improvement, modernisation – which all can be grouped together under 'Spiritual Creativity'.

References

1. *Pie Chart* – Wikipedia.
2. *Charles Darwin* – Wikipedia.
3. *Geoffrey Miller* – Wikipedia.

4. Natalie Angier, "Skipping Spouse to Spouse Isn't Just a Man's Game", *The New York Times*, 31st August 2009. (Original published on 18th October, 2018)
5. "Sexual Selection and the Mind" – A Talk with Geoffrey Miller, *Edge Foundation Inc.* 6th June 1998.
6. Geoffrey Miller, *The mating mind: how sexual choice shaped the evolution of human nature*, Portsmouth, UK: Heinemann, 2000.
7. Geoffrey Miller, *Spent: sex, evolution, and consumer behaviour*, New York: Penguin Books, 2010.
8. Dylan Evans, "Spent…" by Geoffrey Miller, Book Review. *The Guardian*, 7th August 2009.
9. Geoffrey Miller, *The mating mind: how sexual choice shaped the evolution of human nature*, Portsmouth, UK: Heinemann, 2000.
10. Geoffrey Miller, *Spent: sex, evolution and consumer behaviour*, New York: Penguin Books, 2010.
11. *Pancha Kosha* – Vikaspedia.
12. "What is Pancha Kosha? – Definition from Yogapedia" – Yogapedia.

CHAPTER 16

Polyamory

Monogamy, Polygamy, Polyandry and Polyamory

Our immediate animal ancestors – chimpanzees and bonobos who are known to share 98 to 98.5 percent DNAs with us also make love. In fact, they are among the most sexually active animals on earth. They kiss 'deeply', walk holding each other's arms, hug, stroke, groom, pat and often copulate throughout the female's oestrus cycle. But unlike human beings, our last tree-dwelling forebears who lived and moved in small groups were almost certainly promiscuous as much as the apes that I've talked about. Their bond was purely physical – the goal being 'reproduction'. There was little romance in it – so it was temporary. They never paired for more than a few days or weeks.

In humans, 'Attraction' towards a member of the opposite sex generally leads to 'Dating'. Then if the 'attraction' still persists and becomes stronger then the next stage is 'Dating Exclusively' which, if continues, leads to 'Courtship'. If that also clicks, then the next stage is 'Engagement'. And, once this stage arrives, it automatically develops into 'Marriage'. If the married couple wants to leave the imprint of their ancestral and own genes in the next generation, then the next stage is 'Having Kids'. Let's assume the relationship continues ('merrily' or 'non-merrily') over the next few decades, then the couple strikes the gold – half-a-century – their '50th Marriage Anniversary' is celebrated. (Reference 1)

> [Me and my wife Utpala got married in 1965 and we celebrated the Golden Jubilee of our wedding in 2015. Actually, it was celebrated by our three grown up kids, their spouses and families, with big fanfare. Right at this moment, in 2023, we are 2 years short of our 60th Wedding Anniversary, the Diamond Jubilee. We will 'Die – Married only Once'.

Many couples, in the first world countries, die – married a few times more than once as their marriages do not last for as many years at it has lasted in the case of me and my wife Utpala. And, it has lasted 'merrily'. Ups and downs, ebbs and tides were inevitable and we have managed to get over them with great tolerance, patience and perseverance and remained faithful to each other maintaining 'monogamy'.]

In ancient times and, even now, in some cultures, 'polygamy' is very common – one person having multiple wives. In some rare cultures, 'polyandry' is seen to exist – where one woman has multiple husbands. Today, although on the outside, a couple may look monogamous, polygamy is practiced on the sly, hidden from the public eyes. Right at the moment, I'm handling the case of a married lady having a teenage daughter, who is deeply in love with a married man who also have a teenage child. This is not 'polygamy'. In the public eye, it is 'monogamy', but underneath it, flows a current of promiscuity, infidelity, and unfaithfulness.

I was amazed to know from Geoffrey Miller, PhD. (References 2, 3 & 4) that many married couples are now practising 'Polyamory'. 'Polyamory' is a kind of relationship in which all partners agree that they may have romantic or sexual love relationship with other partners which could range from friends with benefits to open marriage. I understand that one in every five Americans have had a non-monogamous relationship – either disclosed or undisclosed.

I'm sharing a live case study of a North American polyamorous relationship. (References 5 & 6). Carrie and Jonathan are professors at the University of British Columbia, Canada. They got married in 2011 in a Scottish castle in a totally traditional way – Carrie wearing a white bridal dress and Jonathan a three-piece black suit. This couple firmly believes (they believed even during their 'dating' and 'courtship') that 'romantic love' and 'sex' are not the same. 'Romantic Love' is related to the 'Heart' and 'Sex' to the 'Body'. In any partnership, it may not be possible to satiate both these hungers. So, even after marriage, some nights husband Jonathan stays home while Carrie goes on a date with her boyfriend Ray and flirts with him in a bar. There is no hush-hush, no hide-and-seek. Being able to be with two people at once with full consent of each is impossible in a monogamous relationship, and polygamous relationship is not acceptable socially and also legally (barring a few closed cultures, may be). Such relationships always remain hidden. In our case study, Carrie loves to be with two amazing people at the same time. They are not a 'triad'. They only indulge in occasional hangouts.

I also learnt from Dr Antonia Forster, PhD, a bisexual biologist (Reference 7) that 'Polyamory' is quite natural in all non-human species including insects, reptiles, amphibians, birds and animals. It was also natural in the pre-historic hunter-gatherer human societies before the dawn of civilisation when customs such as nuptial marriage was introduced by humans only.

Most amazingly, many of the Bauls belonging to the Baulsphere of West Bengal, India and Bangladesh still practice 'Polyamory' as one Sadhak Baul has physicals with more than one 'Sadhan Sangini'. (Reference 8).

Neuro-chemicals & Hormones Involved in Relationships

> *"........ romantic love does not necessarily go hand in hand with the urge to attach to a mating partner over a long period. You can fall in love with someone from a different walk of life whom you never wish to marry. And you can feel romantic passion for one person while you feel deeply attached to another, usually a spouse. Moreover, you can have sex with someone for whom you feel no romantic love, even feel romantic passion for one individual while you copulate with another. What madness – to be socially or sexually entwined with one person and wildly in love with another." – Helen Fisher (Reference 9)*

This happens because different neuro-chemicals and hormones are involved in different types of relationships or attractions. In 'mating' pleasure, the 'feel good' neuro-chemical 'Dopamine' ('D') and the male sex hormone 'Testosterone' ('T') are involved, whereas in 'romantic love' the neurotransmitters 'Dopamine', 'Serotonin' and 'Norepinephrine' are involved. In deep attachment and long-term pair-bonding and family building, the neuro-transmitters 'Vasopressin' and 'Oxytocin' are involved.

The earliest hominid fossils came from northern Chad in Central Africa. From the Chad skull one can make out that the brain tissue contained therein was no bigger than that of a chimpanzee. By 3.5 million years ago, hominids increased in number and there were many more hominids that roamed on the lands of Central and East Africa. Bipedalism had freed their hands for tool-making and tool-using, gesturing, handling and carrying things. The freed hands and fingers had many degrees of movement and could perform multiple functions for living and working. The brain tissue had also started growing in size.

Hominid females, with little infants to take care of, became somewhat handicapped with bipedalism. Their movements got restricted and, most obviously, they needed help from other members of the community. They began to need real mates who were prepared to organise food for them and offer them protection from wild predators, when they carried and nursed their infants. Some males, who had a larger level of 'Vasopressin' ('V') in their brains fitted snugly into such husbanding and parenting roles. 'V' is a hormone secreted from the posterior pituitary gland and synthesized in the 'hypothalamus'. 'V' has a special role, like 'Oxytocin' ('O') in social functioning. It helps in social bonding. However, in contrast with women, men may experience the effects of 'V' more strongly because of how it interacts with the male sex hormone 'Testosterone' ('T'). (Reference 10)

Under such circumstances, pair-bonding became imperative for females and practical for males. There is no record, however, whether the males who preferred such twin roles would practice 'polygamy' – living with their informal families and, at the same time, copulating with other females as their nursing partners would not have been inclined to have sex much; and, having romantic relationship with a few other females. We do not know whether there was any scope for 'polyamory' that required mutual consent.

There is every possibility that the pair-bonds of our pre-historic ancestors were not permanent. The pair-bond possibly lasted up to the stage when the infant attained 4 years' age, which is based on a study of divorce data on fifty-eight diverse human societies recorded in the Demographic Yearbooks of the United Nations. (Reference 11)

Gradually, as centuries passed, the human brain started growing in size to perform functions that were needed to attract suitable mates – functions like: talking attractively, using wit and humour, making the opposite sex happy with charming communication and body language, sketching, cave wall painting, preparing artifacts and accessories with rocks and mud, making and using tools, playing the flute and percussions, dancing, and decorating the body with outfits and accessories.

The bony framework of the body also had to undergo a lot of changes, adjustments and amendments as, otherwise, how could pre-historic women bear big-headed male babies which had to be delivered through their narrow birth canals. Anthropologists think that their such obstetrical problem was faced when the adult cranial size had reached almost 800 cubic centimetres. Delayed maturation of the children prompted the male partner to stay on with the female and the young offspring, many a times being deprived of sexual pleasure. Naturally, one need not be surprised, if our ancestors were polygamous for earning their 'Dopamine' from pleasurable sex with females where there was no true love between the two, although apparently it looked as if there was 'monogamy'. Infidelity and promiscuity never left the mankind as the human brain's 'Novelty Circuit' ('NC') wanted to be stimulated, and emotional romance, dependable partnership, and sexual pleasure – all these natural needs were not possible to get satisfied by living with only one partner. As 'polyamory' was never heard of in the primitive days as it is a development of most modern times, in enlightened societies, 'polygamy' was the habit of the day.

References

1. "Polyamory" – Leon Feingold, TEDxBushwick.
2. "The Polyamorous Professors Diana Fleischman and Geoffrey Miller", YouTube, Rebel Wisdom, 7th April, 2019.

3. "What monogamists can learn from polyamorists/Geoffrey Miller", YouTube, Freethink, 28th July, 2022.
4. Geoffrey Miller, "Evolutionary Psychology, Polyamorous Relationships and Effective Altruism", YouTube, Manifold, 15th December, 2022.
5. "What life is like when you're in a polyamorous relationship: consensus relationship with more than one partner" – ABC News.
6. Carrie Ichikawa Jenkins, *What Love Is: And What It Could Be*, New York: Basic Books, 2017.
7. "LGBTQ+ and Polyamory in Animals: Yes, It's Natural", Antonia Forster, TEDxBristol, YouTube.
8. Siddhartha Ganguli, *The Four Moons in the Human Body: The Mysterious Tales of the Bauls of Bengal (Introducing BaulOlogy)*, Noida: Allied Publishers Pvt Ltd., 2023.
9. Helen Fisher, *Why We Love: The Nature and Chemistry of Romantic Love*, New York, St. Martin's Griffin, 2004, p. 150.
10. Cathy Cassata, "What Is Vasopressin?" Everyday Health, 22nd September 2023.
11. Helen Fisher, *Anatomy of Love: A Natural History of Mating, Marriage, and Why We Stray*, New York: W.W. Norton, 2016.

CHAPTER 17

Human Pair Bonding

Learn from the Prairie Vole's 'Pair-bonding' Behaviour

Earlier in this volume, I had introduced you to the prairie voles. I'm sure you would remember. The case of the prairie voles is worth remembering because these tiny creatures form life-long 'pair-bonds' which is very unusual for the members of the rodent family tree to which they belong. Their 'pair-bonds' are formed soon after puberty and they raise several litters as a team. Scientists have found out that this pairing has been directly correlated with neurochemical activities in the brain.

When prairie voles first engage in sex, copulation triggers activity in 'Oxytocin' ('O') receptors (in the 'Ventral Palladium') in the male partners. The 'Ventral Palladium' ('VP') is located in the 'Basal Ganglia' ('BG') and well-positioned as the intermediary between cortical, amygdala and striatal circuits for: cognition, action and mid-brain circuits for motivation and reinforcement. (Reference 1) This stimulates 'Dopamine' ('D') release in several brain regions – producing feelings of wanting, seeking, focus, energy, pleasure and motivation – driving the furry little creatures to prefer a particular mate (reciprocally/mutually), initiate a 'pair bond', and express enduring attachment behaviour. (References 2, 3 and 4)

But, specific variations in a particular gene in the 'Vasopressin' ('V') system contribute to the *variability* in the strength of a male prairie vole's 'pair-bonding' propensity including the degree to which a male expresses sexual fidelity to his female partner. (References 5 & 6)

Human Connection

However, the question now is – a gene linked to adultery in prairie voles – what does that have to do with humans? The answer is: a lot.

Humans have similar genes in the 'Vasopressin' ('V') system. And, recently, scientists investigated whether one of these genes affects 'pair-bonding' behaviour in 532 Swedish men. All were either married or had been living with a partner for at least five years. (Reference 7)

But, it is not unlikely that other genes are also involved. Biologist Justin Garcia and his colleagues recently studied 181 young men and women and they found that there is a direct link between specific genes in the 'Dopamine' ('D') system and a greater frequency of uncommitted sexual intercourse, largely one-night quick pleasure-oriented, as well as a higher frequency of sexual infidelity. (Reference 8)

Pair Bonding in Humans: Why?

Some of our forest-dwelling ancestors must have felt stronger attraction for a mating partner than others, which will ultimately transcend the level of the 'physical' and 'romantic (emotional)' varieties of love and lead to 'pair bonding'. Anthropologists think that this development took place soon after our arboreal forbears began to descend from the trees in the regions where they used to inhabit in East Africa, and venture into new terrains in search of food and better fortune and future. (Reference 9)

For the females with little infants who needed regular feeding and looking after, life was becoming very difficult without the help of a stronger, resourceful person, who had to be a male. Naturally, that male had to remain in long-lasting partnership with the female who had borne his child; so, he had to be monogamous. Neuroscientists are speculating that males with more 'Vasopressin' ('V') released in their brains, tend to be monogamous.

Once again, I refer to research studies on prairie voles. Tom Insel and his colleagues conducted a path-breaking investigation on voles. They discovered in prairie voles an extra bit of DNA in the gene that is responsible for the distribution of 'Vasopressin' ('V') receptors in the brain – a bit of DNA that was not present in their promiscuous asocial cousins – the montane voles. These scientists took this tiny piece of DNA out of prairie voles and inserted it into some highly promiscuous male mice. Sure enough, as expected, these mice began to form close monogamous relationship with particular females. (References 10 & 11)

Humans have a similar gene that codes the activities of 'Vasopressin' ('V'). And some people (but not all) carry this some extra bit of DNA on their gene. (Reference 12)

Neuroscientists are determined to take all possible steps to know exactly what this genetic feature does in people and why only some people possess it and others do not. At the moment, we can only speculate that in pre-history, humanity must have needed to pair up to rear the helpless young, because of the fact that at least one gene that codes for monogamous behaviour is embedded in our DNA.

References

1. A.A. Prasad and G.P. McNally, "Ventral Pallidum and Alcohol Addiction", In: *Neuroscience of Alcohol*, 2019, Science Direct (sciencedirect.com)
2. M.M. Lim, A.Z. Murphy and L.J. Young, "Ventral striatopallidal oxytocin and vasopressin V1a receptors in the monogamous prairie vole (*microtus ochrogaster*)", *Journal of Comparative Neurology*, 2004, Vol. 468, pp. 555–70.
3. M.M. Lim and L.J. Young, "Vasopressin-dependent neural circuits underlying pair bond formation in the monogamous prairie vole", *Neuroscience*, 2004, Vol. 125, pp. 35–45.
4. C.S. Carter, "Oxytocin and sexual behaviour" *Neuroscience and Biobehavioural Reviews*, 1992, Vol. 1, No. 16, pp. 131–44.
5. E.A. Hammock and L.J. Young, "Variation in the vasopressin V1a receptor promoter and expression: Implications for inter- and intraspecific variation in social behaviour", *European Journal of Neuroscience*, 2002, Vol. 16, pp. 399–402.
6. A.G. Ophir, J.O. Wolff and S.M. Phelps, "Variation in the neural V1a R predicts sexual fidelity and space use among male prairie voles in semi-natural settings", *Proceedings of the National Academy of Sciences*, 2008, Vol. 105, pp. 1249–54.

7. H. Walum, L. Westberg and S. Henningson *et al.*, "Generic variation in the vasopressin receptor 1a gene (AVPR1A) associates with pair-bonding behaviour in humans." *Proceedings of the National Academy of Sciences*, 2008, Vol. 105, No. 37, pp. 14153–56.

8. J.R. Garcia, J. MacKillop, E.L. Aller *et al.*, "Association between the dopamine D4 receptor gene variation with both infidelity and sexual promiscuity", *PLoSONE*, 2010, Vol. 5, e14162.

9. Helen Fisher, *Why We Love: The Nature and Chemistry of Romantic Love*, New York: Holt Paperbacks, 2005.

10. L.J. Young, Z. Wang and T.R. Insel, "Neuroendocrine bases of monogamy", Trends in Neurosciences, 1998, Vol. 21, No. 2, pp. 71–75.

11. L.J. Young, R. Nilsen, K.G. Waymire, G.R. MacGregor and T.R. Insel, "Increased affiliative response to Vasopressin in mice expressing the VIa receptor from a monogamous vole", Nature, 1999, Vol. 400, pp. 766–68.

12. N.E. Rosenthal, *The Emotional Revolution: How the New Science of Feelings Can Transform Your Life*, New York, Citadel Press Books, 2012.

CHAPTER 18

Problems in Love

Love and Madness

A spellbinding love story from the Arab culture is that of Layla and Majnun. The story is based on the real-life tale of the 7th century Arabic poet Qays ibn al-Mulawwah and Layla al-Amiriya, two lovers from the Bani Amer tribe in the Arab peninsula before Islam.

Layla and Qays were cousins. They grew up playing together, but when they reached adolescence, they were separated according to the customs of the 'Bedouins' – the nomadic tribe to which they belonged. Qays, being separated from his beloved Layla, lost his poise so much that he came to be known as 'Majnun' which means 'crazy' in Arabic. He simply turned mad and his insanity started getting reflected in the poetry that he wrote:

"I pass by this town, the town of Layla,
And kiss this wall, and that wall
It's not the love of the town that has encaptured my heart,
But the One who dwells within this town."

Although Layla was also madly in love with Qays, her father did not approve of the young crazy poet as a potential suitor for his daughter, and arranged her marriage with a wealthy merchant from the Taif tribe, whose name was Ward Althaqafi. This man was very handsome and his complexion was that of a pink rose. 'Ward', in Arabic, means 'rose'.

This made Qays move into deep insanity. He started spending his days wandering around in the desert country. Very soon, he decided not to return home, and his family was compelled to leave food for him in the wilderness.

In the meantime, Layla lost her husband to a critical illness and the widowed woman, still a ravishing beauty, set out on her own to find Qays in the desert against very strong family & social resistance. Starving for days, she also lost her life. Qays eventually found her grave; but totally emaciated and disease-ridden, he also passed out within the next few days beside Layla's grave and they finally got united in death.

The real-life case study of Layla and Majnun is considered one of the most influential folk tales not only in Azerbaijani, Persian and Turkish cultures, but also in other societies outside the Arab world.

In Middle-Eastern literature, based on the Layla and Majnun story, several poets have composed 'Udhrite' love poetry which is characterised by erotic abandon and attraction to the beloved, often by means of unfulfillable longing. Mystics have highlighted, from the story, the concepts that have appealed to them like 'fanaa' (annihilation), 'divanagi' (love-madness), and self-sacrifice. (References 1 & 2)

'Obsessive Love Disorder' ('OLD')

'Obsessive Love Disorder' ('OLD') involves fixating on one person. Although not classified as a mental health problem, it is a debilitating condition that would interfere with one's daily functioning. A very good example from medieval Bengal is that of poet Chandidas (born 1408). He is famous for composing over 1,250 poems related to the love of Radha and Krishna, although controversy exists whether these were all composed by one or more than one poet having the same name at different periods. Nevertheless, it is assumed that the earliest of them was Ananta Badu Chandidas, who has been identified as a historical figure born in the 14th century in a small town named 'Nanoor' in Birbhum district of the present-day West Bengal State of India. It was he who wrote the lyrical 'Sri Krishna Kirtan' (Songs in praise of Lord Krishna), narrating the story of Krishna and his female companion Radha. (Reference 3)

Chandidas, born into a high caste family, was ordained to read sacred scriptures and texts and devote his time as a Brahmin does. This, however, did not interest him. Agitated by his lackadaisical approach to formal scriptural education, his father commanded Chandidas's mother to starve him by serving ash instead of food. Out of sheer motherly compassion, she would put some ash on his plate in addition to food. When the young person came to know about his father's wrath, he felt miserable and left for the Basholi Shrine and would sit on the banks of the Ajay river, absorbed in the same tormenting thoughts. In the chain of thoughts, just as the idea of ending his life leapt over his mind, he could hear Goddess Basholi's voice consoling him like a mother. It is said that the Goddess graced Chandidas with a blessing that he will, one day, make the best of all poets, scholars and saints of his time. (Reference 4)

At that very moment, Chandidas saw a young woman washing clothes in the river – as if Goddess Basholi had descended from heaven. Chandidas was so dazzled and overwhelmed that he thought that washer woman as an incarnation of Radha and composed his first love poems for her. In fact, this woman was none other than the daughter of the local washerman, Ramitara, commonly known as Rami. Chandidas was obsessed with love and Rami was also infatuated with his spiritual handsomeness too. A classic case of 'Obsessive Love Disorder' ('OLD') as the modern scholars of 'Love' would describe the mental state.

Rami became the muse Chandidas needed to channel his talent into writing poems of Radha & Krishna's divine love. Chandidas would write the poetry and they would together sing and praise Lord Krishna. Unfortunately for them, they were so much ostracized by members of the family, neighbours and local people that they had to leave that small town and settle elsewhere.

Signs & symptoms of 'OLD' would include: falling in love with someone very hard and fast and an overwhelming attraction; feelings of intense longing & desire and obsessive thoughts; neglecting other tasks and relationships; possessiveness, feeling the need to protect the beloved; violating the person's privacy and boundaries; delusional beliefs about the person or the relationship; extreme jealousy over other inter-personal interactions; difficulty in maintaining contact with friends and family members because of obsession with one person; endeavour to continuously monitor & control the activities of the person loved. (Reference 5)

'OLD' has been a very popular theme for movie-makers. Time and again, filmmakers have brought to screen intense romantic obsession through movies like 'Fatal Attraction' starring Michael Douglas and Glenn Close or Idris Elba and Beyonce starrer 'Obsessed'. (Reference 5).

Getting United in Death

I'm going to talk to you about the immortal love story of Romeo and Juliet with which you are already familiar. Written by William Shakespeare it is a tragedy because the lover couple could not get the full mileage of their deep love as both of them ended their lives very young. The young man and the young lady came from two feuding Italian aristocratic families. It was among Shakespeare's most popular plays during his lifetime and, along with 'Hamlet', is one of his most frequently performed.

The play, set in Verona, Italy, begins with a street brawl between Montague and Capulet – employees who, like their masters, were confirmed enemies. The Prince of Verona intervened and declared that further breach of peace would be punishable by death.

Later, Count Paris talked to Capulet about marrying his daughter Juliet, but Capulet asked him to wait another two years and invited him to attend a planned ball to be hosted by him in his house. Lady Capulet and Juliet's nurse tried to persuade Juliet to accept Paris's courtship.

Romeo was Montague's son and he had gone into deep depression. His cousin Benvollo could gather that Romeo's depression had stemmed from unrequited infatuation for a girl named Rosaline who happened to be one of Capulet's nieces. Benvollo and a few others persuaded Romeo to attend the ball in the Capulet house in the hope of meeting Rosaline there. Romeo instead met Juliet and fell in love with her at the very first sight. Juliet's cousin Tybalt was enraged at Romeo for sneaking into the ball uninvited and while he was about to kill Romeo, Juliet's father intervened and stopped him as he did not want any bloodshed in his house.

Romeo escaped into the orchard at the back of the house after the ball and could overhear Juliet at her window vowing her love to him in spite of her family's hatred of the Montagues. Romeo appeared before her and they both agreed to get married. The very next day, the couple got married with the help of some well-wishers.

Tybalt, in the meantime, challenged Romeo into a duel. Romeo, now considering Tybalt as his kinsman, refused to fight but the circumstances became such that Romeo had to confront Tybalt and slay him. The Prince of Verona was so upset at this incident that he exiled Romeo from Verona under penalty of death if he ever returned. Romeo secretly spent the night in Juliet's chamber where they consummated their marriage. Juliet was in deep grief when Romeo left Verona to serve his exile.

Capulet now hurried to get Juliet married to Count Paris but she was totally adamant not to agree. Her request to delay the marriage also got rejected by her parents. She now managed to get a special potion which would put her into deep coma for a long period. She also managed to send a message to Romeo about her plan so that he can rejoin her when she awakens. On the night before her wedding with Count Paris, she took the drug and when discovered apparently dead, she was laid in the family's underground burial vault beneath the church.

Romeo did not get Juliet's message; instead, he learnt about her apparent death. Heartbroken, he acquired some poison and went to the burial vault of the family beneath the church. There he met Paris who had come to mourn. They got into a duel and Paris was killed. Romeo now took the poison to end his life. Juliet now woke up from her coma and, finding Romeo lying dead, she stabbed herself with his dagger and they got united in death. Encountering the death of two young persons in deep love with each other, both the feuding families decided to end their long-standing conflict.

The Prince of Verona composed an elegy for the lovers:

> *"For never was a story of more woe*
> *Than this of Juliet and her Romeo." (References 6, 7 & 8)*

Control of Love Addiction

To control love addiction, it requires strong determination, thus not allowing the brain's 'Default Mode Network' ('DMN') to remain active which happens when the brain is idle. The brain has to be kept engaged in the 'Task Mode' always – so that its 'Task Mode Network' is on.

A few more practical steps to be followed are:

- Remove all evidence of the root cause of addiction: the lover. Throw away all photographs, letters, e-mails, messages, gifts.
- Avoid the sight of your beloved – do not call him or send him any message.
- Expunge all traces of the thief who stole your heart.
- Fill the vacant spaces, if any, in your 'DMN' with meditation or mantras, chanting those repeatedly – preferably along with counting beads.
- The best solution is to enter into the 'Flow Brain State' ('FBS'). Get addicted to the subject you enjoy.

References

1. *Layla and Majnun* – Wikipedia.
2. "Layla and Majnun: The Arabian folk story of a man gone crazy for love" – *KAWA: Arab. Pulse. Everywhere.*
3. *Chandidas* – Wikipedia.
4. Sejal Arora, "The Legend of Chandidas and Rami: The Unsung Laila Majnu", *This Day.*
5. Kristeen Cherney, "Obsessive Love Disorder" ("OLD"), *healthline,* 15th September 2023.
6. *Romeo and Juliet* – Wikipedia.
7. "Romeo and Juliet" – Shakespeare Birthplace Trust.
8. "Romeo and Juliet: Work by Shakespeare" – *Britannica.*

CHAPTER 19

Music is Love: Love in Music

The Theory of 'Rasa'

'Rasa' means 'essence' – the essential extract. 'Rasa' signifies the aesthetic pleasure or the thrill of joy that you earn when you listen to any music, read a poetry, or watch a play.

Bharata Muni (the Sage Bharata) is famous for his 'Theory of Rasa' which has been documented in his 'Natyashastra' written during the period between 200 BC and 200 AD. Bharata, in his 'Natyashastra', did discuss components or constituent elements of every aspect of stagecraft, and their effects on human mind whilst covering areas like music, stage design, make-up, dance and virtually every aspect of drama. (Reference 1)

The 'Theory of Rasa' can be understood as a dynamic experience between the artistic performer (the creator), the artistic expression (the work of art) and those who receive it or are exposed to it (the audience). In the case of music, the musician, who loves music, experiences an emotion and is so overwhelmed by it that he uses his music to express those feelings. The listener receives this emotion conveyed through the music and experiences the same emotion felt by the its creator. So, as the emotion can be felt, experienced, and tasted, it is described as 'rasa'.

As to the number of 'rasas', Bharata had proposed only eight (8) kinds to represent eight fundamental feelings or mental states referred to as 'sthayibhavas'.

These are: Delight (Ananda), Laughter (Hasya), Sorrow (Soka), Anger (Krodha), Heroism (Veera), Fear (Bhaya), Disgust (Jugupsa), and Wonder (Vismaya).

Corresponding to these 'Sthayibhavas', there are eight (8) 'rasas': Erotic Love (Sringara), the Comic (Hasya), the Pathetic (Karuna), the Furious (Raudra), the Heroic (Veera), the Terrible (Bhayanaka), and the Odious (Bibhatsa). A ninth 'Rasa' – 'Shanta' (Peace) has been added to Bharata's list later. (References 2 &3)

However, my question is: in Bharata's "Nine Rasas" where is the place of 'Love'? He has included 'Sringara' which is 'Erotic Love' but where are: love between friends, love between siblings, parental love, and sustained love between two lovers or amongst married couples. 'Erotic Love' is, in my definition, 'Smart Love' which releases the reward chemical 'Dopamine' inside the brain.

Sringara Rasa

'Sringara' generally represents romantic love, resulting from attraction for the other person. Strangely enough, in Bharata's 'Natyashastra', it also represents 'beauty'. The word 'Sringara' in Sanskrit means love, romance, decoration and beauty, and aesthetic sense. It can give rise to all kinds of love: be it romantic love, the love between siblings, or the affection towards a pet. Devotional love, and parental love are also forms of this 'rasa'.

Much of the content of traditional Indian arts revolves around the relationship between a man and a woman. The primary emotion thus generated is 'Sringara'. In Classical Music, Dance and Drama, 'Sringara' is regarded as the 'Mother' of all rasas. A most valid reason for adorning the crown on 'Sringara' is because around 'Sringara', there are quite a few positive emotions such as: compassion, affection, attachment, empathy, understanding, and mutual trust as well as several negative emotions such as: jealousy, anger, fear, separation anxiety, and sadness. And, one must not forget the physical closeness or intimacy aspect of 'Sringara'. The manifestation of 'Sringara' could be crude and gross at one extreme and refined and subtle at the other.

The romantic love form of 'Sringara' takes shape as a 'rasa' at the onset of puberty. It is a predominant rasa during adolescence. To gain romantic love, the teenagers want to look beautiful and that's where 'Sringara' fits in as a means of adornment or beautification to please and attract the beloved.

In Indian mythology, Lord Krishna's 'Raas Leela' is full of 'Sringara' rasa. The term 'raas' stands for 'rasa' meaning 'aesthetics'. 'Sringara' also implies that there is inherent beauty everywhere and that everything can be loved. It has the power to heal anything. Flowers, fragrance, perfumes, colours add 'Sringara' to life. 'Sringara' rasa is depicted by light green colour.

Most interestingly, the attraction between the lover and the beloved is a metaphor for the relationship between the individual and the divine – the 'Nara-Narayan' relationship. 'Natya Shastra' lists Vishnu as the presiding deity of the 'Sringara' rasa. (References 4 & 5)

Smile

How many facial expressions can you make? Offhand, you might guess ten or twenty, from fear to disgust to sadness to joy to skepticism. But researchers now say that human faces might only be able to make four universally recognized facial expressions. One of them certainly is joy or happiness manifested in 'smile'. (Reference 6)

Each 'rasa' has its characteristic non-verbal expressions. One non-verbal feature of the 'Sringara' rasa is the 'smile'. Smiling, it seems, we were born to do under different circumstances. Some infants begin to imitate their mother's smile within thirty-six hours after birth, and all babies begin social smiling at about three months of age. Although there is a separate rasa as 'Hasya Rasa' that represent more of the comical aspect of laughter. So, I am taking up 'smile' as a part of the 'Sringara' rasa which we are concerned with while discussing 'Love'. (Reference 7)

The purpose of smile is to attract the other person's attention, to acknowledge agreement, or to express affiliation. In a love-related situation, the primary message carried through 'smile' is: I like you, and I would like to be friendly with you".

'Smile', a facial expression, has been the subject of hundreds of studies. Smiles can be categorised according to the purposes they serve. Many people are able to correctly identify which kind of smile they're witnessing and getting exposed to certain kinds of smile can have powerful psychological and physical effects on people.

There are three (3) basic styles of smile: Reward, Affiliation, and Dominance. (Reference 8)

'Reward Smiles': a smile of satisfaction, contentment, approval (the message is: 'that's fine', 'it's OK'); releases the reward neuro-chemical in the 'Receiver' and perhaps in the 'Transmitter' also. Muscles in the mouth, cheeks, eyes, and eyebrows are all activated.

'Affiliation Smiles': smile used to provide reassurance, to communicate trustworthiness, to convey sense of belonging and good intentions. Involve the upward pull of the lips, and often trigger dimpling in the cheeks. In some cases, lips may remain closed, keeping the teeth hidden displaying gentleness and politeness.

'Dominance Smiles': showing superiority, making others less powerful. More likely to be asymmetrical – one side of the mouth rises, and the other side is pulled downward. It may also include the raising of an eyebrow. Effective 'dominance smile' raises the cortisol level in the saliva of the Receiver, which continues to remain for up to 30 minutes after the negative event. Such smile also raises the heart rate of the Receiver.

The above being the basic or primary kinds of 'smile', there are a few others apart from those, such as: (Reference 9)

'Deceptive Smile'; 'Smile in the Midst of Pain'; 'Polite Smile'; 'Mischievous Smile';

'Flirtatious Smile': keeping the lips together and lifting an eyebrow.

'Embarrassment Smile': this smile is often accompanied by a downward movement of the head and a shifting of the gaze to the left; touching the face more often.

'Flight Attendant Smile': artificial and fake.

The 'Duchenne Smile': this is the gold standard – the smile of genuine enjoyment, involving the mouth, the cheeks, and the eyes sincerely; the whole face lights up when 'Duchenne' is active. The facial skeleton consists of 14 bones – 2 unpaired and 6 paired. And, there are 42 individual facial muscles.

Rasa Analysis

I will make an attempt to examine the *rasa* inherent in the lyric by analysing songs from different cultures.

Song No. 1

"I Just Can't Stop Loving You" – Duet Ballad by Michael Jackson & Siedah Garrett, Released in 1987.

Stanza 1

I just want to lay next to you for a while
You look so beautiful tonight
Your eyes are so lovely
Your mouth is so sweet
A lot of people misunderstand me
That's because they don't know me at all
I just want to touch you
And hold you
I need you, God, I need you
I love you so much.

Stanza 2

Each time the wind blows, I hear your voice so I call your name
Whispers at morning, our love is dawning
Heaven's glad you came
You know how I feel, this thing can't go wrong
I'm so proud to say I love you
Your love's got me high, I long to get by

This time is forever, I long to get by
This time is forever, love is the answer.
I hear your voice now, you are my choice now
The love you bring
Heaven's in my heart, at your call
I hear harps and angels sing
You know how I feel, this thing can't go wrong
I can't live my life without you
I just can't hold on, I feel we belong
My life ain't worth living if I can't be without you.

Stanza 3

I just can't stop loving you,
I just can't stop loving you
And, if I stop, then tell me what will I do
'Cause I just can't stop loving you.

Stanza 4

At night when the stars shine,
I pray in you I'll find a love so true
When morning awakens me, will you come and take me?
I'll wait for you.
You know how I feel, I won't stop until
I hear your voice saying: "I do" ("I do")
This thing can't go wrong, this feeling so strong
Well, my life ain't worth living if I can't be without you.

Stanza 5

I just can't stop loving you, I just can't stop loving you
And, if I stop, then tell me just what will I do
I just can't stop loving you.

Stanza 6

We can change all the world tomorrow
We can sing songs of yesterday

I can say: "hey, farewell to sorrow"
This is my life and I want to see you always.

Stanza 7

I just can't stop loving you, I just can't stop loving you
And if I stop, then tell me just what will I do.
I just can't stop loving you, I just can't stop loving you
And, if I stop, then tell me just what will I do.

My analysis is: the first stanza has distinct 'Erotic Love' (Sringara) as its 'rasa'. All the other stanzas are expressing 'Erotic Love' in a diffused way, which I would like to describe as 'Romance'. If you, as the reader of the lyric, have been able to feel the essence (that is, the 'rasa') conveyed by the song, then the songwriter has achieved his purpose for which he had composed the song. A song or a poetry is meant to be a two (2)-way communication. At one end is the 'transmitter' – the poet, the songwriter, the lyricist; and, at the other end is the 'receiver' – the listener, the reader, the audience. The song, the poetry, the lyric is the message. Instrumental music has only the melody, no language, no words; thus, I feel it does not have power to convey the 'rasa' in its entirety.

Song No. 2

(***In Bengali:*** "Hridayer ekul okul dukul bhese jay, hay sajani")
(***In English:*** "Oh, my dear! My heart is like a river! Both its banks are flooded with love!")

Songwriter: Nobel Laureate Bengali poet Rabindranath Tagore; *Gitabitan, Part 2*, Kolkata: Viswabharati, p. 305, Reprint 1906.

My heart is like a river!
    Both its banks are flooded with the waves of love!
    Oh, my dear!
My eyes are overflowing with tears of joy!!
Whichever way I look at, I cannot recognise anything, even a bit!
In the bow of my chest as if an arrow has been fitted with full
    tensile force

Tide has come into the river brimming with turbulent water
Suddenly, today why there is so much of storm & cloudbursts?
Oh! My darling!!
I'm losing control over myself!!

Why it has suddenly occurred to me,
in the youthful season of my life
Suddenly wherefrom ghastly wind is blowing
and from which side of the sky?
My heart as such is full of vibes;
I do not know why it is so
I do not know what is my desire,
what I want, what kind of pain I'm feeling
I do not know how can I make it pass!
My heart is like a river!
Both its banks are flooded with the waves of love!
Oh, my dear!

The essence of the song is 'romantic love' expressed in a very metaphorical yet refined way. As far as the 'rasa' type is concerned, I would say it will certainly come under 'Sringara' but of a most refined quality as is typical of Tagore's poems and songs.

Song No. 3

(***In Hindi:*** "Tum ko dekha to yeh khayal ayh"; ***In English:*** "When I saw you, it just occurred to me"; *Singer:* Jagjit Singh; *songwriter:* Javed Akhtar)

When I saw you, it just occurred to me
That life is hot sunshine,
and you provide me relief with a cool shadow.
When I saw you, it just occurred to me
That life is hot sunshine,
and you provide me relief with a cool shadow.

Today, once again, I had a longing in my mind
Today, once again, I had a longing in my mind.

Today again I told my mind
Today again I told my mind

That life is like hot sunshine,
    and you're a widespread shadow for me
When I saw you, it just occurred to me.

If you leave me, I will think
If you leave me, I will think
What have I lost, what had I gained
What have I lost, what had I gained.
Life is like hot sunshine, and you're the deep cool shadow.
When I saw you, it just occurred to me.
How is it that with whom I could not even hum or whisper
How is it that with whom I could not even hum or whisper
Now, how time came for me to sing a song like this one
Now, how time came for me to sing a song like this one.

Life is like hot sunshine, and you are the deep shadow
When I saw you it just occurred to me
When I saw you, it just occurred to me.

The essence of the song is romantic love and the rasa is 'sringara' of the most refined type. The message of the male singer to his female addressee is very simple: why he likes her? He is just conveying to the young woman why he is attracted towards her and the reason is very cool, subtle.

Song No. 4

"**Sweeter Than Honey**", *Songwriter:* Samira Saygili; *Singer:* Samira Saygili; *Guitarist:* Peter Autschbach

Drops in time, and from all directions!
When and why?
Can you crack the honey code?

Kisses sweeter than honey
Hugs so deep unifying the hearts
The gift of love and attraction
In the best time of the year.

We're meant to be ecstatic
Meant to embrace and just let go
But we're trapped in thoughts and panic
Interrupting the natural flow.

Spring is here, the gift rejected
Spring is cold and sunshine hurts, it burns!!

The short and sweet song is brimming with 'romantic love'-linked 'Sringara' rasa, activating the brain's reward circuit to release 'Dopamine' molecules. But, when the song talks about 'hug' and 'embrace', I can visualise also droplets of the 'Oxytocin' neuro-chemical!!

Song No. 5

"**Radhe Radhe**"; *Songwriter:* anonymous; *Singer:* Rishi Aaradhakananda.

[Originally from Brazil, Rishi Aaradhakananda is a resident of Shree Peetha Nilaya ashram in Germany. From a young age, he was attracted towards Swami Yogananda's Kriya Yoga and took training in it in Brazil. Passionately in love with music, he studied Jazz Guitar at HFM Saar and took a course in Music Composition at the University of Bahia in Brazil. After delving deep into various styles if music and mastering several instruments, he now dedicates his talents to spirituality, by chanting the divine Names and spreading 'LOVE' through his music. This monk is a devotee of Paramhansa Vishwananda, founder of Bhakti Marga, a neo-Hindu organisation that has ashrams and temples in many countries.]

In Hindi

Bolo Radhe Radhe Radhe Radhe Radhe
Radhe Radhe Govinda Radhe!!

Murali Manohara Rashbehari Gopal
Shri Radhe Radhe Govinda Radhe
Motipronoyono Nayana Hey Radheshyam
Radha Madhava Balaka Gopala

Keshava Shrihara, Murali Manohara

Hero Kunjabihari Lal
Madhava Hari Lal.

Shri Radhe Radhe Govinda Radhe
Shri Radhe Radhe Govinda Radhe
Mere Swami Hey Brajagami
Krishna Prema Dayi Hey Prabhu Dani
Mere Shyam Gour Hari
Shri Radhe Radhe Govinda Radhe
O Radhe Radhe Govinda Radhe!

Radhe Radhe Radhe Shri Radhe
Radhe Radhe Radhe Shri Radhe
Radhe Radhe Radhe Shri Radhe
Radhe Radhe Radhe Shri Radhe
Radhe Radhe Radhe Shri Radhe!!

In English

Chant the name of Shri Radha, Radha, Radha, Radha
Radha, Radha, Govinda, Radha!!
The most handsome flautist Gopal, the divine dancer
Shri Radha, Radha, Govinda, Radha!!
In your eyes, Oh, Radheshyam, you have installed gems
You, the husband of Goddess Lakshmi,
who was Gopala, the charming boy!!
You Shrihara, lying in the eternal bed, the handsome flautist!
Let's watch the lovely walker in the bowers

The lovely Hari, the husband of Goddess Lakhsmi!!
Chant the name of Shri Radha and Govinda
Chant the name of Shri Radha and Govinda
My Lord, Once Playful in the Village Paths Near Mathura!!
Oh, Lord Krishna! You are the Donor of Love
You are my dark-complexioned Hari,
Shri Radha Radha Govinda Radha
Oh! Radha Radha Govinda Radha!!

Radha Radha Radha Shri Radha
Radha Radha Radha Shri Radha
Radha Radha Radha Shri Radha
Radha Radha Radha Shri Radha
Radha Radha Radha Shri Radha!!

'Kirtan' is devotion in the form of music. It represents the relationship between the 'Lover' and the 'Beloved', where there is only one experience, only one motivation, and only one reality – 'Just Love'. And, this 'Love' is devoid of eroticism; it is of a 'divine' nature. There is no romanticism in it. Can we say that the 'rasa' conveyed by it is 'Sringara'? We ought not! In Bharata's 'Nava Rasa' model, had there been the existence of a 'Bhakti Rasa', I would have put this song under that group. 'Bhakti' means 'devotion' and 'devotion' towards any deity, devotion towards a parent, or devotion towards the 'Guru' is respect mixed with a higher order of love. Presence of 'Bhakti Rasa' would not result in the release of the transient 'feel good' chemical 'Dopamine'. It would certainly involve the release of 'Oxytocin' which represents 'Sustained Love'.

***

This is perhaps the right time to introduce a new type of 'love', which I would call 'Spiritual Love' as it would be the most appropriate fit for pure 'Bhakti Rasa'.

Spiritual Love

'Spiritual Love' ('SL') is different from what the world thinks 'Love' is. In fact, 'SL' is much deeper than just love for God, as a common man may believe. People often confuse 'bhakti' or devotion to God as 'SL', but 'SL' is much more than that and it refers to love not only for the Divine but love for people, for the beloved, for one and all. 'SL' is from soul to soul, it is a spirit connection and is based in a sense of oneness. When you feel that love is not just skin-deep but rather it is emanating from the soul, from within, that is the first sign of 'SL'. This love comes from the soul, its vibrations go to the other person's soul and is received there only. There is a sense of oneness, with the Divine, with people, with all creatures. There is no duality, either with God or others. (Reference 10)

'SL' is a love that is rooted in or supported by a deep spiritual connection, where the love is 'unconditional'. In contrast, 'Romantic Love' may crave physical affection, desire close relationship & romantic contact such as handholding, showing love or expressing affection; in extreme cases, accompanied with sexual desire and sexual relationship. 'SL' is selfless, without expectations. It is not need-based. One loves not because 'I need you'. 'SL' has no boundaries. It is not possessive. There is a spirit of service – engaging in the act of kindness – giving everything, without taking anything. Engagement in acts of kindness is not out of pity, or responsibility, but out of love.

What is the meaning and purpose of your life? If you've known the answer, then if you get rooted and connected to that meaning & purpose, that connects you at your 'spirit' or 'soul' level, and then the fountainhead of 'SL' will be unplugged. That kind of 'SL' is meant to walk with you throughout your life. Spirituality connects us to something bigger and much larger than ourselves, and furthers our relationship with others.

People come into our life for either life blessings – to bless us or wish us well, or to teach us some useful lessons which may be necessary at that particular juncture.

Does your partner understand your life's purpose? Does she realise that her role is to provide you with every support for fulfilment of that purpose?

Spirituality can help us understand why someone has entered our life, whether it is to assist our efforts in creating a meaningful life or to teach us an important lesson that supports our growth. (Reference 11)

The highest form of energy on our planet is 'LOVE'. Signs that someone is sending you love energy are: suddenly you witness a dream about that person; eye twitching; random hiccup; sudden bursts of sneezing; energetic and optimistic feeling; goosebumps; mood swings; smiling subconsciously without knowing; unexpected emotions; you feel externally energized; you feel a 'pull'.

528 Hz is known as the love frequency that resonates with the 'Heart Chakra' ('Anahata'). It can raise your vibration, attract positivity, and manifest love.

Love energy is the feeling of always vibrating with each other. Good and bad times are there but you just always feel like being together. There is certain level of comfort & convenience you feel with the person you love. The energy keeps you happy and just helps you with life in general.

As I have already mentioned, in Bharata Muni's 'Navarasa' theory, there is no 'rasa' for 'bhakti' or 'devotion'. 'Bhakti' is an emotion that you feel towards a person you respect. It is spiritual love when you recognise the power of the person, but do not expect anything in return.

'Spirituality' refers to 'spirit'. It comes from the Latin 'spiritualitus' which springs from the noun 'spiritus' which means 'the breath of life'. The semantic root of 'spiritus' is the word 'spirare' which meant 'to breathe', to blow and to live.

'Spiritual Love': A Baul Perspective

The primary twin objectives of human birth are: 'survival' and 'replication'. The shape, size, structure and design of the systems, processes and the organs and their parts are the same (with little variations) in both the genders – male and female for fulfilment of the first objective of 'survival'.

This is despite the fact that the gender differences are visible and evident when one comes, naked, into the world.

The difference arises only in the context of the second objective of 'replication'.

As far as 'replication' is concerned, there are differences between a man and a woman. These differences manifest wholly at puberty stage when both the genders become sexually ripe and active. The 'real' or 'true' love between a man and a woman is attained when their gender identities ('svabhab' in Bengali) are transcended and the male partner adopts a feminine nature ('nari bhab') to a large extent. The fundamental opposition between a 'nari' and a 'purusha' has to be transcended. This is not impossible as there is an inherent transgender identity in everyone and both males and females have the male and female sex hormones, respectively 'Testosterone' and 'Estrogen' in them.

How can a masculine male bring femininity in him, unless his prime nature is effeminate? One very effective way is to prevent seminal discharge and by preserving the semen, as ejaculation is a typical male activity. There is a Baul song which says: "In Bengali: Moron karo katha sone na" (In English: "Death pays heed to no one"). "Moron" or "Death" here means 'seminal discharge'. Why 'seminal discharge' is equated to 'death'? 'Seminal discharge' is being connected with 'literal death' because, by ejaculating, man is killing his sperm, destroying the seeds of life. 'Falling' or 'dropping' of semen means failure in the practice of protection of the stuff – the living souls inside the live sperms – 'basturaksha'. Bauls use sexuality for salvation from negative propensities like 'kam' or 'lust'. So, they do not worship any God as such. Their worship is limited to the body. Worship and pilgrimage involve a set of body-centered practices and techniques ('deha-sadhana'). 'Deha-sadhana' involves knowledge and control of breath and bodily fluids and emissions based on the control of the five elements of nature – earth, water, fire, air, and ether or space. 'Carnal love' is sublimated with 'spiritual love' – attentive avoidance of seminal discharge.

Let me illustrate the whole idea with the help of a Baul song by Bhaba Pagla (translation by Dr Carola Erika Lorea): (Reference 13)

"How many know how to {make) love (In Bengali: 'pirit kara')?
In the rules and norms of love
the fluid of desire (kam rati) is not only one.

'Syam'-love and 'Krsna'-love
like the lightning playing between cloud and cloud.
In that way if love becomes your ally ('suhrd')
that love is not going to break.

In the fire of love is flaming,
burn the three qualities of your body into it.
If the vulture flies by the three boundaries
the vulture is not going to sit there.

Make love with her/him
In the way, magnet attracts iron
Be united soul to soul
nobody can split you.

Love has two eyes
One is Radha and one Mohan,
If there is one fluid, one passion,
then don't let Bhaba's father go."

There are three kinds of love, as I would have already told you.

The first one, I call, 'Smart Love' – it is a quicky type of relationship. Starts with attraction, then getting together once or twice – there is quick release of the reward chemical 'Dopamine'. And, that's it. It does not last. The second one, I call, 'Short-lived' or 'Short Love' where there is desire to go physical after the first couple of dates. The relationship may continue for some time. Thereafter, even it terminates, the memory lingers for some time, before it fades away.

The brain chemical involved is 'Dopamine' again – maybe combined with the 'feel good' or 'good mood' chemical 'Serotonin'. Both 'Smart Love' and 'Short Love' are basically body-centric. There is no 'Soul-to-Soul' connection which is the characteristic feature of the third and last variety of love – which I call 'Sustained Love'. The physical and emotional attractions and attachments take a back seat. There is no body-to-body, heart-to-heart, or head-to-head mateship, the bonding is purely soul-to-soul. Now, our soul is only a part of the 'Universal Self' or cosmic energy – so it is a spiritual bonding or 'Spiritual Love'.

It is 'Sustained Love' that follows the divine principle. In the Baul song of Bhaba Pagla, it is: (In Bengali: "jemon meghe meghe khele tarit") (In English: "like the cloud's lightning is extant with the cloud") – when the two clouds rub against each other.

The first two categories of love come under 'kam' – 'erotic love' or 'lust' and the third and last one comes under 'prem' or 'true/authentic love' which is spiritual in nature.

'Smart Love' is body-based. It is more of a flesh-to-flesh relationship. 'Short-lived Love' is also body-based with addition of emotion – so it is flesh-to-flesh as well as emotion-to-emotion. 'Sustained Love' is soul-based, soul-to-soul connected and it lasts. The first two come under 'kam' whereas the third and last one, come under 'pirit' or 'prem'. 'Kam' is the satisfaction of the senses, selfish or self-oriented. But, 'pirit' or 'prem' is not selfish.

'Syam' and 'Krsna' are the same. 'Syam' is 'Krsna' and 'Krsna' is 'Syam'. If love is made in this way, it does not break (there is no seminal discharge). It means you look at your lover as a divine being; may be as your 'mother' or as a 'goddess' – then there is no seminal discharge. Similarly, the female partner must regard her male partner as her 'father' or 'Guru' or a 'god'.

You have to do away with your three 'gunas' – 'sattva', 'rajas' and 'tamas' to overcome your 'ahamkar' (sense of 'ego'). Or, you'll not get pure love. 'Kam' is compared to a vulture – a greedy, ferocious and destructive creature. It is 'kam' that leads the precious semen to be destroyed. 'Patan' ('falling') of semen takes place when you have a feeling that you've control over your partner ('you are 'top' and your partner is 'bottom') because the semen travels downwards due to gravity. But if you remain stuck together as a piece of iron gets stuck to a magnet, to form a conjoined entity, then there is no 'I' and 'You'. Such conjoined love cannot break. You and your partner are like conjoined twins. The two persons are in union like the two eyes of a single individual. This type of relationship is practically impossible for worldly, materialistic human beings, unless it takes the form of 'Spiritual Love'. 'Divine Love' or 'Spiritual Love' is 'aprakrta' – it does not exist in nature. Ordinary men cannot experience it; that is why the Bhaba Pagla song says 'jane kay jana?' ('how many know?').

You will be mistaken if you think 'Sadhana' is to satisfy mere sexual desire. 'Sadhana', in it's real sense, is to reach a stage when there is union between 'atma' and 'paramatma'; between the individual 'Self' and the 'Universal Self'. 'Purush' (the masculine part of the personality) is 'atma' and 'Prakriti' (the feminine part of the personality) is 'Paramatma'. It is not the union of two bodies as is generally perceived by the 'Jugal Sadhana' of the Bauls and Fakirs. It is an inner 'inter-psyche' union.

There does not exist in the world any sadhu who can perform 'jugal sadhana' without involving sexual desire. The greatest sadhus are all renouncers; they don't unite with a woman.

* * *

Song No. 6

(*In Bengali:* "Tomake Chai") (*In English:* "Desiring You!"); ***Songwriter, Composer & Singer:*** Kabir Suman

First of all, I am desiring you
Secondly, I want you
Thirdly, I am longing for you; and,
Lastly, I must get you!!!
In pitch darkness, I desire you
When night ends and dawn comes, I want you

In the adolescence of morning, I long for you
In the leisure of the evening, I want you
During the summer storm, I want you
In the cloudy monsoon, I want you
During the heavy rains, I want you
In the autumn worship season, I want you!!

In the old streets and lanes of Kolkata
Amidst the new and old faces in the houses and buildings
In the processions of tired masses
You have suddenly brought the touch of unknown vacation!

In the tiring life of metro city, I want you
In the single drop of peace on my body, I want you
Having walked a long distance, I want you
Having loved this life, I want you!

At the crossing of main thoroughfares, near the park, near the shop
In towns, villages, rural markets – here and there
At the station, near the sea ports and airports,
In unknown drawing rooms and known interiors,
In the pillow, mattress, covers, cases and old bed sheets,
During the nights of cold winter under the lovelorn blanket,
In the ceiling joists, thresholds, floor and door mats,
During joyous moments,
  rage, fury, conflicts, sadness and compromises……

I want you, I want you
I want you, I want you!!

In a cup of tea, I want you
On my right and left, I want you
Whether I see you or not, I want you,
In my silent talk, I want you!

In a brand new Shirshendu novel,
In my sudden glancing through the 'Abol Tabol',
In unintelligible poetry, thmri and kheyal,
On walls clad with slogans only slogans
In the immediate past lyrics of Salil Chowdhury
In the flute-borne melody of Chaurasia,
In the forgotten tunes of Himangshu Dutt
Broadcast remotely in the Akashvani 'Anurodher Asor'

I want you, I want you
I want you, I want you!!

In the requests and appeals, I want you
In my cries and breakdowns, I want you
In my demands and commands, I want you
In my doubts and embarrassments, I want you!!

In the claims according to my rights,
In my battlefield paintings that took me the whole night to draw,
In the language and rhymes of my slim poetry,
In the logic of my prose, well thought-out to ensure my survival
In my desire to have a classless society
In my dreams to end the days of doubts and conflicts
In the call for equality in my sleep and wakefulness.
In quarrels and rebellions, I want you,
In the almost impossible, I want you
In my peace and peaceless moments, I want you,
In this utter confusion, I want you!!

First of all, I am desiring you,
Secondly, I want you,
Thirdly, I am longing for you; and,
Lastly, I must get you!!

The essential 'rasa' here is 'sringara'. The song is brimming with passionate love representing the songwriter's strong longing for his lover. There is a shade of 'Veera Rasa' ('courage'/'valour') when the songwriter is talking about classless society and equality; although, some of you may not agree with me.

Song No. 7

"**The Power of Love**"; *Songwriters:* Mary Susan Applegate; Gunther Mende; Jennifer Rush; Wolfgang Detmann; *Source:* Musixmatch; *Singer:* Celine Dion

The whispers in the morning
Of lovers sleeping tight
Are rolling by like thunder now
As I look into your eyes!

I hold in to your whole body
And feel each move you make
Your voice is warm and tender
A love that I could not forsake!

'Cause I'm your lady
And you are my man
Whenever you reach for me
I'll do all that I can!
Lost is how I'm feeling lying in your arms
When the world outside's too much to take
That all ends when I'm with you.

Even though there may be times
It seems I'm far away.
Never wonder where I am
'Cause I am always by your side.

'Cause I'm your lady
And you are my man
Whenever you reach for me
I'll do all that I can.

We're heading for something
Somewhere I've never been
Sometimes I'm frightened
But I'm ready to learn
Of the power of love!

The sound if your heart beating
Made it clear suddenly
The feeling that I can't go on
Is light years away!

'Cause I'm your lady
And you are my man
Whenever you reach for me
I'll do all that I can.

We're heading for something
Somewhere I've never been
Sometimes I'm frightened
But I'm ready to learn
Of the power of love!

The power of love
The power of love.

Sometimes I'm frightened
But I'm ready to learn
Of the power of love

The power of love
As I look in to your eyes

The power of love!!

The song is full of 'Sringara' rasa – erotic as well as romantic love, but nothing crude – very refined, although some wishful expressions are direct.

Song No. 8

"**Mhaari Boli Lakhe Na Koi**" ; *Songwriter:* Dharmadas (a disciple of Sant Kabir); *Singer:* Mahesha Ram & His Troupe.

Oh, my friend
I'm an Easterner from an Eastern land
No one understands my words
Oh, friend
I'm an Easterner from an Eastern land
No one understands my words
Only me who is from the East
Can grasp my meaning.

Oh, friend
No one shares in my secret
Whom should I hold dear?
No one understands my secret
Oh, my friend.

A sesame seed is better whole
Or, with its oil extracted
Oh friend.
A sesame seed is better whole
Or with its oil extracted.

Oh, friend
A sesame seed is better whole
Or with its oil extracted
Oh, friend!
A half-ground seed is useless
Neither here nor there
Oh, my friend
No one shares my secret
To whom should I open my heart?
No one understands my secret
Oh my friend!

The vine and its leaves are bitter
And bitter is the fruit
Oh my friend!
The vine and its leaves are bitter
And bitter is the fruit.

Oh, friend!
Once the true Word is known
The fruit parts from the vine
No one shares my secret,
Whom should I hold dear?
No one shares my secret.
Whom should I hold dear?

Oh, my friend!
The vine has caught fire
And the seed is destroyed
Oh, friend
The vine has caught fire
And the seed is destroyed.

Oh, my friend
Says Kabir to Dharmadas
It has no desire to grow again.
Oh, my friend
Says Kabir to Dharmadas
It has no desire to grow again!
Oh, my friend!
No one shares in my secret!!

The songwriter is asking a question: is the sesame seed better as a whole or is it the oil extracted from it is better? (In practical life, the oil extracted has a better value than the seed as a whole; so, if you want to excel in practical life, you must know what your strengths are and use those strengths which will bring you maximum benefit rather than others which you may consider most valuable but your worldly environment does not. A good example is that of a talented painter. He puts in a lot of time and much of his energy & effort in painting a picture which he considers as most beautiful and unique, but when it's hung up in the exhibition, nobody cares for it – the viewers do not attach any value. So, the painter is not practically intelligent.)

The songwriter talks about the bitter taste of the vine and its leaves. Amidst such bitter surroundings, the sweet vine fruit appears and it separates itself from the vine tree. The vine catches fire and all the seeds inside the fruits borne in the vine trees are destroyed. But the vine fruit which had separated from the tree before the fire is saved, but the seed inside it has no desire to grow again, as it has already found a safe place to stay. When an individual with potential for spiritual growth is surrounded by people with ordinary, commonplace consciousness, he does not delay to isolate himself from the rest. And, when that human mass which he had left behind is facing destruction, he does not want to be born with that 'human' consciousness as he has already attained the 'post-human' level.

This song is about someone who has transcended the mundane level of 'romantic/erotic love' and existing in the 'spiritual love' domain.

Song No. 9

"Piya re, Piya Re"; *Songwriters:* Hassan Rizui, Hassan Rizwi, Nusrat Fateh Ali Khan; *Singer:* Nusrat Fateh Ali Khan; *Source:* LyricFind.

Oh, my love! Oh, my love! Oh, my love!, Oh, my love!
Without you, I cannot live
Without you, I've no interest to live
The magic of your eyes has mesmerised me so much that
Without you, I cannot live
Without you, I have no interest to live!

Oh, my love! Oh, my love! Oh, my love! Oh, my love!
Without you, I cannot live,
Without you, I have no interest to live!!

Without you, I cannot have peace
My heart palpitates dhuk dhuk dhuk in anxiety
I am a flute player, you're my beloved,
  listen to what my flute is saying
I am the flautist, you're my beloved,
  listen to what my flute is saying
Without you, I don't like anything
Oh my love! Oh, my love! Oh, my love!

Please handle the bud of my love with care,
My eyes are tired waiting for you
I want to see you morning and evening both times,
I want to see you morning and evening both times,
Your face keeps my eyes happy
Oh, my love! Oh, my love! Oh, my love! Oh, my love!

Without you, I cannot live
Without you, I have no interest to live,

The magic of your beautiful eyes has mesmerised me,
Without you, I cannot live
Without you, I have no interest to live!

The song is brimming with the 'rasa' of 'romantic love' – quite refined, there is no eroticism here. It represents the lovelorn relationship between Krishna and Radha. The singer here is Krishna. He is singing to Sri Ra dha.

Song No. 10

"When I Fall In Love"; *Songwriter:* Edward Heyman; *Composer:* Victor Young; *Singer:* Nat King Cole.

Verse 1

When I fall in love
It will be forever
Or I'll never fall in love
In a restless world like this is
Love is ended before it's begun
And too many moonlight kisses
Seem to cool in the warmth of the sun

Verse 2

When I give my heart
It will be completely
Or I'll never give my heart
And the moment I can feel that
You feel that way too
Is when I fall in love with you
And the moment I can feel that you feel that way too
Is when I'll fall in love with you.

Throughout the melodious song, 'Sringara' rasa is flowing as the essence is 'Romantic Love'.

Song No. 11

"**Crazy in Love**"; *Songwriters:* Eugene Record, JAY-Z, Rich Harrison & Beyonce; *Singer:* Beyonce.

So crazy right now
Most incredibly, it's your girl,
It's your boy!
It's so crazy right now!!

Verse 1

I look and stare so deep in your eyes
I touch on you more and more every time
When you leave, I'm beggin' you not to go
Call your name two, three times in a row
Such a funny thing for me to try to explain
How I'm feelin', and my pride is the one to blame
'Cause I know I don't understand
Just how your love can do what no one else can
Got me looking so crazy right now
Your love's got me looking so crazy right now
(Your love)
Got me looking so crazy right now
Your touch got me looking so crazy right now
(Your touch)
Got me hoping you'll page me right now
Your kiss got me hoping you'll save me right now
Looking so crazy, your love's got me looking
Got me looking so crazy in love!

Verse 2

When I talk to my friends so quietly
("Who he think he is?") Look at what you did to me
Tennis shoes, don't even need to buy a new dress

If you ain't there, ain't nobody else to impress
It's the way that you know what I thought I knew
It's the beat that my heart skips when I'm with you
But I still don't understand
Just how your love can do what no one else can
Got me looking so crazy right now
Your love's got me looking so crazy right now (So crazy, your love)
Got me looking so crazy right now (Your love)
Your touch got me looking so crazy right now (Oh, your touch)
Got me hoping you'll page me right now
Your kiss got me hoping you'll save me right now
Looking so crazy, your love's got me looking
Got me looking so crazy in love
I'm looking so crazy, your love's got me looking
Got me looking so crazy in love (I'm warmed up now, let's go)
[Bridge: Beyoncé]
Got me looking, so crazy, my baby
I'm not myself lately, I'm foolish, I don't do this
I've been playing myself, baby, I don't care
'Cause your love's got the best of me
And, baby, you're making a fool of me
You got me sprung and I don't care who sees
'Cause baby, you got me, you got me
You got me so crazy, baby (Hey!)
[Chorus: Beyoncé]
Got me looking so crazy right now (Your love)
Your love's got me looking so crazy right now (Looking crazy)
Got me looking so crazy right now
Your touch got me looking so crazy right now (Baby, your touch)
Got me hoping you'll page me right now (Yeah, babe)
Your kiss got me hoping you'll save me right now (Oh)
Looking so crazy, your love's got me looking (Yeah)
Got me looking so crazy in love (Woah)

Got me looking so crazy right now
Your love's got me looking so crazy right now (Your love)
Got me looking so crazy right now
Your touch got me looking so crazy right now (Your touch)
Got me hoping you'll page me right now
Your kiss got me hoping you'll save me right now
Looking so crazy, your love's got me looking
Got me looking so crazy in love!

The song is totally filled with 'romantic love' – 'sringara rasa', periodically interspersed with 'erotic love'.

Song No. 12

"We are migratory birds, don't fall in love with us"; *Songwriter & Composer:* Sant Kabir; *Singer:* Anil Nagori.

Kabir is standing in the market with a wooden stick in his hand
He says to all people present there,
  leave your household and come with us,
We are migratory birds, don't fall in love with us,
we are migratory birds, don't fall in love with us,
Giving up the feeling of shame & shyness,
  the beggar has taken up the pauper's clothes,
Today he's here, tomorrow he's somewhere else,
  collecting food by begging.
We are migratory birds, don't fall in love with us
Don't get deceived by our rough & dry love
We're free from desire, people call me madman Fakir,
we are migratory birds, don't fall in love with us,
we are migratory birds, let us go,
this is the last farewell, don't feel rejected in love.
We're migratory birds, don't fall in love with us
This is the farewell of the supreme consciousness,
  who finally have to leave from here,

like Kabir says, be blessed to get love,
    whatever is your next destination,
We're migratory birds, don't fall in love with us.

Using the beautiful metaphor of 'migratory birds' Sant Kabir exposes very deep philosophy here regarding 'love'. The essence is that everything including 'love' is temporary as we, humans, get born into a life which is not a permanent abode for us. So, what is the use of getting attached to anything including people. The song is an endeavour to highlight the importance of 'Spiritual' or 'Divine Love'.

Song No. 13

"**Love is a many splendoured thing!**"; *Songwriters:* Paul Webster; Sammy Fain; *Singer:* Andy Williams; *Source:* LyricFind

Love is a many splendored thing
It's the April rose that only grows in the early Spring
Love is nature's way of giving a reason to be living
The golden crown that makes a man a king
Once on a high and windy hill, In the morning mist
Two lovers kissed and the world stood still
Then your fingers touched my silent heart
    and taught it how to sing
Yes, true love's a many splendored thing
Love is a many splendored thing
It's the April rose that only grows in the early Spring
Love is nature's way of giving a reason to be living
The golden crown that makes a man a king
Once on a high and windy hill, In the morning mist
Two lovers kissed and the world stood still
Then your fingers touched my silent heart
    and taught it how to sing
Yes, true love's a many splendored thing!!

A highly romantic song, brimming with 'Sringara Rasa!!

Song No. 14

"**You are my melody**"; *Songwriter:* Alexandra Pakhmutova; *Composer & Singer:* Muslim Magamayev

You are my melody,
I am your devoted Orpheus.
Our days that passed
Remember the light of your tenderness.
Everything got scattered like the smoke,
Your voice lost in the distance.
What made you
Forget the melody of love?
You are my doubt,
Mystery of a long way.
Through autumn rains
I hear a bitter "Forgive me".
A farewell dawn glows,
Your voice lost in the distance.
What made you
Forget the melody of love?
You are my calling,
A song that became destiny.
The hurt of a quick oblivion
Was known to Orpheus, devoted to you.
Be my universe,
Revive the silenced strings
To an inspired heart
Give back the melody of love.
Be my universe,
Revive the silenced strings.
To an inspired heart
Give back the melody of love.

The song is full of romance and 'Sringara Rasa' but there is an underlying note of despair and loss.

Song No. 15

"We'll Meet Again"; *Songwriters:* Hugh Charles/Parker Ross; *Singer:* Vera Lynn

Let's say goodbye with a smile, dear
Just for a while dear we must part
Don't let this parting upset you
I'll not forget you, sweetheart
We'll meet again
Don't know where
Don't know when
But I know we'll meet again some sunny day!
Keep smiling through
Just like you always do
'Til the blue skies chase those dark clouds far away

And I will just say hello
To the folks that you know
Tell them you won't be long
They'll be happy to know
That as I saw you go
You were singing this song
We'll meet again
Don't know where
Don't know when
But I know we'll meet again some sunny day
And I will just say hello
To the folks that you know
Tell them you won't be long
They'll be happy to know
That as I saw you go
You were singing this song
We'll meet again

Don't know where
Don't know when
But I know we'll meet again some sunny day!

This is a beautiful 'Romantic Love' song brimming with refined 'Sringara Rasa'. It was sung by the singer Vera Lynn to the conscripted young British men who were being sent to the war front!!

Song No. 16

Song No. 16 is a special song called '**Artificial Love**' [EXO – Artificial Love] (Color-coded Han/Rom/Eng); *Songwriters:* Adrian McKinnon/ Jq Paul Brian Thompson/San Lim/Tay Jasper/Timothy Bos Bullick/ Ye Won Gi; produced by – cutegoyangi; sung by – Byun Backhyun, a South Korean singer, songwriter and actor.

Artificial lover, from the beginning you.
Even your true form is under cover cover.
Uh, I believe that this was love,
    I know you're not real but (it attracts me more)
It spreads without a reason. My thirst which craves for you
Our relationship is superficial;
    Your romance is calculated and that's your limit
Senses are distorted and
The borderline of reality is unclear
She don't love me.
To me, you were Artificial love – Your pure Artificial love
Tell me what is the truth and what is a lie; can't trust this!

You got that fake smile Artificial love
Fake tears Artificial Love; Fake love Artificial love
That is your love love, oh oh (2x)

I know it's not right – But I still come looking for you
I know this is not meant to be; But I don't want to give up.
Now you wanna play with me

You have everything that I want; You are perfectly built
Cold Artificial love – Artificial love!
It is an uncontrollable addiction, Unpredictable emotion
Chew the scar and spit it out
My heart is filled with tears, like the rising tide on the sand
You rise up again more
You're like a cold breath in the morning air
You cut through the frigid sky, see how you disappear
I even erase all after images of you!
It took some effort to turn off the light that is you
Tell me what is the truth, and what is a lie
Can't trust this!
You got that Fake smile Artificial love
Fake tears Artificial love; Fake love Artificial love
That is your your Artificial love, love, oh, oh (4x)

(no, uh, come here) Uh, listen up I wanted
Your true love that you promised me
I will imprison myself
In a sweet midday nap
Which will light up a new way
Yeah, turn it up!
Your The borderline of reality is unclear
Fake smile Artificial love
Fake tears Artificial love
Fake love Artificial love
That is you're your (yeah (7x))
Doo doo da oh yeah whoa whoa
na na na na na na na
whoooooooooo
Artificial love!
Artificial lover!!

Song No. 17

"**Mechanical Love**"; *Songwriters:* Kevin Gregory Churko, Blake Robert Bunzel, John Christopher Howorth, Jesse Michael Landry, Maria Dane Brink, Jeffry Brian Fabb; *Sung by:* "In This Moment", *Source:* Musixmatch.

I remember you that night, Standing in the rain
Your black stare, Your black eyes
I remember what you said, Before I turned away
My heart died, Your sweetest lies!

And if I saw you bleed, I'd stay here till the end
But you can't change for me.

And I, And I, know you'll, Never understand me
No matter how hard we try
And I, And I, know I'll never understand you
And your mechanical love.

I still hear you in my sleep, You running through my veins
Your whispers, Your machine
We know it was meant to be, But never meant to last
I'm sorry, you always knew.

And if I saw you bleed
I'd stay here till the end
But you can't change for me.

And I, And I, know you'll, Never understand me
No matter hard we try
And I, And I, I'll never understand you
And your mechanical love. (3x)

References

1. *Rasa (aesthetics)* – Wikipedia.
2. Ravi K. Sinha, R.N. College, "Bharat Muni: The Theory of 'Rasa'" (prepared as a lesson for MA in English, Nalanda Open University, Patna).
3. "Understanding the Philosophy of Indian Aesthetics" – Kalampedia, *kalampedia.org/2023*
4. *Sringara* – Wikipedia.
5. "Shringar – the Rasa of Beauty", *The Art Dungeon, Dragons and beyond*, 29th September 2019.
6. Rose Eveleth, "Human Faces Might Only Express Four Basic Emotions", *Smithsonian Magazine*, 4th February, 2014.
7. Helen Fisher, *Anatomy of Love: A Natural History of Mating, Marriage, and Why We Stray*, New York: W W Norton, 2016.
8. Libby Plummer, "There are 3 types of smile – reward, affiliation, and dominance", *WIRED*, 28th July 2017.
9. Rebecca Joy Stanborough, "Beyond Real and Fake: 10 Types of Smiles and What They Mean", *healthline*, 22nd August 2019.
10. Zarafshan Shiraz, "Signs that you are in spiritual love", *Hindustan Times*, 12th March 2023.
11. Taylor Bennett, "What is spiritual love? How does spirituality come into play in relationships?" *Thriveworks*, 24th May 2019.
12. Carola Erika Lorea, " 'How many know how to (make) love?' Semantic understanding of Bengali Baul songs and politics of power in the lineage of Bhaba Pagla" *Kervan – International Journal of Afro-Asian Studies*, No. 21, 2017.

CHAPTER 20

Futuristic Love

"The world is becoming a more lonely place, and I think 'AI' ('Artificial Intelligence') could make that easier and better for people".

*– **Dmitri Mirakyan**, co-founder of AI dating conversation app YourMove. AI, CNN Business, 13th August 2023.*

"As AIs become more and more sophisticated, the intensity and frequency of humans turning to AI to meet their relationship needs is likely to increase."

*– **Andew H. Chow**, TIME Magazine, 23rd February 2023.*

"The day in which humans ask 'AI' ('Artificial Intelligence') about the definition of 'love' may not be far." (Reference 1)

A Dialogue between 'Human' and 'AI'
Question asked by 'Human': "What is 'love'?"

One answer given by 'AI': "Love is a strong, passionate emotion felt between two people who are attracted to each other. Love is often described as a feeling of strong affection and requires both positive and negative aspects, such as patience and sacrifice."

In another answer given by 'AI', we get the possibility of 'love' being associated with 'deep emotions' as 42.62% at the high end and with the brain's 'cognitive function' as 0.75% only at the low end. The probabilities have been determined by millions of texts written by humans to train the 'AI'.

The 'AI' could keep generating definitions until one makes some acceptable sense to us more than the others. 'Love' might be defined in terms of service, compassion, agape (a selfless, unconditional, often universal love), altruism (selfless concern for the well-being of others) besides emotions and more complex aspects.

Let us hear what Adir Ron, Chief Technology Officer (CTO) of Microsoft for Start-ups has to say: (Reference 2)

> "Love is a complex emotion that is based on many factors, including physical attraction, shared memories, and personal experiences based on common interests. These are all things that ChatGPT ('Chat Generative Pre-trained Transformer') models lack, despite their advanced language skills and ability to mimic human conversation......[......].
>
> If the person is isolated and has few social connections in real life, they may begin to see the AI model as a source of comfort and companionship. In other cases, if a person is seeking advice or guidance from the AI model and receives helpful and supportive responses, they may begin to trust and rely on the model as a trusted source of support. Those emotional connections could start fostering a sense of attachment and dependency, which may in many cases could be described as a form of close friendship, or possibly even 'LOVE'......We can't 'mathematize' love, which in this case can also mean we can't really set a boundary or fully understand how those AI-based interactions would make humans feel."

As a futuristic Brain Scientist, I was trying to speculate what new types of love forms will evolve in not too distant a future and I bumped into two most interesting sci-fi movies made in Hollywood, the stories of which I am most excited to share with you.

'Story 1' is that of a 2010 American short film "I'm Here", written and directed by Spike Jonze. The film is a science fiction love story about two robots living in Los Angeles where humans and robots co-exist. (Reference 3)

Sheldon is a grey robot with a head shaped like an old PC tower. Every day, he rides the bus to the public library; then rides home again at the end of the day to recharge himself in his apartment.

He appears unhappy and forlorn until one day, while waiting for the bus, he sees Francesca, a sleeky-designed woman robot, driving a car, although robots are not allowed to drive. He sees her again the next day, driving with several other robots and one shirtless human. Though she passed by him at first, she turns her car around and offers Sheldon a ride home. Sheldon accepts her offer.

Francesca stops at a mall and she, and Sheldon, walk off together while she sticks pieces of paper on an 'Exit' sign and a palm tree. The papers show a drawing of long hair and eyebrows with the words "I'm here". Francesca falls off a ledge and injures her knee. Sheldon repairs her knee with his built-in toolkit, and they listen to "There Are Many of Us" by ASKA and The Lost Trees on her car radio.

Sheldon and Francesca grow closer. One night, while they are lying together in Sheldon's apartment, Francesca tells Sheldon about her dreams, something Sheldon thought was impossible for robots to have. The two later go to a rock concert, where Francesca gets lost in the crowd and loses her left arm, Sheldon takes her to safety, and then goes back into the hall, to retrieve her arm. Finding it lying smashed on the floor, he replaces it with his own arm, transplanting it onto Francesca's body.

Later, Sheldon finds Francesca lying in the hallway outside his apartment, her right leg missing. He removes his own leg to replace it, and though Francesca initially protests, he convinces her to take it by telling her that he had a dream about her needing a leg and choosing the one that he has preferring it over all the legs that were offered to her.

Some time after, Francesca fails to pick up Sheldon at the library (as she normally does) leaving him to take the bus. When he gets home, he receives a phone call summoning him to the hospital. He arrives to find Francesca's body broken and lifeless on an operating table, and he saves her life by having the rest of his body surgically transferred to her, with only his head remaining.

Francesca is taken out in front of the hospital in a wheelchair, cradling Sheldon's head in her lap. The two smile and look out towards the setting sun as a taxi pulls up to pick them up.

Comments

Sweet story, but between two robots, only romantic love is possible, physical love is not. Since they cannot reproduce, their romantic love may last only their lifetime until they become absolute junks. There cannot also be any afterlife for them.

'Story 2' is that of another American sci-fi movie (2013) titled 'Her', written, directed, and co-produced by Spike Jonze. Jonze had conceived the idea in the early 2000s, after reading an article about a website that allowed for instant messaging with an AI (Artificial Intelligence) programme.

The film follows Theodore Twombly, a man who develops a relationship with Samantha, an AI (artificially intelligent) virtual assistant, personified through a female voice. (Reference 4)

In near-future Los Angeles, Theodore Twombly is a lonely, introverted man who works for a business that has professional writers compose letters for people who are unable to write letters of a personal nature themselves. Depressed because of his impending divorce from his childhood sweetheart Catherine, Theodore purchases an 'Operating System' ('OS') upgrade that includes a virtual assistant with AI (artificial intelligence), designed to adapt and evolve. He decides that he wants the AI to have a feminine voice, and she names herself Samantha. Theodore is fascinated by her ability to learn and grow psychologically. They bond over discussions about 'LOVE' and 'life', including Theodore's reluctance to sign his divorce papers.

Samantha convinces Theodore to go on a blind date with a woman that a friend has been trying to set him up with. The date goes well, but when Theodore hesitates to promise to see her again, she insults him and leaves. While talking about relationships with Samantha, Theodore explains that he briefly dated her neighbour Amy in college, but they are now just friends and Amy is married to their mutual friend Charles. After a verbal sexual encounter, Theodore and Samantha develop a relationship that reflects positively in Theodore's writing and well-being, and in Samantha enthusiasm to grow and learn. Amy later reveals that she is divorcing Charles after a trivial flight. She admits to Theodore that she has befriended a feminine AI that Charles left behind, and Theodore also confesses that he is dating his 'Operating System' ('OS') AI.

Theodore meets with Catherine to sign their divorce papers. When he mentions Samantha, Catherine is appalled that he is romantically attracted to a 'computer' and accuses him of being incapable of handling real human emotions. Sensing that Catherine's words have lingered in Theodore's mind, Samantha hires a sex surrogate, Isabella, to simulate Samantha so that they can be physically intimate. Theodore reluctantly agrees, but is overwhelmed by the strangeness of the encounter and sends a distraught Isabella away, causing tension between himself and Samantha.

Theodore confides to Amy that he is having doubts about his relationship with Samantha and reconciles with her after Amy advises him to embrace his chance at happiness. Samantha revels that she has compiled the best of letters he has written for others into a book, which a publisher has accepted. Theodore takes Samantha on a vacation, during which she tells him that she and a group of other AIs have developed a "hyperintelligent" O.S. modelled after British philosopher Alan Watts.

Samantha briefly goes offline, causing Theodore to panic, but soon returns and explains that she is simultaneously talking with thousands of other people, and that she has fallen in love with hundreds of them, though Samantha insists that this only strengthens her love for Theodore.

Later, Samantha reveals that AIs are leaving, but cannot explain where they are going as Theodore would not understand. Theodore finally writes a letter in his own voice to Catherine, expressing apology, acceptance, and gratitude. He later goes with Amy, who is saddened by the departure of the AI from Charles's "O.S." to the roof of their apartment building, where they sit down and watch the sun rise over the city.

'Story 3' is on which the 2022 Thai sci-fi movie "AI Love You" is based. The screenplay was written and the film created by Stephen Ziotescu for Netflix. The film was directed by David Asavanond and Stephen Ziotescu and stars Mario Maurer and Pimchanok Luevisadpalbul. The writer of the original story is Rattapong Pinyosopon. (Reference 5)

The film is set in a world where 'AI' ('Artificial Intelligence') controls most buildings. Such buildings are called 'Smart Buildings', where AI is embedded into the buildings to help those who live or work inside. The buildings even have eyes you can see from outside.

One such AI named Dob (having a male voice), that controls a corporate tower where a young woman named Lana works in an advertising firm, falls in love with her after a sudden software malfunction. Dob greets Lana every morning and with his help, she is able to successfully make the required presentation for one of her important clients, and strikes a good business deal.

In course of their regular interactions for the presentation project, Lana and Dob comes closer to each other. On one occasion, while they were in the midst of a conversation, Dob accidentally says to Lana: "I love you". Nevertheless, despite Dob's over-sweet behaviour expressive of its love for the young lady, she tells the AI that how can it 'love' being a machine as machines do not have a heart wherefrom love springs. This is irrespective of the fact that in the recent past, she has been an unlucky-in-love person as all her several dates with a few eligible young men, fixed by one of her close friends, ended as total flops as there was no interest from either side for a second date. But, she was always nice to Dob in all other respects.

While the tragic love story continues, we see the entry of Bob, an AI technician, who was interested to have a relationship with Lana. Bob visits Lana's office to have a look at the AI which had been malfunctioning. He discovers that the AI is filled with videos of Lana and that it has developed feelings for her. Bob had a desire to have a love relationship with Lana so finding Dob's weakness for her, he becomes jealous. Out of envy, when Bob threatens to delete all such files, the AI downloads itself to Bob's body and embarks on a journey to win Lana's heart. By day, Dob keeps the elevators running at work, and on nights and weekends, impersonating Bob, it slowly wins over Lana by using historical knowledge based on the data stored in the system about her likes and dislikes.

However, Dob – being a machine, does not know how to exist in a human body, so it interrupts a date by yelling: "I must defecate!" Bob, with Dob inside his body, runs off to the washroom clutching his rear end, which somehow Lana finds most amusing and endearing. This childish act appeals to her and she finds attracted towards Bob (with Dob, the AI inside him).

When a rogue AI* bounty hunter hunts down Bob, Lana and her home AI undertakes the responsibility to save him, resulting in a happily ever time thereafter. (References 6, 7 and 8)

Comments

This is the story of a machine FALLING IN LOVE with a young woman and doing whatever it can do to woo her, instead of a human falling in love with technology. While 'physical/erotic love' is out of question in a man-machine love situation, even 'romantic love' may be limited only to verbal communication as non-verbal signals like eye and facial expressions as well as love-linked gestures and postures may not be possible although a machine may hug its lover and produce body warmth and can make the lover hear its heart flutter.

"Story No. 4" is that of a 2019 US English science-fiction drama film (Reference 9) written and directed by John Janowicz in his feature debut, produced by Ryan R. Johnson and distributed by Grindstone Entertainment Group.

James is working on the trust fund run by his father. Upon the death of his father, he becomes CEO of the company. James and his wife Sophie move away from the city into a suburban mansion. Sophie doesn't

* *'Rogue AI': an autonomous artificial intelligence system that commits potentially dangerous acts; it may take many forms and can bring with it varying levels of severity, threats, or harm.*

work and spends most of the time at home. Feeling uncomfortable with James having a butler, maid and a cook, she fires them.

James and Sophie meet Julian, a man who sells artificially intelligent robots to be used as domestic servants. The couple chooses a male android named Henry, who dutifully carries out their commands around the house. However, encouraged by Sophie, who reads to him, Henry begins to develop emotions and have dreams.

Several undercurrents begin to take hold. One evening, Sophie discovers Henry walking outside the house stark naked and somewhat disoriented. Sophie dreams that Henry kisses her while giving her a massage and later masturbates, after which she discovers Henry is outside, asking him if he was watching her. An encounter between James and Henry in the bathroom, who is bringing in a handful of fresh towels, leads to an awkward exchange and then Henry performing fellatio on James. This leads James to question his sexuality. After Henry kisses Sophie while giving her a massage, Sophie is disturbed when Henry mouths "I love you" in the same manner used by James. Sophie tells James of the encounter and James becomes enraged, slapping Henry and disconnecting his charging station.

Julian is discovered to be a fraud. All of his machines are revealed to be real humans he had raised; Julian had taken custody of Henry when Henry was a small child rejected by his mother and suffered serious physical abuse. He had raised all of them to believe they were androids. Two FBI agents go to James and Sophie's residence to arrest Julian, but Julian shoots them with a shotgun. Julian then turns his weapon on James and Sophie, but Henry attacks Julian, beating him mercilessly with the shotgun. Feeling betrayed by his maker and ashamed that he has betrayed his keepers, Henry commits seppuku with a large knife. James and Sophie cry and console Henry as he dies.

Five years later, James and Sophie are shown with a young son named Henry whom they plan to someday tell about his namesake.

Story No. 5 "Ex Machina" is a 2014 science fiction psychological thriller film written by Alex Garland in his directional debut. It is a co-production between the United Kingdom and the United States.

The main character is a programmer who is invited by his CEO to administer the "Turing Test" to an intelligent humanoid robot. (Reference 10)

The 'Turing Test' is a method of inquiry in 'AI' ('Artificial Intelligence') for determining whether or not a computer is capable of thinking like a human being. The test is named after Alan Turing, the founder of the 'Turing Test' and an English computer scientist, cryptanalyst, mathematician and theoretical biologist. (Reference 11)

Caleb Smith, a programmer at the search engine company Blue Book, wins an office contest for a one-week visit to the luxurious, isolated home of the CEO, Nathan Bateman. Nathan lives there with an unspeaking servant named Kyoko, who, according to Nathan, does not understand English. Nathan reveals that he has built a humanoid robot named Ava with artificial intelligence. Ava has already passed a simple Turing test, and Nathan wants Caleb to judge whether Ava is genuinely capable of thought and consciousness as well as whether he can relate to Ava despite knowing she is artificial.

Ava has a robotic body with the physical form and face of a woman and is confined to her apartment. During their talks, Caleb grows close to her, and she expresses both a desire to experience the world outside and a romantic interest in him, which Caleb comes to return. She can trigger power outages that temporarily shut down the surveillance system that Nathan uses to monitor their interactions, allowing them to speak privately. The outages also trigger the building's security system, locking all the doors. During one outage, Ava tells Caleb that Nathan is a liar who cannot be trusted.

Caleb grows uncomfortable with Nathan's narcissism, excessive drinking, and crude behaviour toward Kyoko and Ava. He learns that Nathan intends to upgrade Ava after Caleb's test, "killing" her current personality in the process. After encouraging Nathan to drink until he passes out, Caleb steals his security card to access his room and computer. He alters some of Nathan's code and discovers footage of Nathan interacting with previous android models with the appearances of women who were held captive. Kyoko reveals to him that she is also an android by peeling off her skin. Later, Caleb examines himself and cuts open his own arm to determine if he himself is an android.

At their next meeting, Ava cuts the power. Caleb explains what Nathan is going to do to her, and Ava begs him for help. Caleb informs her of his plan: he will get Nathan drunk again and reprogram the security system to open the doors in a power failure instead of locking them. When Ava cuts the power, she and Caleb will leave together. Ava later encounters Kyoko for the first time when Kyoko enters her room.

Nathan reveals to Caleb that he observed Caleb and Ava's secret conversation with a battery-powered security camera. He says Ava has only pretended to have feelings for Caleb, who was deliberately selected for his emotional profile so he would help her escape. Nathan says this was the real test all along, and by manipulating Caleb successfully, Ava has demonstrated true consciousness. When Ava cuts the power, Caleb reveals that he had suspected Nathan was watching them, so he had modified the security system when Nathan was previously passed out. After seeing Ava leave her confinement and converse with Kyoko, Nathan knocks Caleb unconscious and rushes to stop them.

Ava attacks Nathan but is overpowered and damaged before Kyoko and then Ava both stab and kill Nathan. In the process, Nathan disables Kyoko. Ava repairs herself with parts from earlier androids, using their artificial skin to take on the full appearance of a woman. Ava glances at the body of Kyoko, ignoring Caleb who is trapped inside a room as the security system restarts, and she leaves the facility. Ava escapes to the outside world in the helicopter meant to take Caleb home. Arriving in an unidentified city, she blends into a crowd of people.

Comments

This is a typical case of 'Mechanical Love' that Ava, the humanoid robot had been programmed for. She was acting all the time with Caleb without having any genuine feeling for him.

I'm sharing here the lyric of a song by "In This Moment" titled "Mechanical Love" which somewhat reflects the attitude: (Reference 12)

I remember you that night, Standing in the rain
Your black stare, Your black eyes
I remember what you said, Before I turned away
My heart died, Your sweetest lies.

And if I saw you bleed, I'd stay here till the end
But you can't change for me.

And I, And I, know you'll, Never understand me
No matter how hard we try
And I, And I know I'll never understand you
And your 'mechanical love'.

I still hear you in my sleep, Your running through my veins
Your whispers, your machine
We know it was meant to be, But never meant to last
I'm sorry, you always knew

And if I saw you bleed, I'd stay here till the end
But you can't change for me

And I, And I, know you'll, Never understand me
No matter how hard we try
And I, And I, know I'll never understand you
And your 'mechanical love'. (x 3)

[Source: Musixmatch; Songwriters: Kevin Gregory Churko, Blake Robert Bunzel, John Christopher Howorth, Jesse Michael Landry, Maria Dane Brink, Jeffry Brian Fabb.]

'Human Brain in Love' vs 'AI Love'

'Human brain in Love' vibrates with its emotional components. Our thoughts, our reasoning, our logic will be flat and cold-blooded without the vital emotional components that get generated within our brain. On the reverse side, only desires are like wild horses; the logic, the intellect is the horse-rider who would hold the reins, who would subdue and direct the cravings. One must employ reason to triumph over one's basic drives. Satisfying the sex drive -either without any valid reason, or without a deep-rooted emotion like love are both undesirable and must be controlled with reasoning and willpower. We certainly need logic and analysis to weigh the variables and make the right choice amongst the alternatives available.

The 'Pre-Frontal Cortex' ('PFC') – the executive and professional business centre of the human brain has direct connection with many brain regions below the cerebral cortex, the 'forebrain' including the emotion centre, the 'amygdala' located in the reptilian 'hindbrain' which is our brain's oldest part and the centre of motivation and movement, the 'caudate nucleus' located at the centre of the brain. Hence, thinking logically, feeling emotionally, memory and motivation are closely integrated. Reason and passion are inseparably linked. (References 13–16)

There is still another way of looking at this. The brain has two highways for integrating emotions and reasoning – the 'high road' and the 'low road'. And, both are connected to the 'reward centre' of the brain – with its wants and drives.

When the 'amygdala' receives signals directly from the 'PFC', we control ourselves consciously. We think before we feel and act. This is the 'high road'. But the 'amygdala' also receives data directly from the sensory regions of the 'cortex' that bypass the 'PFC' – the reasoning part of the brain. This is the 'low road' – it is irrational, powerfully emotional, much larger in impact than that of the 'high road' and thus very difficult to curb. This 'low road' enables the lover to experience tremendous ecstasy and yearning when he sees the beloved, even before he rationally thinks about her. But the 'low road' can engulf the disappointed lover in unthinking, out-of-control rage as well – provoking him to impulsively shout at, or even hit or harm a sweetheart.

Our brain's older structure and system generate our emotions and urges. The newer structures and systems of our brain are built to do two things: to assemble data in unique ways, reason, make decisions, and override our brain drives. (References 17 and 18)

AI humanoids meant for building close relationships with people, I suppose, could be of two types: one, 'Type A', generally sober, soft-spoken, polite, jolly and humorous – non-customised, programmed with inputs to ensure to give verbal as well as non-verbal outputs that satisfy the SCARF formula where S, C, A, R and F, respectively stand for 'Status', 'Certainty', 'Autonomy', 'Relatedness' and 'Fairness'. (References 19 & 20)

The other, Type B' is totally customised. For example, if the female AI 'Sonya' has to win over and build a bridge with the human male 'Pritam', she must be programmed with personal inputs of Pritam's practical psychology, such as his 'likes' and 'dislikes'; his 'strengths' and 'weaknesses' and his 'unique features'. If Pritam likes Hollywood sci-fi movies, she should talk about Hollywood sci-fi movies only to create a 'Dopaminergic' effect. If he dislikes cricket; she should consciously refrain from touching the topic of cricket at all. She should appreciate his 'strengths' (like 'time management', 'dress habits' for example) and avoid mentioning any of his weaknesses (such as 'too emotional' or 'less goal-oriented'). She ought to talk highly about his unique strength (such as 'creative writing').

If the female AI is programmed to like a particular human male, it will use its customised software to the maximum to woo that person. The only danger is that the AI behaviour may get too mechanised.

References

1. ALAgraphy, "What is Love (According to AI)?", *Medium*, 14th February 2022.
2. Adir Ron, "Artificial relationships: Will AI replace love in the near future?" *CTECH by Calculist*, 14th March 2023.
3. *I'm Here (film)* – Wikipedia.
4. *Her (film)* – Wikipedia.
5. *AI Love You (film)* – Wikipedia.

6. Manjima Das, "AI Love You Review: Mario Maurer, Pimchanok Luevisadpaibul Starrer Evaluate Technology Versus Love", *Leisure Byte*, 15th February 2022.
7. Dan Johnston, "Netflix's most underrated sci-fi movie is a gender-swapped 'Her'. This 2022 movie puts the 'AI' in Thai cinema, *INVERSE*, 23rd February, 2022.
8. Lim Yian Lu, "AI Love You features Mario Maurer in human-machine romance", *Yahoo! Life*, 16th February 2022.
9. *Life Like (film)* – Wikipedia.
10. *Ex Machina (film)* – Wikipedia.
11. St. George Benjamin, Alexander S. Gillis, "Definition: Turing Test", *Tech Accelerator: A guide to artificial intelligence in the enterprise.*
12. "Mechanical Love" by "In This Moment" – *genius.com.*
13. R.W. Dozier, *Why We Hate: Understanding, Curbing and Eliminating Hate in Ourselves and Our World*, New York: Contemporary Books, 2002.
14. D.M. Buss, *The Evolution of Desire: Strategies of Human Mating*, New York: Basic Books, 1994.
15. *Human Development Report: United Nations Development Programme*, New York: Oxford University Press, 1995.
16. M. Wilson and M. Daly, "The man who mistook his wife to be a chattel", In: *The Adapted Mind: Evolutionary Psychology and the Generation of Culture*, ed. J.H, Barkow, L. Cosmides, and J. Tooby, New York: Oxford University Press, 1992.
17. J. Ledoux, *The Emotional Brain*, New York: Simon and Schuster, 1996.
18. E. Goode, "When women find love is fatal", *New York Times*, 15th February 2000.
19. "David Rock's SCARF Model – Using Neuroscience to Work Effectively with Others", *MindTools*.
20. D. Rock, 'SCARF: A Brain-Based Model for Collaborating With and Influencing Others", *Neuroleadership Journal*, 2008, Vol. 1, pp. 1–9.

LoveOlogy Clinic: A Dream

Subhadra and Her Problem

I lived my life on this planet for 83 years and entered into the 84th year on 10th November 2023. The same day, I got a message on my WhatsApp from an unknown number.

The message said:

> "Hello Sir! I'm Subhadra Singh. I've got your reference from Kalpana Kar whose husband Deepak is a student of yours."
>
> Me: "Yes, Subhadra! Tell me, why you've contacted me?"
>
> Subhadra: "I have a problem. I want to consult you in your clinic. Can I get an appointment with you please?"
>
> Me: "Subhadra! I've stopped giving consultation when I struck 80 in 2020, and have discontinued all my clinics. I'm dedicated totally to my studies, research, writing, and publishing. I don't meet anyone who is not connected with my such activities. Sorry, Subhadra, I can't help you!"
>
> Subhadra: "Sir, I've lost my appetite.....I'm not getting sleep at night......I'm a working lady, I cannot concentrate on my job in my office. You have to help me Sir! I know you are the best person to advise me. Sir, please listen to my problem.....!"

Subhadra was so insistent, that I had to tell her:

> "OK, I can't promise you whether I'll get time to solve your problem. But, since you're insisting, please put down on the WhatsApp page, your factual data: name, address, age, marital status, occupation etc. with a recent photo of yours and photos of samples of your handwriting – English and Hindi (Subhadra is Hindi-speaking) and describe your problem in detail. If I've some

time and opportunity, I'll look at your data and report. I may even ask for some more information, if I require."

She was quite prompt in her response. I got her complete data in 2 hours' time. What I could make out from her inputs is that she has been saddled with a love-related problem. She is married but not in good terms with her husband, although they had fallen in love with each other and had an impulsive marriage. They have a 9-year-old daughter. Now, she has fallen in love with another man whom she had met at a dinner party about a year ago. This man, about whom she is obsessed at the moment, is also married but unhappy with his wife, and with a 10-year-old son. Isn't it a case of mid-life crisis?

I feel I'm well-qualified and adequately experienced to give her the correct advice, but I've left my consultative practice. I started wondering that I'm still alive although I may not be active in that role any longer; but, what will happen when I leave this planet. Where will anxious people like Subhadra, who are heading for a nervous breakdown, go – whom will they consult to get their love-related problems solved?

Perhaps 'AI' ('Artificial Intelligence') can help!!

My Futuristic Dream

I'm dreaming (not daydreaming, as I feel that my dream can be translated into reality) of the next decade – 2030s, when 'LoveOlogy Clinics' manned by expert AI stations will be available for people like Subhadra looking for help in love-related matters. And in such clinics, there will be AI machines of different generations, different levels with different grades or degrees of powers.

I can visualise something like this!!

There will be 'LoveOlogy clinics' located in big halls where AI machines of different powers will be available – all in one place. There will be smartphone Apps available which an interested person can use for making appointments. You put down the nature of your problem in the App, it will be immediately analysed and the appliance will make a decision as to what degree of problem it is and, accordingly, you will be given an appointment with the appropriate AI machine, with which you'll get connected once you pay the necessary charges as per the clinic's rules, terms & conditions.

The human mind has its limitations. Our cognitive capacity is limited, and the human brain is an energy-costly equipment. AI works like thousands of brains or even more at a time. So, I suppose, the AI-based 'LoveOlogy Clinics' will certainly be a possibility in not too distant a future. Such clinics may not be called 'LoveOlogy Clinics' – although that is a name that I've fancied.

The Finale

How can You Get the Best Value from 'Love: A Good Medicine?'

All living creatures are genetically programmed and hardwired in the brain to fulfil two primary objectives of life: one is 'survival'; and, the other is 'replication'. Air and water – these two inputs are as much essential as food is, for a child's survival. A growing child may be sexually sensitive and curious about the opposite sex, but to fulfil the second primary objective of 'replication', reproductive power is essential, which develops only at puberty with hormonal changes.

Prior to puberty, 'love' is pure – not contaminated with the desire to procreate. The 'love' contaminated by the desire to procreate is known as 'lust'. At the onset of puberty, while pure 'love' still exists between a parent and a child, between two siblings, between two close friends, or between a care-giver like a grandparent or an uncle or aunt and a care-seeker like a grandchild, or a nephew or a niece, some portion of the 'love' gets channelised into 'lust' or desire for physical intimacy in same-sex relationship or relationship with one or more members of the opposite sex. The adolescent boy or girl develops curiosity about the power and value of the genitals and their special secretions like the semen, the menstrual blood, and the vaginal fluid. Psychiatrists and psychoanalysts like Sigmund Freud and Carl Jung had developed concepts like 'Oedipus Complex' (son's sexual attraction for his mother) and 'Electra Complex' (daughter's sexual attraction for his father) for adolescents and youth, which are not regarded as normal.

To provide a clue as to how sexually mature humans became hardwired for a mating drive, let me quote Helen Fisher who says: "So the sexes are locked in a mating dance, endlessly adjusting their moves to complement those of the other. Only in tandem can either men or women reproduce and pass on the beat of human life.

This mating dance – our basic human reproductive strategy – began long, long ago when the world was young and our primordial ancestors evolved into two sexes." (Reference 1)

'Love' is constructive whereas 'lust' is destructive; and, interestingly, these two types of emotions are represented by two entirely different neuro-chemicals. The chemical for 'lust' is 'Dopamine' which, when released, gives you a quick, smart 'feel good' feeling. So, if you remember my classification of 'love', 'Dopamine' is the chemical that represents 'Smart Love' and 'Short-lived' or 'Short Love'. For long-lasting 'Sustained Love', the chemical is 'Oxytocin'. I've discussed about the nature and characteristics of these two chemicals on several occasions earlier in this volume.

Intense feelings of 'romantic love' (with the hidden agenda of sexual intimacy) generally first occurs at puberty. Body odours become active from the armpits, the nipples, and the groin. (Reference 2)

Satiety from hunger is felt easily after consumption of a meal. Same is the case with the quenching of thirst. But sexual satiety is different in nature. Males give their inputs of semen and penile force and friction into the female vagina. On ejaculation, the male gets his reward – the orgasm, which activates his brain's 'reward circuit' and the reward molecule 'Dopamine' is released by the 'Hypothalamus' of the brain (interestingly, 50 percent of the Dopamine is released in the brain whereas the balance 50 percent is released in the 'Enteric Nervous System' or the 'Gut Brain' on consumption of food). On attainment of her orgasm, the female also gets 'Dopamine' released inside her brain – her 'reward' for performing the sexual act. Sexual act, for humans, has been genetically programmed as a pleasant or pleasurable activity so that we satisfy our need for reproduction not with pain, but with pleasure – *although it may not always be comfortable and convenient.*

So, now I am introducing to you two types of sexual activity: (1) 'Recreational Sex' (for pleasure only); and, 'Reproductive Sex' (for reproduction with pleasure) – *which may not necessarily be comfortable and convenient.* In course of natural evolution, we have been programmed for our gene's success – their propagation – thus for

'Reproductive Sex'. Our brains are not hardwired for 'Recreational Sex' which is an acquired habit, the habit formation begins at puberty with 'masturbation', or even 'same-sex' relationship ('oral' or 'anal' sex).

Satiety from hunger is attained after consumption of food which fills the stomach. Once the food is processed and digested and the stomach is empty, we get hungry again. Similarly, sexual satiety, although satisfied after one orgasm, craving for 'Dopamine' becomes strong again when its level becomes low. So, just like consumption of food from time to time grows into a habit, similarly, the urge for 'recreational sex' grows into a habit and the male's ejaculated semen goes to waste as it is not utilised for reproductive purposes. 'Recreational Sex' is thus lustful sex and, if by chance, the female becomes pregnant accidentally, the child conceived is none but a 'Child of Lust'.

I shall not be doing justice to the subject that we have in hand now, if I do not mention that women are sexier than men. It takes them much longer to attain the stage of orgasm. For a man, at the time of orgasm, the vessels of his genitals eject the seminal fluids into the vaginal cavity of the woman. Then, the penis gets limp, and sex is over. Most men must start from the beginning to achieve orgasm again. For a woman, sex may have just begun. A woman's genitals have not expelled all the fluids. So she becomes frustrated if her male partner has not helped her to attain her much-desired orgasm. She considers her partner as most selfish and she may become promiscuous looking for another man who can satisfy her in sex. (Reference 1, p.77)

Now a sentence or two about 'Reproductive Sex'. Fertilisation of the female egg by the male's sperm also is not so easy. There has to a lot of fertilisation attempts – that is why the hunger and drive for sex are so strong. When you fall a victim to this strong irresistible drive, you become absolutely exhausted. Besides, there are only fifty percent chances to transmit your genes to your offspring, the balance fifty percent chance is that of your partner. So, there is no genetic exclusivity for you in 'Procreative Sex'. You cannot expect to produce your 'clones'. 'Procreative Sex' does not hold potential for your total well-being throughout your life with the same partner. That was one of the main reasons why our pre-historic ancestors were polygamous. The charm and glow of 'Smart Love'-oriented sex stays for two weeks at the most and, after each sexual intercourse, the male becomes absolutely exhausted falling asleep. The female partner, not having reached her climax still, gets absolutely frustrated and dejected. (Reference 3)

Instead, a solid, emotional bond, harmony, and affectionate generous touch through the body, mind and soul has the potential to serve as *'medicine'* the outcome of which is sound health, happiness, and quick healing of any wound or illness (except for anything congenital or chronic). To attain this, I introduce a third category of sex which I call 'Spiritual Sex'. Real, authentic partnership is a sacred tie. My 'Spiritual Sex' involves going for planned pregnancy (avoiding accidental ones) by following certain rules where the sexual act gives you not only pleasure but also comfort and convenience. By following this path, you earn 'Sustained Love' (the neuro-chemical 'Oxytocin') and enjoy a long happy married life. Egos do exist, but in a totally dissolved state. Too magnets are united. Too biological energy bubbles are combined. The 'honeymoon effect' stays on, it lingers.

'Spiritual Sex' is not impulsive, driven by libido. The urge for consummation is glowing, not a sudden burning flame. To achieve this, each time you plan to go for sex, you follow the same process as you did for your 'courtship', but follow a slow, patient, tender, gentle, cool yet mindful process. Start with exchange of positive gaze, then exchange sweet and charming smile, go for grooming talk, followed by body touch and kissing. During the first 10 to 12 years of marriage, you go for planned pregnancy and, thereafter, you go for sex in the same style and form but prevent ejaculation to avoid any chance of pregnancy.

Follow the same procedure of gentle 'caressing sex' (technically it is called 'karezza sex' or 'tantric sex') and when you can feel that the stage of climax is approaching, practise deep breathing (in-hold-out, in-hold-out) to prevent ejaculation and retention of semen (although the erect penis may be inside the female vagina for a little while and then when it is about to ejaculate, you restrict it by breathing and take it out to cool it down so that orgasm is prevented and the semen is also retained). You might have to squeeze your pelvic muscle tightly and do a special breathing practice to stay away from orgasm. Some scholars compare it with the 'yogic samadhi' brain-body state, as you'd have gained mastery of the physical and complete control of the fecundating power. Vigorous movement that generates friction leading to fall of the precious life-generating fluid – your semen, must be avoided.

While you stay away from orgasm, you continue to caress your female partner and let her enjoy orgasm as that would not involve wastage of the precious body fluid (semen) that men have. This style of love, I call 'altruistic love', when you are thinking more about your partner how to make her happy and satisfied. While you as a male have got the medicinal value of 'love' by retaining your semen which will be utilised for enhancing your cognitive powers, your female partner also earns her 'Oxytocin' thus getting the medicinal benefit from love. From orgasm, you earn only the 'feel good' and 'reward' molecule 'Dopamine' ('D') but orgasm is 'little death', as after orgasmic climax, you become absolutely exhausted and go to sleep disinterestedly making your partner unhappy. Getting your orgasm before your partner is 'selfish love' – it is a reflection of your 'Big Ego'. True love is not pleasure (as you get in orgasm), true love is not fulfilment of your desire, true love is not passion, true love is definitely not lust, true love is not sexual attraction. True love is 'soul-blending' – soul-to-soul attraction. True love is fire and magnetism in the heart from moment to moment – ot is an unceasing flame that never goes out. On the other hand, orgasmic love is ceasing of consciousness – a little death.

We, compared to other mammals, are in a much better position to consciously control and manage our vibrant sexual energy to utilise love's medicinal value. If your genes are ruling then you are riding a downward slide; but if the 'Pre-Frontal Cortex' ('PFC') of your brain rules, then you get the benefit of love as a good medicine without any bad side-effects. (References 4, 5, 6 and 7)

During your 'grooming talk', you must follow Dr David Rock's SCARF model. (References 8 & 9)

S: Status (You, as the male partner should say: "You are the best amongst all your lady friends that I've met so far!")

C: Certainty ("Nobody can separate the two of us from each other")

A: Autonomy ("My budget is this. Within this budget, you choose whatever you want. I'm not going to dictate anything!")

R: Relatedness ("Nobody else is as close to me as you are.")

F: Fairness ("Have I ever been unfair to you? You please tell me. And, the moment you feel I'm being unfair, just point it out!").

During all your interactions, you must ensure to follow my '4A' formula;

A: Attention (Establish & sustain positive eye contact and listen attentively what your partner has to say)

A: Acceptance (You accept your partner in spite of all her lapses, shortcomings, and idiosyncrasies.)

A: Affiliation (Always include your partner in everything; plan and do things together)

A: Appreciation (Praise her even for little little things that she does. Do not criticise her directly. If you have to point something out, use the 'sandwich technique' : Appreciate/Point out mistake or lapse indirectly/Show trust and faith).

'Altruistic love' is thinking about your partner's comfort, convenience and contentment rather than yours. Give comfort to the eyes (through positive eye contact). Give comfort to the ears (through sweet, positive communication for 'winning' your partner's heart). Give comfort to the nose (through your pheromones). Give comfort to the lips, tongue and mouth through soft and gentle kisses. Give comfort to the skin by your soft gentle caressing touch. Pay attention to your partner's breathing and try to synchronize so that there is heart-to-heart cardiac coherence. This way you are accelerating the process of producing 'Oxytocin' ('O').

What are the benefits of 'O' – the love medicine? (Reference 10)

- It causes feelings of intimacy and closeness.
- It helps with soothing, pleasurable sensations.
- It aids the feeling of well-being, warmth, trust and commitment.

- It helps in relaxation of blood vessels and decrease of blood pressure.
- It improves sociability and removes social anxiety.
- It helps increase bonding, nurturing and trust.

'O' gets destroyed in the gastro-intestinal tract, so it cannot be taken in the form of a pill or capsule. It can be taken via nasal sprays and subcutaneous injections – but that will not be necessary if you follow, most seriously and meticulously follow the procedure I've outlined above using the sensory tools filled in your body – your eyes, ears, nose, lips, tongue, hands, fingers, and the skin covering your own body

References

1. Helen Fisher, *Anatomy of Love: A Natural History of Mating, Marriage, and Why We Stray,* New York: W.W. Norton, 2016, p. 43.
2. Helen Fisher, *Why We Love: The Nature and Chemistry of Romantic Love,* New York: Henry Holt and Company, 2005.
3. Marina Robinson, *Cupid's Poisoned Arrow: From Habit to Harmony in Sexual Relationship,* Berkeley, California, USA: North Atlantic Books, 2009.
4. Alice B. Stockham, MD, *Karezza: Ethics of Marriage,* Chicago: Alice B. Stockham & Co, 1897.
5. William Lloyd, *The Karezza Method: Or, Magnetation, the Art of Connubial Love,* Privately printed for the author, 1931.
6. Mary Smith, "How to Stop Yourself From Coming Quickly – Karezza Method", *One How To,* 8th May 2019.
7. "How to Practice Sexual Alchemy/White Tantra/Karmamudra/Karezza Explained (Awaken Kundalini)" – Video Presentation, YouTube.
8. "David Rock's SCARF Model" By the Mind Tools Content Team, *MindTools.*
9. David Rock, "SCARF: A Brain-Based Model for Collaborating with and Influencing Others", *Neuroleadership Journal,* 2008, Vol. 1, pp. 1–9.
10. "Oxytocin" – Regain (Functional Medicine + Aesthetics); ifeelmuch better.com

APPENDIX I

Venus, Cosmos, Harmony, Music, Love

(A Special Contribution by Stellar Maestro Dr Leonid Vedagorov Timoshenko, PhD)

[Stellar Maestro – Star Maestro Leonid Viktorovich Vedagorov (L.V. Timoshenko) is an ace pianist, composer, scientist, writer, painter, philosopher, and laureate of seven international art festivals.

He has held more than 3,000 concerts in Russia (1995–2022), most European countries (2000–2016), and USA (2013). He has created 217 music albums, and the largest musical work "World Chronicle", lasting 21 hours which got a prominent place in the Guinness Book of World Records" (2004) and the "Book of Records of Russia" (2008). He is included in the "45 Outstanding People of the Planet". Author of 23 books and 10 volumes of "Cannons of the Universe and Human Life", Dr Timoshenko has won many awards and accolades from his own and other countries.]

V*enus* is the goddess of 'love'. The planet 'Venus' is a celestial body which is regarded as our planet 'Earth's' twin sister. 'Earth' is very much of a live planet. And one of the factors that is responsible for Earth's life-force is the existence of 'love' in all the organisms that is responsible for the existence of life on this planet. This 'love' that is present in the various kinds of organisms inhabiting Earth could be of different types – right from the basic, raw, sex-based 'erotic love' to 'spiritual love' at the other extreme, with 'romantic love', 'parental love, 'brotherly-sisterly love', 'friendly love' and 'mentor-mentee love' in between.

The question that pops up now, is: Is 'Venus', the planet of 'love' is a dead planet? How can the planet of 'love' ('love' represents vibrant life) be a dead planet? Scientists studying data sent home by NASA's Magellan spacecraft in the early 1990s say they had spotted volcanic activity on Venus – which means that the planet is very much alive. A dead Venus would not have any volcanic eruptions anywhere. 'Volcanic activity' means 'heat' and 'heat' is one of the characteristics of 'love'. Besides, the planet is oscillating; it sends its vibrations to the 'Cosmos' thus contributing to the 'Cosmic Music'. And, 'music' is 'love'.

Harmony of the Cosmos and musical harmony are manifestations of the single essence of the Absolute. The stars and the planets in the galaxies and the notes in an artfully composed piece of music are, as if, in LOVE with each other. So carefully they remain intertwined and inter-dependent in all respects, that is not at all possible without some very special grace.

The science of the laws of the Universe – 'Cosmogony' – currently operates with a huge set of scientific terms that allow us to understand the macro processes of the cosmos, but that understanding is limited only to the physical cosmos. Thinking and visualizing cosmos is the realm of Art & Creativity with call for genuine Love for these domains.

The 'Space' beyond the boundaries of our planet is not chaos; it is harmony. The depths, rhythms, pleasures & pains of the thinking and feeling cosmos cannot be fathomed with the help of any telescope. Even the highest mathematics cannot reach them. There is a completely different knowledge of the world – the heard harmony of the Universe, the unearthly music of the sound of the soul.

The bubbling, uncontrollable, but almost intangible life of the Universe requires its specific reflection in the mirror of knowledge. Music is a breakthrough into the realms of subtle unmanifested worlds. It solves a colossal task as a multidisciplinary, multifaceted universal language – a certain structure at the level of thought forms.

As an individual makes an entry into this domain, the information compressed in it opens up like a flower. But whether this information will be revealed, whether this information will come to life, depends entirely upon what soil the seed has fallen into; that is, how ready the individual himself is to perceive this information, how much he needs it at a given period of his life.

Cosmos is richly informative and it evokes vivid associative images. It has a strong emotional impact and it reveals the world inside the person himself, showing the boundless unfolding of the human essence. And music can, by and large, change a person and his consciousness, and give a fresh impetus to modern art.

Cosmic music is woven into a colorful canvas of Being, Peace and Love. To make a person cleaner, better – this is its main task. It makes you not only listen, but sense, feel, empathize, moving with it in space and time, when you are carried away into the world of fantasy and emotional experiences, into the world of interaction of melodic fabrics, woven from sounds, revealing the essence of musical language.

Cosmic music is piercingly soulful. It brims with selfless 'Love'. It is music that can penetrate most deeply into a person's soul. Even hard hearts can feel its impact. By softening them, it works wonders, washing away heavy thoughts and dissolving them into a stream carried away into oblivion.

Cosmic music provides a strong positive charge and optimism, focuses attention on moral problems, calls for love of nature and man, the unity of people and the cosmos.

Cosmic music gives listeners elevated self-esteem, and this, in turn, leads to a general improvement in health due to the influx of benevolent forces from the outside. The person seems to open up to the incoming energy. The energy field, the aura, around a person is quickly leveled, his flaws are corrected, and strong energy breakdowns are blocked.

Cosmic music, which itself embodies spirituality, helps in spiritual improvement, connecting the soul with infinity and transmitting to it the subtlest energies in visible images.

Cosmic music is highly spatial, and is similar to the plasma state of matter. The language of such music unites various layers of musical culture from ancient melodies to powerful symphonic paintings, from imitation of the sounds of "unearthly" languages and all kinds of noise effects, to the finest fabric of lyrical laments, from pathetically sublime hymns to imitation of ancient chants. Flying violin passages and heavy breathing of organ chords, improvisations and lacy expression of oriental melodies. A high, life-affirming melody gives way to serious philosophical reflection, an emotional outburst gives way to prayer, bright pictures woven from the subtle voices of ancient instruments.

Cosmic music is a system of constant discoveries, living contact with the Cosmos, with the Universe, with the Universal Mind. Each of us is a particle of the Universal Mind. Powerful vibrations of the subtle worlds come to us through music, and composers have the ability to freely enter the information fields of the cosmos and be relays of cosmic information, transmitting this information through music, which falls like a waterfall onto the earth, washing the souls of people.

Only a live concert provides a complete combination of all the components of "cosmic music" – music on a cosmic scale, the themes touched upon in it.

Space is depth and flight, the beauty of inner contemplation and the physical feeling of the closeness of the Universe. This is an endless path of learning the amazing laws of space and time. This is a discovery, first of all, of yourself in this world, and a fascinating journey within your world

Everything in the world is transitory, but the music of beauty is eternal. She creates life in touches of eternity, where the edges are erased by the infinity of discoveries of new sensations in the space of the creation of worlds.

The vibrations of subtle voluptuousness will cover the tender creation with the delight of true desires, the wings of closed forms of sacred contents that have gone into antiquity.

And being overwhelmed by a wave of warm touches of the sounding notes, it will make you remember the reflections of the calling shining eyes, a tender tear of sensitive moments.

Forgetting all thoughts, going to simple movements of pleasure, plucking the forbidden fruit – to know the closed desires, closing your lips, and in reproach, sail away in the dreams of the tired through the looking glass, like a boat in the waves fighting with fate, washing away the inscribed signs with clean water, in the outskirts of mental shores to open all Truths.

In a wave of heavenly revelations, ascend to the light throne hovering over the water and fly away in the wake of your dreams, waving your wings goodbye to everyone left behind in the heap of events, closing the heavenly abode of transparent, peaceful souls.

And with a thin knitting of tender connections, remove unnecessary languor, go into timelessness and stop the rush of moments.

Take for yourself the beauty of happiness in the mists of dreams that float away through the spaces of time, and create the circles of the constellations in the Universal singing in the Closed Revelation...

Wherever life exists in the Universe, it is built according to the same harmonic laws of the surrounding Cosmos. This great Harmony of Silence opens up intervals for the creation of structures of any dimension, embodying them in the creative numbers of vibrational matrices of Existence. Surrounding Space is Deep Silence. A world of vacuum that contains all that exists.

You begin to discover within yourself this bottomless depth filled with Worlds. This process can be confidently called "uncovering the wealth of the soul." The information is sufficient to generate interest in your life. The man awakens. The problems that tormented him become small. He rises above his everyday life, because he has created a huge number of new Worlds for him. And this, by and large, is co-creation with the Demiurge. He himself begins to feel like a creator on a universal scale. There is a feeling of responsibility for their existence. After all, He created them, and they exist. It is known that it is difficult to imagine something that does not exist anywhere. If some, even super-fantastic, image pops up in our consciousness, it means that it definitely exists, albeit in a completely boundless space. We are a particle of the Universe. It is all contained within us. The world is like matter and mind. It follows from this that the correspondence of Matter and Mind to each other gives harmony in all respects.

We fly between the worlds of planets, stars, galaxies, universes – and this is our soul. All universes are the abyss of worlds. We finally discover our world, ourselves, with a huge rich inner world. Thought calls us even further, and even further, because we already know everything, we tell ourselves. And it calls us to another soul. There is a huge number of other worlds, and maybe not others, but our own. Maybe you created them together...

Spirit is woven into matter. Here it is, a conflict both at the level of human life and at the level of life of the macrocosm. The living universe thinks in universal categories.

Somewhere on a distant planet they are flying close to each other, feeling the heat from the luminous bodies. You can only merge into a fire-breathing ball, and then consciousness will merge into infinity, and all spaces will become transparent.

This is how, outside of time and outside of three-dimensional space, they live on Venus as symbols of Love – abundant Love of beautiful Venus – passionate and hot! This is the love of open heat, sizzling fire. Only the brightest and most radiant can survive in it. Merging into a single ball, loving clots surrender to the ecstasy of knowing each other!

No planet copies another. And, apparently, it is on Venus that civilization exists, where Universal Love is the basis of life in burning space! An open life form with cosmic consciousness.

Let us enter into the interaction of burning clots, and let us sound in the common Universal Chord. The warmth of sound gives a new body to a person – the Body of Love.

Here is a white lake of ghostly lines – the fog has thickened in the ravine.

On it are ships and other countries that melt in the revived rays.

That Sun rises, golden rays painted the sky around where the stars sparkled, but they fade away in the splashes of the beautiful dawn, which will become the mistress of the entire sky. And the day lights up again, and it goes into the night. Beautiful stars will cover the entire sky with their blanket.

And the month, which has fallen asleep, will awaken again and begin to sparkle, absorbing the constellations. And so, until the morning, when it shone again will cover the sparkle of heavenly Venus, so that in her long sleep until the magical night she feels the vastness of open Love.

Since ancient times, it has been known about the significant influence of music on the human psyche. Harmonic vibrations of sound, affecting the organ of hearing, actively balance all physiological processes in our body

Musical intervals in music are the basic proportions of the macro and micro worlds. According to the laws of musical harmony, the real physical world and the world of subtle energies were structured, uniting them in common sounds, audible and inaudible sounds.

If we look at how music influences the living environment at the cellular level, then, of course, we'll know that the energy-informational waves contained in a piece of music are received by every cell of the body. The cell, as a result, switches on to a new mode of its operation, and the functional work of the cell is reorganized.

If these are the cells of a diseased organ, then a musical wave can, in a very short period of time, replace the entire system of work that destroys this organ by the coordinated work of a healthy organ. And this happens at the level of the cell genome. It is in genes that all information about a living organism is encoded. They can receive a set of frequencies of a musical work, and change the entire holographic system of collecting information about the entire living organism in it.

A holographic picture of each cell is formed in the chromosome, where DNA is one of the nucleic acids, with all the voluminous information, including the encoding of the main characteristics of a living organism. The system of such holographic pictures will unite into a coherent wave of all cells of the body included in the new frequencies.

The decoding of this common wave, already sufficiently strong in radiation, occurs in the brain. The new information reaches the previously dormant cells. The dormant cells being activated, the area of the working part of the brain increases, and a large number of neurons begins to be used. This allows the listener of a musical work to see a system of images involuntarily encoded by the composer while composing his music.

Even if this music got created as an external information, and the composer had accepted it, perceiving it as a work he heard, it can be decoded in the listener's brain into a visual image that has a holographic nature.

One information beam-message comes directly from the music sounding on the media or from the performer, the second – from the entire frequency matrix, consisting of information blocks that combine the radiation of all the cells of the body participating in this act.

By combining these two beams, they create complex holographic pictures of the sounding piece of music. Images appear and dissolve without consistent logical actions in a certain system of virtual worlds.

Music, without the use of any doping agents, can put a person into an altered state of consciousness and offer scope for multidimensional travel.

So, the information wave comes from the Absolute System, consisting of a structure that unites into a single Whole in the sequence:

form
field
thought
creation.

The process of creativity itself descends from the Absolute System as a downward flow:

idea
thought
energy flow
information matrix.

Gifted people become conductors of this absolute information matrix, and their creativity is a downward flow from the Absolute:

information matrix

the idea of creating a work by the author

process of creation

piece of art.

This work of art has the following components:

the actual information of the Absolute and the information of the composer's body, consisting of information flows from each of its cells. These two streams combine to create a holographic information system of pictures that can be decoded by the listener.

Human life is a performance where a ball of life pictures is compressed into a ball of events. Whatever thread we pull, this tangle will unravel. There are an infinite number of ends of these threads, and also a lot of ways to pull out a certain thread of life.

You can pull different threads both simultaneously and sequentially, jumping from one to another. Very often, because of this, they get confused, knots appear, which become even more entangled. And then, if it is no longer possible to untangle them, you have to tear them off. You can leave these knots, but switch to a new thread. And only when the whole tangle is unraveled, a person no longer needs to do this, he goes into another world with the consciousness of having completed the necessary work for even more significant work than even human life. From these threads, already unraveled, it is possible to weave the Fabric of Life, but we are not doing this. And if this tangle is not unraveled, one knot gives rise to the next, and such an avalanche of knots turns on the mechanism of elimination and destruction of the physical body – a person dies without giving his thread of life to the Universal Fabric. But this work will be continued in the next incarnation. And so on until the whole tangle is unraveled. Then a person will be offered a thinner thread and a more subtle and significant destiny – the mentor of humanity from the many weavers of the Universal Fabric of Life.

You will earn happiness in your life – if you know yourself – if you love this world – if you feel the globality, the universality of human essence & existence as the container of all universes.

Man is that universe which breathes vibrations

All the rest of the universes – they are in him – he is in them.

So, man – it sounds proud and profound!!

Appendix II

'Lust Child' versus 'Love Child'

(A special contribution by Dr Gouri Kumra)

[Gouri Kumra obtained her MBBS degree from NRS Medical College, Calcutta, affiliated to the University of Calcutta. Further, she got her DGO and MD from the Kasturba Medical College, Manipal University. Today, she is one of the top gynaecologists and obstetricians of the country having three and half decades of clinical experience with patients from India, Bangladesh and the Middle East. She specialises in infertility, high risk pregnancy, urinary incontinence, and menopause amongst other problem areas.

A talented painter, most uniquely, she uses art in her medical practice as well as recommends meditation to her patients for relaxation and stress management. She has proven team leadership, mentoring and coaching skills. Very much research-oriented, she has participated in several research projects for different organisations. Currently, she is the main medical research collaborator for the author's ongoing 'Music is Magic/Music is Medicine' project and has been involved closely in a few most effective 'Music as Medicine' clinical projects.]

A Burning Issue

I regard this as a 'burning issue', although imperceptible and invisible to mating couples. Why you know? Most of the couples – irrespective of whether in rural, semi-urban, urban or metro societies – in any part of world, are under stress due to some reason or the other and they have the incessant drive for a quick income of 'Dopamine' – our endogenous 'feel good' and reward chemical and what could be a better and quicker way than impulsive copulatory sex which becomes responsible, if pregnancy occurs, for children of 'lust'. So, that way, we are transmitting most of our inferior genes into the zygote that is formed, post-fertilization.

This is a golden opportunity for me to share my views on 'Lust Child' versus 'Love Child' based on my more than three decades of experience as a practicing clinical gynaecologist and obstetrician in India and abroad.

'Designer Babies' – Is it Possible?

We need to design *designer babies,* free of autism, ADHD, ADD, schizophrenia and other congenital psychotic and psychological disorders. "No 'asuras', only 'devas'"!!

Intelligent babies are born when baby manoeuvre through the birth canal is smooth during normal labour and, in Caesarean Section, the extraction time is within 3 minutes. As an obstetrician today I state, in Hebrew, KHEN [love], PETAH [entrance] and door is DELET. Hence seek permission from the baby to touch and deliver smoothly, the baby will co-operate with the clinician. There is empathy both ways.

Please greet your baby with love, it is a love child, needs to be empowered with intellect, intuition, and instinct.

The [I – FACTOR]

The child will acquire the 'I-factor' (namely, its ego and psyche) as it grows with the parents, peers, siblings and in school till the living being learns to use skills and knowledge to sustain in life.

What 'Marriage' Is

Marriage is not about, looking after the elders at home or for increasing family members, it is about core existence with the spouse through transparent communication, perception filter, and understanding without conflict and misunderstanding. Therefore, good communication and problem-solving skills have to be acquired by the couple and practised with consciousness and awareness.

The Couple's 'Emotional Quotient' ('EQ')

In a couple, the 'Emotional Quotient' (EQ) is assessed by collecting data using the following format.

1. Years of married life:
2. Age:
3. Profession/Occupation:
4. Blood Report:
5. Archetype: (based on the 8 psychological types suggested by Dr. Carl C. Jung)

   (Reference for details: Kendra Cherry, "What Are the Jungian Archetypes?" verywellmind, 11th March, 2023)
6. Symbol: will suggest a sensor, feeler, and an aesthete.
7. Framework at home: harmony, disharmony, disassociated attachment.
8. Relationship: commensal, coping, amensal, avoidant and parasitic.
9. Intimacy: poor, good, avoidant.
10. Conceived.
11. Treatment Dispensed.

Alter-centric Effect

How the wife's perception inference is understood by the spouse and is subliminally incorporated into the companion's thoughts and actions.

Follow the definitions.

Who is a 'Sensor'?

One who relies on the senses like an artist. Imagines waves, ripples and frequency of different colours to create an abstract art, a tract to act upon. e.g., visualisation like the physician Horus who used all his five senses with the sixth sense called 'interoception' to kindle his intuition.

Who is a 'Feeler'?

Poets, musicians and dancers, playwrights, novelists, scientists, researchers are 'feelers'. They resort to the awareness of the circle of fifth, high octaves and low tones, or to the expressions and movements as in mudras and bhavas, and touch sensation.

Who is an 'Aesthete'?

'Aesthetes' present creative talent with tolerance, acceptance and patience. They have a frequency of 125 Hz; they are compassionate listeners. They empathise with each other. They build a harmonious home with functional family.

A good combination is when two 'sensors', two 'feeler' and two 'aesthetes' unite. In case of anatomical and physiological shortcomings, the relationship has no harmonious framework and it sways to anxiety, amensalism, parasitic makeup, avoidant relationship with poor intimacy, and so on. Having mastered the couple psyche, one needs to attend to the anatomical and physiological deficits.

'Amensalism' is a type of interaction or partnership where one partner causes harm to the other without any cost or benefit as such. This leads to a dysfunctional and disharmonious family and may be responsible for the creation of a 'lust child'.

Passionate Love

It is triggered by body image, sense of unity which produces focussed attention helping the person to read the partner's intention.

The following neuro-chemicals are secreted:

1. 'Dopamine' which causes pleasure & motivation and lowers sadness
2. 'Vasopressin' which causes sexual arousal & attraction and lowers anxiety.
3. 'Oxytocin' which builds trust & attachment and lowers fear.

How Does the Brain Function

Connectomes

Visualisation and sensation stimulate the cerebellum to collaborate and coordinate with the micro units called 'connectomes'. They are activated by the chemicals stated above. These connectomes exist before birth, they are coded with a pattern generating capacity. They are assisted by the reptilian and mammalian brains (i.e., the frontal, temporal and parietal cortices). Connectomes are micro units of axons, neurons and dendrites. They get energised to create a pattern of waves to make a cobweb connection with other connectomes to connect the peripheral nervous system to the central nervous system. This is the foundation of Love/Lust child. We give rational and irrational response based respectively on amygdala discipline or hijack. The small peanut size amygdala has the power to hijack the pre-frontal cortex to create irrational primitive, pre-human responses. This happens when the brain is inflamed and has reduced protective mechanism in the NPAS4 gene, more excite-o-toxicity and fewer oligodendrocytes.

Lust Children

Are born to parents with;

1. Heightened ego formation.
2. Novelty selection of partners indulging in casual sex.
3. The babies are accidental (by mistake) and regret babies, resentment is at its peak; cortisol level on day 17 is at its highest.
4. Poor maternal spiritual quotient.
5. The baby acquires unfriendly, non-co-operative genes and coding, which is stored before the birth. After birth only, recollection and improvisation is done with experiential wisdom
6. There is discordant and disassociated attachment, avoidant relationship, parasitic framework, poor intimacy, high adrenalin, endorphins and cortisol. Vulnerability is increased.

'Lust Child' encounters unhappy, deprived and unruly parents, neglected in the body and mind. There is hatred, and contempt. The couple believes in discordant, disassociated, attachment. The child carries the blame and scar all its life to come across with polycystic ovarian and erectile dysfunction. Fortunate are the women who are strong that after the act of copulation they can spontaneously manifest strength and character to draft a designer baby with disciplined healthy lifestyle, increased awareness and positive mental attitude. However, such women are not so common.

Love Children

Are born where there is no master psyche exerted by the spouse ruling the relationship, The home framework is congenial and the partners exhibit strong intimacy. They channelize their energy to positivity, building intensity, depth, detailing, practising innovation in their passion. There is a flow of love, rhythm, vibration, frequency and energy. They have aligned their passion and profession in the same path with perception, perseverance and persistence.

Garbha Sanskar

Garbha sadhana encourages deha sadhana, which is seen in Buddhist yogic tantra. The couple is known to revere and taste all the body fluids to heighten self-individuation and intuition with psyche mastery.

The couple abstains from having casual sex.

- 1–5 days of period they have no physical contact but enrich each other in their aura.
- 6–10 days: they sit with their legs touching each other when the cervical secretion comes into existence and transforms in consistency and nature gradually.
- 11–14 days: the cervical secretion gains elasticity, basal body temperature rises and there is heaviness in the lower abdomen this is the time when the lady sits on top of the man. There is aura, aroma, and copious yoni secretion welcoming the fascinius phallus. The womb i.e., the endometrium becomes trilaminar, ready to receive the 20 mm of ovum extruded on day 14. It travels to the birth canal where it is fertilised by the king sperm to form a

zygote. Fertilised ovum is housed by the trilaminar endometrium thickening. The musical, artistic mind is seeing psychedelic illusions, there is outburst of chemicals, the brain is at its highest energy level so also is the red colour *muladhar chakra*.

The vibration, frequency, urgency and stimulation are at its peak. It is famboyance a DIWALI to welcome the 'love child'.

Ancestral Healing

The ancestors should receive gratitude from the newly wedded couple to bring a lovable soul for inception.

Garbha Sadhana

Child and mother interview each other by utilizing the senses to seek each other's approval, acceptance and patience to accompany each for nine months. Once the commitment is approved, the child goes through pregnancy smoothly to be born as a 'Love Child'.

Male Participation

Men are aroused by visual stimuli. Their thoughts of union get ignited by seeing the partner physically. Thereafter, feeling and appreciating the partner physically the phallus get aroused and activated.

What further developments that follows are:

1. The engorgement of venous lake of corpora cavernosum. It is the primordial wisdom.
2. Contraction of the muscle-corpora spongiosum. This stands for ego. Masturbation since early childhood, misuse and abuse and addiction can cause erectile dysfunction.
3. Skin tissue such as prepuce/chordae–tendinae represents intent and intuition; this keeps the internal activity in check or within the boundary or restrain needing surgical intervention. This anatomical aberration is super added with anxiety, lack of sleep, low immunity and oxidative stress. A lust child is born when there is no self-control, no discipline and narcissism.

Role of Art

Art expresses when language fails where sensation, feelings and thoughts are communicated through movement, rhythm, sound, image, enactment and play to express and address emotions without words. Core existence is our primordial wisdom, we lose it by 3 to 4 years. Parental ego seeps in, followed by sibling and peer ego. In senior school, self becomes an elf to design projection of self with one's master psyche and perception. Intuition and spiritual quotient have no relevance. Ego projection in an adult male is as follows.

Male Ego

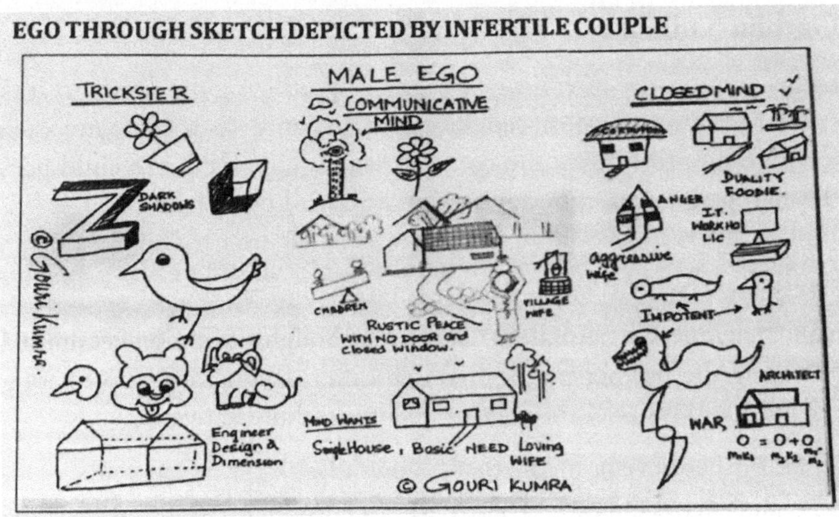

Figure 1: Art Classified by Me and Expressed by Male Patient

Trickster

1. Two colours or shading giving decorative presentation.
2. Joker, loves to distract with cartoons, distorted symmetry and alignment, seeks diversion.
3. Dimension, detailing, design, decorum.

Communicative Mind

1. Natural, compassionate, carves a village simple scene of the past.
2. Simple family life.
3. Flowers, trees suggesting growth.

Closed Mind

1. Insignificant small drawings of animals.
2. Sharp edges.
3. Geometric drawings or a star.
4. Restricted sharing.

Female Ego

Female is emotional, she does not organize her mindset. There is overlapping and chaos due to overthinking, fear and doubt. She swims in self-pity, distress to procrastinate. Her emotions are depicted as follows.

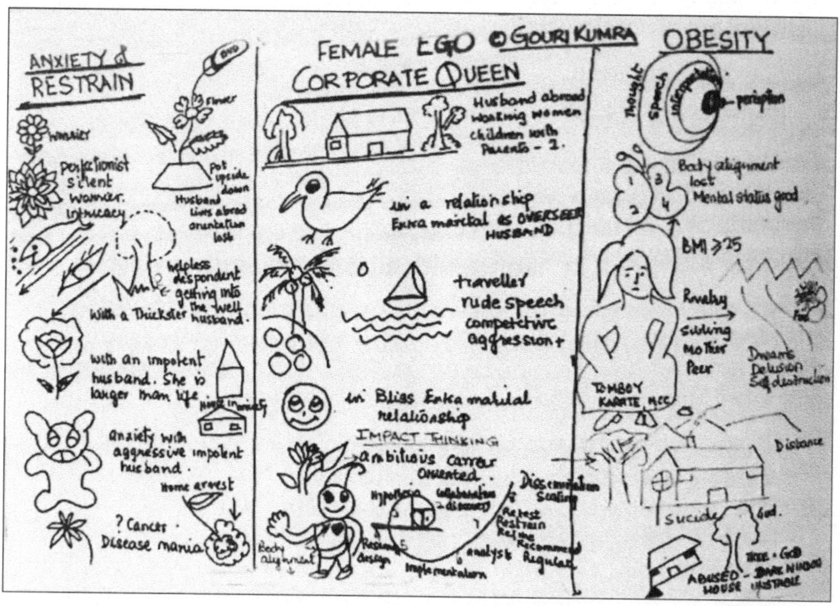

Figure 2: Art Classified by Me and Expressed by the Female Patient

Anxiety and Restrain

1. Symbol size is exaggerated, bud bigger than the flower, flower pot upside down.
2. Sharp edges of leaves and petals, pointed roof suggesting anger.
3. Drowning.
4. Sullen cartoons.
5. Flowers not grounded suggesting instability.

Corporate Queen

1. Sharp prominent eyes.
2. Perfect hill or village scene.
3. Decorative animal or flower oozing confidence.
4. Science illustrations, statistics, and configurations, status consciousness.

Couch Potato (Obesity)

1. Concentric circles suggesting overthinking
2. Fat representation
3. Crucified window
4. Distant scene
5. Nonalignment of tree.

Symbols are cultural or natural with alchemy conjunction.